TOURISTS _and_ TRADE

TOURISTS _and_ TRADE

Roadside Craftsmen
and the Highway Transforming Craft

BRUCE A. AUSTIN

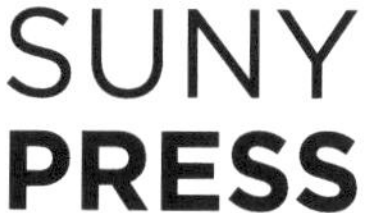

Published by State University of New York Press, Albany

For information, contact State University of New York Press, Albany, NY
www.sunypress.edu

Library of Congress Cataloging-in-Publication Data

Name: Austin, Bruce A., 1952- author.
Title: Tourists and trade : roadside craftsmen and the highway transforming craft / Bruce A. Austin.
Description: Albany : State University of New York Press, [2023] | Includes bibliographical references and index.
Identifiers: LCCN 2022041857 | ISBN 9781438493312 (hardcover : alk. paper) | ISBN 9781438493305 (ebook) | ISBN 9781438493299 (pbk. : alk. paper)
Subjects: LCSH: Vending stands—New York (State)—Upstate New York. | Handicrafts—New York (State)—Upstate New York. | Roadside marketing—New York (State)—Upstate New York.
Classification: LCC HF5459.U6 A97 2023 | DDC 381/.1809747—dc23/eng/20220916
LC record available at https://lccn.loc.gov/2022041857

10 9 8 7 6 5 4 3 2 1

Contents

List of Illustrations   vii

Acknowledgments   ix

Introduction   1

 1   A Short, Pretty Straight Road   17

 2   See-It-Made   35

 3   Sheltered Space   45

 4   Tap, Tap, Tap   63

 5   The Business Plan   75

 6   Drivers   89

 7   Passengers and Passages   105

 8   Billboards   125

 9   Less Copper, More Shoppe   147

10   No Shortcuts   157

Conclusion   171

Notes 187

References 217

Index 239

Illustrations

Figure 1.1   Clarence Wemett in his "Motorette."   20

Figure 1.2   Hand-drawn stick figures depicting the four
Roadside Craftsmen.   21

Figure 3.1   Roadside Craftsmen's interior display room.   51

Figure 3.2   Fulper Pottery's "Potter and His Wheel" logo.   59

Figure 4.1   Arthur Cole, the Avon Coppersmith.   66

Figure 5.1   "Touring" card game.   79

Figure 6.1   Bloomfield Pottery brochure depicting
Guy Daugherty.   92

Figure 6.2   Ceramist Guy Daugherty's signature.   95

Figure 6.3a–d. Signatures marking Roadside Craftsmen's ceramics.   96

Figure 6.4   Trade card for Bloomfield Art Pottery.   96

Figure 6.5   Copper plaque by William Nelligan.   102

Figure 7.1   Roadside Craftsmen's satellite shop in
Cooperstown, NY.   133

Figure 7.2   Woodcroftery box.   119

Figure 8.1   Cover for the 1930s Roadside Craftsmen retail
catalogue.   128

Figure 8.2   Interior spread, 1930s Roadside Craftsmen retail
catalogue.   128

Figure 8.3　Back cover, 1930s Roadside Craftsmen retail catalogue.　129

Figure 8.4　Cover for the February 1957 Roadside Craftsmen price list.　130

Figure 8.5　Avon Coppersmith logo.　134

Figure 8.6　Stationary holder by Avon Coppersmith.　135

Figure 8.7　Avon Coppersmith sales brochure.　137

Figure 10.1　The "spirited workers" of Roadside Craftsmen.　167

Figure C.1　Bookends by the Avon Coppersmith.　181

Acknowledgments

Helping to deepen, broaden, and sharpen my understanding of the two craft shops and their surrounding context was an unconnected army of researchers, librarians, archivists, and collectors. I benefited from and am grateful for their unselfish counsel. The book is informed by them, and I thank them: Amie Alden, the Avon Preservation & Historical Society, Kathy Busby, Tamar Carroll, Tom Cole, Megan Culbert, Giuseppe de Piero, Joe DiTucci, Amelia Fontanel, Jennifer Freer, Bridget Gleeson, Cami Goldowitz, Robert Goller, Grant Hamilton, Zack Hensley, Maureen Kingston, Dave Kornacki, Jon A. Kornacki, Susan E. Kowalczyk, Laurie Lounsberry McFadden, Doug McFarland, Bryan Mead, Verna Mullen, Dave Nesbitt, Hannah Parshall, William Reece, Robert C. Rust, Sandy in Clarence (New York), Bill Shaw, Jody Sidlauskas, Judi Stewart, Holly C. Watson, Dawn Wayne, Aaron Weber, Laurel C. Wemett, Lee J. Wemett. The text was improved by Kathleen S. Smith who copy edited an early version of the manuscript. A. Sue Weisler graciously provided original photography.

A one-semester sabbatical granted by the College of Liberal Arts, Rochester Institute of Technology, allowed me time to write. A College of Liberal Arts Faculty Research Grant funded a portion of the manuscript preparation costs. I am grateful for both.

Introduction

The intersection of the American road, its roadside, and car culture is easily sentimentalized when the past is viewed from the present. Back then (whenever "then" was) things were simpler, better, even if they were not. "Back then," automotive air conditioning was "4-40": four windows down, forty miles an hour. In ninety-degree weather, that system's inadequacies became clear at the first stop sign. Happily, modernization removed such hardships. Ushering in a new century, few things were unambiguously more modern than automobiles. Yet, mistiness persists with retrospection on the faded romanticism of yesteryear. The folksy, poetic corniness of sequential Burma Shave signs, for example. Or the cramped coziness of uninsulated tourist cabins set next to a lake—or a gas station. The same gauzy nostalgia explains some of today's enthusiasm expressed by collectors bidding on kitschy, cartoonish early twentieth-century roadside advertising signs, replete with—by current standards—their amateurish persuasive appeals.

Maudlin memories, nurtured and held hostage by glossy, colorful coffee table–style books.[1] Their compelling photographs depict inventive and eccentric, curious, and occasionally perplexing roadside architecture. Visual magnets for passing motorists, the structural oddities were outlandish attractions intended as much for themselves as for what might be inside: something just weird enough to distract drivers' attention from the task they were supposed to be performing and toward the purely optional curbside. And sometimes nearby, oversized lath and plaster figures—real or imagined—are stationary, mute observers beckoning the traffic flowing in front of them. High or low, "camp" as though intended to inspire Susan Sontag.[2] Memorialized in songs, movies, novels, pop art, and photography, the (mediated) world of yesterday's cars, the roads they were driven on, and the roadside driven by are symbols of American culture appropriated by the present even though experienced only in the past.

The story presented here revisits the intersection, this time further crowding it with additional avenues: a can of worms where narratives of transportation infrastructure and automobility (chapters 1 and 2) meet small-scale business and decorative arts history (chapters 3 through 9), funneling traffic in handcraftsmanship in a new direction (chapter 10). The intersection's location is in two small, upstate New York farm villages separated by about fifteen miles on the same highway.

Set in the economic turmoil of the Great Depression, an oil merchant initiates and underwrites two craft shops, Roadside Craftsmen and Avon Coppersmith, employing a business model widely adopted seven decades later for a much different highway. The shops jump-start the evolution of Craft from lower- to uppercase and their makers from talented but mostly uncompensated amateurs to professional artists. Whereas most Craft histories locate Craft's elevation and professionalization to the third or even fourth quarter of the twentieth century, the narrative presented here identifies a much earlier date. The preposterous story is practically ripped from the script of a 1930s Hollywood screwball comedy, such as *My Man Godfrey* (1936),[3] though this one's ending was not predictable.

Like the movies, quirky characters populate the present story. They almost seem delivered by Central Casting: Clarence Wemett, a successful petroleum businessman who takes a fancy to homespun crafts created by artists he places on public display as though sideshow performers; Art Cole, a well-established metalsmith at a famous copper shop, who quits his job mere months before a quarter of the US workforce loses theirs; and Guy Daugherty, a potter with an exotic backstory who is persuaded to exchange temperate southern climes for wintry upstate New York. Theirs is a story of inefficient, labor-intensive handwork amid a highly mechanized and Taylorized industrial environment. Outwardly, the men resembled the ordinary but functional structures housing their workshops: Roadside Craftsmen's was an abandoned, century-old church, while Avon Copper-smith's was little more than a tool shed. Neither building was remotely like those in the coffee-table books referenced above. None of the actors set out to change the world, not even the small corner Craft occupied. Neither publicity-shy nor promotionally averse, their names pop up in news reports with some frequency. Each with a polychromatic biography, none sought self-aggrandizement. Newspaper stories about them serve the interest of the business enterprises, not the owner's or craftsmen's egos.

"Modesty" does not fully capture the essence of their personalities and the stoicism connoted by "reserved" may be a bit too deep into the cowboy movie hero stereotype: men who say little because they have little to say. In the end, Hollywood portraits of this story's principals would be more impressionist than representational.

Portions of the story, like some of Hollywood's, seem goofy. Goofy ideas are not a commodity in short supply nor is there much demand for them. Because, well, they are goofy and, unsurprisingly, frequently unsuccessful. In East Bloomfield and Avon, the two craft shops launched as the Depression tightened its decade-long grip on the nation. Roadside Craftsmen's and Avon Coppersmith's products appreciatively looked backward for aesthetic inspiration while the decorative arts experienced the tension of contradictory design styles: the comforting but derivative Colonial Revival and the jazzy, machine-age Modernism.[4] At the same time, the businesses predicted a novel, if fanciful, optimistic model for consumer behavior. Hollywood-like in its contrariness, at precisely the wrong time for such things to happen, the improbable business idea achieves traction. The Roadside Craftsmen/Avon Coppersmith story weaves together threads from an anachronistic decorative arts style and those of a future composed of concrete and cars. The story's craftsmen produce discretionary products for a consumer market characterized by 25 percent unemployment, and their story is a chapter in the prehistory of modern Craft. The shops' longest-lasting contribution is the most subtle: a critical historical bridge that spans objects individually created for personal use to the work pioneering a national movement professionalizing, commercializing, and ultimately raising and enhancing Craft's status.[5] Not single-handedly, of course. Rather, as part of a geographically dispersed, uncoordinated "movement," one that did not coalesce until the postwar years and under the aspirational and financial stewardship of another New York visionary, Aileen Osborn Vanderbilt Webb. The shops' narrow stories tell a wider one of Craft's ascension and professionalization.

This is not a Great Man story. This is a Great Idea story, even if it is not entirely a Great *Original* Idea story. It is a risk-filled story of entrepreneurial capitalism begun in the depths of the Depression. The scenario looks backward to handcraftsmanship and for aesthetic guidance while staring forward to industrialism for profit, all encapsulated within a fraught context of economic uncertainty and a "bifurcated political and social environment."[6] Clarence Wemett's idea was manifested first at Roadside Craftsmen and then a few years later at Avon Coppersmith. Both were located at two nearby, tiny dots on the printed map of western New York: East Bloomfield and East Avon, respectively. The two craft operations are connected by Wemett's initiative, his financial underwriting and business model, and by the conjoined New York Route 5 and US Highway 20. The shops share overlapping highway and automobility history, concomitant developments in personal leisure and its "expenditure" on travel and tourism, and each is an extension of an element of the American Arts and Crafts movement. It is a story tied to a novel form of small-scale commerce, staffed by talented craftsmen. Members of a dwindling set of professions, their skills and creativity were touted as virtues as much for the craft (products) as the customers. Work was a form of theater, where craftsmen performed for customers on a commercial stage. Only with the benefit of hindsight do we say this is a story about elevation: raising public awareness and the status of Craft from the unnoticed and ordinary to appreciation and reverence for the material culture, never mind the "art," created.

Despite the commonality of financial underwriter, their geographic proximity and chronology, and an identical if unarticulated business plan, the Roadside and Coppersmith narratives for the most part are not interwoven and instead run parallel and largely independently. Neither shop was the first or only such enterprise. Others existed elsewhere, some earlier, many more later, but few survived as long. That the two craft shops were driven by the same individual underscores his entrepreneurship and suggests the merits of product diversification for similarly motivated, affiliated industries: attracting the business of itinerant travelers. To be sure, a dash of serendipity was involved: in this case, being at the right place with a good idea but at seemingly the wrong time. For bad luck to become good required the company of nerve and the wherewithal to execute and sustain: because at the moment of inception, each must have been seen by most observers as risky silliness. Only by the privileged but selective clarity afforded by 20/20 hindsight would one judge the enterprises an idea benefiting from "good luck."

Wemett understood symbiosis well before the term became a cliché, and he knew enough to stay out of the way while staying the course. When launching his enterprises, the manufacturing world had evolved well beyond the point where crafts might have been understood as emblematic, Luddite-like revolutionary forms of protest against the imposition of the machine and the disposition of the craftsmen. The machines were firmly in place and the craftsmen long displaced. There are no heroic proletarians toiling anonymously in dimly lit, windowless sweatshop factories, producing cookie-cutter products for customers they would never meet. In most ways, in fact, the small-sized cast of Wemett craftsmen's story is just the opposite. Roadside Craftsmen's and Avon Coppersmith's workplaces were created as though intentional responses to complaints about the nineteenth-century industrial revolution's depersonalization: where craftsmen were tied to their labor and as separated from their work as they were their customers. Both Wemett enterprises were designed to foster close personal relationships between craftsmen and customers; virtues mirroring precisely often discussed but rarely achieved elements espoused by American Arts and Crafts—the early twentieth-century design movement underpinning Roadside and Coppersmith but that had long passed from popularity.

The story begins with Wemett's late-1920s "tin can" tourist road trip to the American South, a fortuitous excursion that inspired both Roadside Craftsmen and Avon Coppersmith. On the road, Wemett became fascinated by a demonstration of clay throwing and pottery making. "See-it-made" became the marquee feature he emulated on Route 20—New York's throughway before there was a thruway. Coincidentally, the rural highway threaded between East Avon and East Bloomfield acquired federal status shortly before the two craft shops launched. Its two lanes, Wemett envisioned, would carry a caravan of cars, each filled with potential customers. "See-it-made" demonstrations at Roadside and Coppersmith would be magnets, Wemett believed, drawing drivers from the highway and into each shop as customers for the craftsmen. Italicizing the appeal, at Roadside Craftsmen, the potter and woodworker "performed" their craft-making outdoors during warm weather in the fresh air and under covered pavilions for all those who drove by to see.

This is much less a story about art and one more about commerce, though not at the sacrifice of creativity. For in the process, the two craft enterprises inadvertently nudged Craft's status upward. The story's commercial thread extends the contrarian impulse guiding the shops' establishment. The businesses commercialized traditionally home-bounded craft objects made of metal, clay, wood, and fiber—humble media used to produce functional products. Unbeknownst to those then working at their craft in the midst of the Depression, Craft was at a transformational point in its evolution, objects migrated from necessity toward luxury, albeit tinged with a hint of nostalgia. It was an ambiguous, somewhat uneasy place for creator as much as customer. Prior to the industrial revolution, after all, "craft" was treated as a verb describing a behavior. Later it became a noun referencing objects people themselves made or traded other goods for in order to make living more hospitable, easier, and convenient.[7] In 1930, craft objects were neither assigned the label of "art" nor fit under its umbrella. But the establishment of the two businesses enabled, propelled, and empowered the transitional period for Craft well before the discipline, the work, and its media sought or were elevated further up the art hierarchy and to a museum's pedestal. The commercial inspiration that produced Roadside's and Coppersmith's business success first relied on an appeal to and exploitation of customers' better, loftier, other-directed motives and qualities: gift-giving. Second, to expand sales beyond the immediate ones, Wemett's commercial acumen was combined with an intuitive appreciation for an emerging if not-yet-articulated theory of interpersonal influence. Together, they enhanced the size and reach of the craft shops' customer base without diminishing the artistic impulse, all wrapped inside an environment where creativity was nurtured and channeled for profit.

Clarence Wemett knew his roadside businesses could not be sustained by relying solely on a local market. He speculated the provincial investment might draw interest from beyond the immediate communities. What would be the merchandise's customer appeal, and how would his shops reach a wider market? His business model for the roadside craft shops predates the one widely adopted seventy years later for an even newer superhighway, the internet: grab a small portion from the huge volume of traffic flow. The craft shops, like the highway next to which they were situated, share an identical prophecy. Each anticipates what was expected to follow: travel and trade. Extraordinary as much for the economic audacity of their timing as the products each produced and the customers they sought, the two businesses survived and sometimes thrived. Both persisted through the Great Depression and a World War, as well as two dominant but divergent decorative styles; in Coppersmith's case, it lasted long enough to welcome hippies. The initiatives were made possible by the foresighted oil vendor who saw business symbiosis among a recently adopted mode of transportation, a more recently paved, skinny highway on which to drive the cars, and a novel form of leisure recreation.

Not nearly as famous, despite being almost a thousand miles longer, US Route 20 was to New York State journalists and their readers what Route 66 was to everyone else in America: an iconic "Main Street," a highway of commerce. Mostly a two-lane strip across the top of New

York, Route 20 was "Scenic" before the city people or Triple-A deemed it as such. Alas, Route 20 was never memorialized by a popular song; and the handsome men in equally attractive Corvettes who sped along its straightaways, banked into gentle curves, and downshifted to climb modest hills did so without the benefit of a TV show. Journalists, though, were undeterred by any perceived second-class status. Traveling Route 20, they later rhapsodized, was a "road to history" forming a "ribbon of memories," one filled with "roadside attractions."[8] Privileging the leisurely, Route 20 was well-suited "for travelers who want to stop and smell the roses."[9] Mary Hedglon italicized Route 20's historical significance for late-twentieth-century readers: "the nation's only remaining [original] transcontinental highway."[10] First a Native American trail, Route 20 became the principal route for American colonists' westward expansion and New York's commercial growth, one heavily populated with mineral spring spas, taverns, and cabin courts.[11] "Since the 1700s," Hedglon wrote, "When white settlers started dribbling through," the seventy-mile stretch where New York Route 5 and US Highway 20 are conjoined, especially, was "a shrine to retail entrepreneurship."[12] Her six-part, 1991–92 series for the *Rochester Democrat and Chronicle* introduced readers to that space, the one within which the present work is also located.

Common to Routes 66 and 20 were roadside businesses. Initially mom-and-pop operations, the amateur retailers sought extra income. By the first quarter of the twentieth-century, businesses lining either side of the highways sprouted in optimistic anticipation of a new, numerically large group of mobile leisure travelers. "Auto-tourists," as the noncommercial drivers became known, required service industries for their machines and themselves, as had the earlier stagecoach, canal, and railroad industries and their travelers. Soon, colonizing Routes 66 and 20's roadsides were nonessential, peripheral businesses of seemingly every kind, tempting those passing by on their way to someplace else to stop. In the southwest, "tourist trap" craft stores catering to the itinerant purported to offer homegrown goods such as Native American weavings, jewelry, and ceramics. Tourists could bring a little bit of their travels home with them—mementos and souvenirs, empirical evidence of their vacations. Still earlier, in the east, the Shakers were both subsistence farmers and commercial entrepreneurs who sold seeds and herbs at roadside stands. Later, a secondary market emerged when antiques collectors prized their furniture and accessories.

In New York State, ideas were peddled at the roadside nearly as often as consumer goods. Mac Nelson's "walking tour" treatment of US

20 across the state documents the remarkable number of establishments selling homegrown salvation, redemption, and political realignment.[13] Equality of the sexes was promoted at John Humphrey Noyes's Oneida Community, east of Syracuse and founded in 1848, the same year the road later marked as Route 20 carried conferees to the Seneca Falls convention on women's rights. The Brotherhood of the New Life (Brockton), established in 1867 by Thomas Lake Harris, sold hay, nursery crops, and fruit, in addition to socialism. Spiritualists took advantage of the traffic Route 20 delivered, including the Fox sisters in Hydesville[14] and those at Lily Dale, farther west. Methodist education took place at the Chautauqua Institution and in Palmyra, Joseph Smith launched his Mormon faith. What later became the Route 20 highway facilitated travel for Auburn, New York "conductor" Harriet Tubman's "passengers" on the Underground Railroad. Utopians, socialists, and religions of many sects and inventions, as much as commercial retail establishments were savvy about locating their physical footprint near New York's Great Road.

Even good, sensible ideas sometimes have to percolate before a confluence of discoveries, processes, and understanding converge for their realization. That imperfection or failure can follow preliminary, tentative attempts is as certain as the aphorism about finding love: You have to kiss a few frogs. Ancient Egyptian mathematician Ptolemy, for instance, is often credited as first to envision motion pictures. With a better understanding of optics, chemistry, and technology, Thomas Edison realized the idea almost two thousand years later. So, too, retail commerce beyond a manufacturer's physical geographic locality awaited developments and improvements in transportation and delivery systems, maturation of the persuasion industry, and, among customers, the affluence that affords disposable income. Roadside Craftsmen and Avon Coppersmith drew business lessons, wittingly or not, from Arts and Crafts movement impresario Elbert Hubbard and other mail-order merchants, though largely without their mediated apparatus. The craft shops adapted earlier business models for merchandising and extended them to the peripatetic. By the third decade of the twentieth century, paved highways and the broad diffusion of automobile ownership personalized and liberated leisure from its once primarily homebound location: a customer base for roadside entrepreneurship Wemett's commerce in crafts at once democratized the product and professionalized its producers.

Road-building and paving impacted virtually every facet of American life, though this may be difficult to appreciate today. Contemporary contemplation of the highways built long ago parallels how so-called "digital natives" think of the internet: "It has always been there, right?" Of course, neither highway nor internet *had* always been there. A glow of understanding for the wide significance of road development begins for some with the "Plank Road" street sign's meaning. A short-lived, mid-nineteenth-century innovation in road surfacing, much more than an enigmatically colorful description, the sign once discriminated between the road paved with boards laid side to side like those at a seashore boardwalk and all the others that were little more than rutted, muddy paths.

While people's leisure time and auto ownership both began expanding in the early 1900s, the proportion of passable highways lagged. "Outrageous" was one 1897 driver's assessment of road conditions across upstate New York on what eventually became Route 20. Four years later, the founder of the Hudson Motor Car Company duplicated the trip, but took the Erie Canal's towpath for 150 miles "because it was better than the roads." As early as the 1820s, New York led the nation in turnpike building.[15] But, by 1916, little more than 10 percent of all American roads "could be described as 'surfaced.' "[16] World War I military needs stimulated construction of improved roadways. President Woodrow Wilson signed the first Federal-Aid Road Act into law in 1916. (History repeats itself forty years later during the Cold War with the 1956 Federal Highway Act that created the Interstate Highway System.) Following the war, and with the initiation of road improvements, "what had been a trickle of tourists grew into a deluge."[17] The twentieth-century novelty was the intertwined personalization of transportation, the integration of automobility on interconnected paved highways, and the availability of otherwise uncommitted time for people to combine the two.

Route 20 began as a private turnpike enterprise. Land speculators, seeking to profit from farmers anxious to expand the market for their crops, pressured the state to develop the road as an "opportunity to participate in commerce."[18] Roadside service industries, including taverns, inns, blacksmith shops, and stables, emerged to meet the travel needs of the stagecoach's passengers and animals: lodging, fuel, and food. Traffic volume on Route 20 increased dramatically and annually between 1930 and 1950.[19] Hard-surfaced highways led to ever more novel, discretionary forms of roadside retailing. By the early twentieth century, "Roadside strip development and billboards grew without control."[20] Abetted earlier by the advent of railroads in the third quarter of the nineteenth century, tourism became an increasingly popular middle-class leisure activity.

Although roadside entrepreneurship was no novelty, the twentieth-century difference for its merchants was twofold: The inventory morphed from cast-off personal possessions that had survived personal utility and surplus crops to goods created specifically for sale and intended for profit to a customer base of itinerant strangers from remote locations. And instead of spontaneous, one-off events, roadside businesses meant continuous, predictable days and hours of operation for vendors as much as customers. The challenge faced by roadside businesses was their reliance on passing customers whose stops at their shops were rarely intended. Roadside Craftsmen and Avon Coppersmith were places customers happened upon rather than sought out. Purchases were more spontaneous than intentional. The two crafts shops prospered without the supportive marketing, advertising, and publication muscle of Arts and Crafts movement merchandisers; theirs was not mass marketing, it was serendipitous, point-of-purchase salesmanship. The one Coppersmith and Roadside market discriminator was *how* its products were produced.

As with highway landscapes, handcraftsmanship is a source of nostalgic affection, appealing to old-time, preindustrial "traditional" virtues and values: quaintly primitive expressions imbued in equal measure with innocence and idiosyncrasy. "Craft" is also associated with utility and purpose, although at least some portion of craft work, like "art," was perfectly functionless, created as robust acts of expression. "Just for nice" is a nineteenth-century Pennsylvania German colloquialism for objects made for the maker's own pleasure irrespective of functionality.[21] Handcrafted products fluidly cross boundaries, muddling definitions among such post hoc categories as "folk art," "naïve art," "self-taught art," "rustic art," "indigenous art," and "outsider art." In each instance, the creator's untutored status modifies the artifact's significance. Traditional connotations of art are softened, diluted, or manipulated and the object's form either "excused" or "explained" by the term preceding it. Nostalgia-motivated buyers—today's or yesterday's—of handcrafted work can alternately view their acquisitions as self-congratulatory lifestyle enhancers, status symbols, or as acts of philanthropy, demonstrating their support for the community and its "natives." Handcraftsmanship may seem uncomfortably incongruous when nested adjacent to the very epitome of modern, industrial efficiency (the highway), as was Roadside Craftsmen and the Avon Coppersmith.

At the same time Roadside Craftsmen and Avon Coppersmith peered into the future, anticipating a novel kind of customer, the two enterprises drew on established educational traditions and from an even older craft "movement." Coppersmith and Roadside are grounded in New York State's history in crafts. The number of New York State Arts and Crafts operations is striking—and teeming with talent. Coy Ludwig's exhibition introduced readers to New York products and people driving the Arts and Crafts movement, including smaller, more intimate manufacturers. The state's educational institutions also emphasized commitment to craft by training talented craftsmen for the workforce: from Alfred University, one of the oldest clayworking college curricula in the nation and Mechanics Institute in the west, to Syracuse University in central New York and Troy School of Arts and Crafts in the east, and downstate at Teachers College at Columbia University and Pratt Institute.[22] But the Avon Coppersmith and Roadside Craftsmen enterprises were initiated at the distant cusp of the Arts and Crafts movement. By the time each shop was founded, the public's taste in decorative art had changed. The most profound influence of Arts and Crafts on Wemett and his two craft shops was not the movement's philosophy; it was on the products, product nationalizing, and craft's customer base. At best, only aesthetic influences lingered.

Roadside Craftsmen and the Avon Coppersmith's story connects the aesthetics and business of the turn of the century's Arts and Crafts movement to Aileen Webb's multipronged postwar activism on behalf of Crafts. Slowly, imperceptibly, Craft's quiet migration began after World War I: some carpenters became woodworkers and some clay-throwers ceramists. Their homework became public work once it moved from occasional front-yard stands to permanent, year-round structures, including those at the roadside. Skill training in Craft, once guildlike and occurring exclusively on the job, evolved to formal education with Craft as part of a curriculum that could be taught, learned, and adopted as a lifetime career.[23] Craft's professionalization occurred in disparate locations, and in fits and starts, until finally coalescing at midcentury under Webb's generous umbrella. But Roadside and Coppersmith were founded well in advance of America House, Mrs. Webb's all-craft Manhattan retail store.[24] Roadside Craftsmen and Avon Coppersmith retained traditional handwork processes, eschewing the industrialization widely adopted by other industries. The shops contrasted with big-city department stores serving urban citizens who arrived by mass transit to purchase mass manufactured goods. Roadside and Coppersmith served unique products to individualized shoppers delivered singly in their automobiles.

The evolution and maturation process that led eventually to Craft's enhanced status did not possess the organizational structure associated with other, better-known social movements. Beginning in the 1940s and nearly single-handedly, Aileen Webb made it her life's mission to spearhead and underwrite the elevation of Craft. She legitimized Craft by linking together the seemingly ordinary with the undeniably exceptional. Her cue was the Arts and Crafts movement that overtly connected the formerly separate world of Art with Craft. There, each element cast a halo on the other, enhancing the other's legitimacy and bridging "the sometimes bitter antagonism between the 'fine' and the 'useful.'"[25] Arts and Crafts conveyed a democratic sense of accessibility and inclusion. The functionality associated with Craft would no longer be relegated or confined to the humdrum. Carefully designed and executed objects held aesthetic appeal without abandoning their utility. The hedonic, psychic rewards previously restricted to Art that was hoarded and jealously guarded expanded to embrace Craft, including its makers and owners.

As thoughtful as she was tireless, Webb adopted a strategy that took four complementary, integrated, and mutually reinforcing forms. She founded a professional organization to encourage collegiality as much as advocacy; a school to teach the Art and skills as much as how to earn a living at Craft; a store located at the heart of the world's retailing capital that exclusively sold crafts; and a museum to certify the objects' movement from sales and cupboard shelves to pedestals and vitrines. At the vanguard, predating Webb's initiatives by a decade, were Roadside Craftsmen and the Avon Coppersmith. They exploited the symbiosis of art and craft by positioning their products as gift items, an appeal to a sense of philanthropy and altruism embraced by all. Differently, the Roadside-Coppersmith Craft story is devoid of patronizing "wealthy people" as silversmith Jack Prip later dismissively if ironically noted about midcentury Craft work.[26] Whereas Webb had an agenda she sought to advance and fulfill, Wemett had a business and financial success as his goal. Roadside Craftsmen and Avon Coppersmith's achievement advancing craft to Craft is that they did so unselfconsciously, for so long, and with the talents of so few.

It is unlikely Wemett or any of the Roadside or Coppersmith craftsmen were aware of the broader drama their narrative was part of and motivated: Craft's movement up the hierarchy and into the province of Art. Aileen Webb's advocacy on behalf of Craft was consciously driven. But a decade earlier, Wemett held no such plan. Any cognizance Wemett had that his craft enterprises were breaking new ground was in a way not so different from the string of gas stations he founded. His businesses exploited and served an emerging group of customers. The craft shops were extensions, satisfying less the motorist's need and more the tourist's interest, or maybe their impulse. For Wemett, handcraft was a means to a business end for which the unintended consequences held more profound virtue. That Craft would see its status raised was a by-product of his initiative, not his intent. This is not to say Wemett was dispassionate about craft; the 1929 motor trip when he was inspired by see-it-made demonstrations belies any such notion. Recounting Wemett's role is less hagiography and much more an examination of innovation, entrepreneurship, and adaptation of business practices for the new age.

The received history of Roadside Craftsmen and Avon Coppersmith is fragmented and fugitive. Aside from products, neither left much from which to learn their stories. Though Coppersmith and Roadside each produced product brochures and what were generously defined as catalogues, they were issued with no apparent publication schedule and, most likely, were only reprinted when extant stock dwindled. But, as Tom Cole, son of Coppersmith's founder, remarked dryly, "The product line didn't change much."[27] No one alive today is a firsthand, from-the-beginning witness. Absent the architectural excesses found in coffee table–style books, their physical buildings, like the products they sold, were inconspicuous and unostentatious. Contemporary Route 20 travelers will find no physical evidence for one, and the other is so well disguised by renovations that passersby are none the wiser. A distant memory for a few, the structure housing Roadside's business goes unnoticed and is unfamiliar to most.

Much that is reported on the following pages is pieced together from scattered, brief, and often mundane reports in local newspapers. The papers were civic boosters and purveyors of minutia and trivia, as the professionalization of journalism as we now know it did not begin until about 1945. Community newspapers published columns devoted to happenings of local consequence and insignificance, liberally mixing the two. Bulleted "community notes" reported on day-to-day occurrences involving their citizens. Who visited whom, who had dinner where and in whose company, who traveled to this place or that, who had surgery or was recovering from what after how lengthy a convalescence: all of these events were itemized, often in Western Union style. Loosely arranged, often by locality rather than theme, the information was usually volunteered by the subject. Rarely was anything momentous reported: tragedies were few and triumphs (no matter their slightness) prevailed. The kind of chit-chat that might today compose a newsfeed on social media, perhaps without the pejorative associated with bragging. Byline columnists were more stenographers than reporters and the columns a kind of over-the-backyard-fence grapevine given permanence by the printed page though intended for consumption as rapidly as their disposal. More a public diary, stitched together they form a selective, quasi-documentary snapshot of a community—or at least the literate part of the community who had the time to note the ordinary. A narrative of the two shops' emergence and persistence unfolds in snippets. Some story arcs doubtless remain invisible.[28]

Previously, Michael Clark and Jill Thomas-Clark published the only longer-form article related to the present study: it focused on Avon Coppersmith.[29] For a number of years, their column, "The Best of the Rest," was a regular feature in *Style 1900*, a magazine serving divergent Arts and Crafts movement interests including commerce in period antiques, the enthusiasm of fans and collectors, and scholarship. "Best of the Rest" essays discussed second- and third-tier movement manufacturers and craftsmen: factories and figures just outside the spotlight occupied by better known brands and personalities. Noting their efforts, Arts and Crafts historian David Cathers called the Clarks "pioneers" for making visible "a vast landscape [of] unknown territory."[30] The histories and biographies contextualized and helped readers better understand the work produced, no doubt heightening awareness, broadening appreciation, and improving commercial values for work otherwise glossed over. Unsurprisingly, the columns focused heavily on "the work": objects and the techniques required to produce them, comparative aesthetics, and the critical lens through which to appreciate them. The Clarks' column exploring Avon Coppersmith was longer than most.[31]

Living in Western New York, I drive New York 5 and US 20 frequently and have passing familiarity with its roadside. The conjoined highway once connected important sites of natural and man-made invention: from photographic film in Rochester to sound-on-film in Auburn and between them the condo-sized nests built by ambitious osprey in the Montezuma Wildlife Refuge. Today, the towns and villages lining the road, once thriving pockets of prosperity, are little more than shells of their former selves. Their evaporated grandeur is documented by elegant, occasionally palatial homes that sell for bargain prices and downtowns of frequently vacant storefronts that no longer see the foot traffic that once made them retail magnets. Sad reminders all of prethruway years of abundance. Annually, for more than thirty-five years, I make the mid-August pilgrimage to the Madison-Bouckville flea markets. For one week, a carnival-like two-mile strip of Route 20 highway is bordered on either side with up to two thousand antiques dealers under tents, while cruising collectors slow traffic to a crawl. An extreme, contemporary example of curbside commerce where both vendor and customer are itinerant.

Objects were my first point of contact with the present subject. Work by the shops popped up as often at antiques stores as yard sales. Typically modestly priced, the objects are little more than curiosities for most: tchotchkes with sketchy histories. I wrote about the American Arts and Crafts movement for a few publications and organized a modest-sized exhibition of work tied to Western New York.[32] Included in the exhibition catalogue is a black-and-white photograph of a pair of hammered copper bookends and a pen tray. All were worked in a woodgrain, hammered pattern; bore a nearly identical, dark brown patina; and looked to have been made by the same hand. But the bookends carried a circular impressed mark, "Rochester Metal Craftsmen/Hand Wrought Copper," though the pen tray was signed "The Avon Coppersmith." The catalogue's thumbnail description of Avon Coppersmith correctly identified Arthur Cole and Walter Jennings's involvement and their relationship to Karl Kipp and Roycroft, though erroneously reported the business's lifespan. As I began the present project, I misread clues promising good but ultimately unfounded stories. "Jennings," for instance, was the maiden name of Clarence Wemett's two wives. A little knowledge went a short way.

Mostly, the present project is motivated by my perception of the nearly singular focus of much published about Arts and Crafts: objects. At a 2017 Buffalo conference,[33] I paraphrased another scholar's comments on a different subject:[34] Arts and Crafts research has gone from humble beginnings to more grandiose beginnings. But it always seems to be making beginnings. The focus on objects and inordinate attention to stars, studios, and surface was at the expense of other avenues of investigation. To broaden the scope of Arts and Crafts research requires transcending what often is the initial attraction: "The Work."[35] The present project shares an interest with two previous studies: the context within which the objects reside.[36]

1

A Short, Pretty Straight Road

The debate proposition minced no words: "Resolved that the study of Latin and Greek is a waste of time." Not "unnecessary" or "old-fashioned"—a *waste of time*. Impertinence may be a quality best reserved for youth, who seem to already have a monopoly on it. Whether such was the case in 1906 when the Livonia, New York High School hosted the debate, we will never know. But we do know Clarence Wemett took the affirmative.[1] Differentiating between iconoclastic, contrarian, and rebellious can be difficult. The related inclination to rub against the grain also can be seen as evidence for innovation, creativity, and a willingness to genuinely ask, "Why not?" Comfortably fitting somewhere in that taxonomy, about twenty years later, Wemett thumbed his nose at a Depression that, unbeknownst to him, would stretch on for a decade and initiated a business selling trinkets to transients for a quarter century.

Reviewing Clarence E. Wemett's life (1885–1961)[2] by reading contemporaneous newspaper reports yields a picture of a respected professional businessman typically depicted in photograph-less stories. The scarcity of media images is just the opposite of what one might expect, and the reports offer only hints about his personality. Known by most, including family members,[3] as "C.E." (to avoid confusion with his older brother, Correl) and "the Boss," he was active from the start, ambitious and entrepreneurial nearly throughout. One 1937 news report characterized him this way: "Clarence Wemett of Hemlock is always doing interesting things. Buying something, building something, remodeling something, originating something."[4] Earlier still, his high school graduation program lists him as speaking on "Requisites for Success," and a 1933 story quotes Wemett's proactive motto: "Don't itch for better business, scratch for it."[5] The article's writer concluded, "Perhaps this policy explains why he is so successful."

In addition to his business interests, Wemett was optimistic, forward-looking, civic-minded, and engaged. His obituary presents him as a member of the Hemlock Methodist Church, Civic Club, Odd Fellows, Board of Education, and director and past president of the neighboring Livonia Union Cemetery Association. A devout man, he was dedicated to his family; his five children all remained close to their Hemlock, New York home and all held lifelong ties to C.E.'s businesses.[6] He and his first wife, Ada, appear often in the society and events columns of local newspapers. A May 17, 1920 briefing in the *Cohocton Valley Times*, for instance, reports on Mrs. Wemett's appendicitis operation at Dr. Lee's Hospital in Rochester, taking care to note she was "doing as well as can be expected." One acknowledges the tautology that prominent people gain prominence by virtue of prominent media presentations, in some cases becoming known for their well-knownness.[7] Still, Wemett's multiple serial business successes, coupled with his near-patriotic devotion to and investment in the region, legitimize his media presence.

Wemett's diverse businesses never strayed far from Hemlock, even as his family trips to distant locations as an adult were dutifully reported on by hometown newspapers. One trip inspired his craft enterprises. Three of his most significant businesses, including those he underwrote and fostered, despite being deeply rooted in Western New York, were all intended to touch destinations much, much farther away. Gas stations propelled Wemett's automobiling customers throughout the Finger Lakes, across the region, and, for some, the nation. Work produced at and sold by Roadside Craftsmen and Avon Coppersmith, though available to the locals in East Bloomfield and Avon, was much more directed to a customer base distant from those in the shops' backyards. And many purchases made at Roadside or Coppersmith by passing tourists were not for the customers' personal use but would end up as gifts. An early, undated brochure for the Bloomfield Pottery, Roadside Craftsmen's original name, assures readers that "a useful gift . . . carries a special charm." Helpfully, the brochure advises tourists that "you will find just such a gift, created in a unique manner at the Bloomfield Pottery." Knowing Bloomfield Pottery's customers might be at remote locations, delivery and transportation costs are listed along with a COD option available with a 25 percent cash deposit. Even Wemett's earliest business—retail hardware stores—was an evergreen industry with legs: the inventory would never go stale or spoil and would almost always eventually find a buyer. From homeowners to farmers, sooner or later, everyone goes to the hardware store. Extant news reports do not reveal how Wemett's initial and subsequent businesses were capitalized, but they do indicate his collaborative inclination. Nearly as often as not, Wemett was a partner; this, too, suggests a personality feature. Although one reason for partnerships is spreading the risk, in Wemett's case a more plausible explanation is the generous one: sharing an opportunity.

A few years after graduating from high school, a one-sentence notice in the January 27, 1911 *Livonia Gazette* reports Clarence was one of the builders of a canning company's house for its superintendent. That experience, and even without knowing whether it was him swinging a hammer, is related to Wemett's first business venture in retail hardware three years later. The *Livonia Gazette* reported[8] that in 1914, with Edward Bacon, Wemett bought the John Beam hardware store in Hemlock where he had once worked. Not long after, his reputation and business interests widened. The same publication recorded: "Clarence Wemett is known over this way as the oil king. The name fits him pretty well. He buys gasoline and kerosene in car-load lots and his tanks distribute it."[9] Beginning "back in the days of kerosene lamps," the Wemett Corporation's (incorporated 1925) products were "delivered by horses and wagons in the summer and sleighs in the winter."[10] Starting with a single gas station in Livonia, Wemett expanded his reach by acting, first, as a distributor for Pennzoil for six or seven years and, later, as a distributor for the Eldred Company for four or five years.[11] Eventually, the "king's" oil empire expanded to more than two dozen Shell gasoline service stations spread across Livingston, Ontario, and Steuben counties.[12] Ten months after being "crowned," the *Wayland Register* favorably referred to him "a hustler" following his purchase of the Webster Crossing, W. G. Johnson hardware business with Hugh Drain.[13] Beginning January 5, 1938, Wemett leased his complete portfolio of twenty-eight stations to the Shell Union Oil Company; as "the largest distributor of Shell products in the state," during 1937 the Wemett Company had paid state and federal gasoline taxes averaging $5,000 a month.[14]

Wemett was a relentless promoter, even if not on the scale of P. T. Barnum. But he did so for the sake of his businesses rather than self-aggrandizement. Wemett's frequent newspaper appearances and his ability to attract attention and generate publicity was typically in service to personalizing his business interests. Sometimes the reports involved "stunts." A 1929 article, for example, described the motorette, "a queer, three-wheeled gasoline vehicle manufactured in Hartford in 1901." Wemett had revived and returned the unusual car to life "after fifteen years of slumber in a barn."[15] Wemett's engagement with the significantly photogenic vehicle, "used daily on the streets of Livonia and Hemlock," neatly dovetailed with his business interests in gasoline retailing. The story—and the tricycle—promotes Wemett's business by inference and without any "hard sell." In addition to his proclivity toward public relations tactics, Wemett was a forward-thinking businessman. He was generous toward his employees and recognized their performance. In January 1950, for instance, even as the Roadside Craftsmen operation began its slide into obscurity, the Wemett Company hosted a dinner for its employees, including those employed at Roadside. Eighteen people gathered at Jean's restaurant in Lima, and bonus checks totaling more than $3,000 were presented for 1949 performance. The article reporting on the dinner notes the company pays its employees' hospitalization insurance, sick and accident insurance, life insurance, and vacation (see figure 1.1).[16]

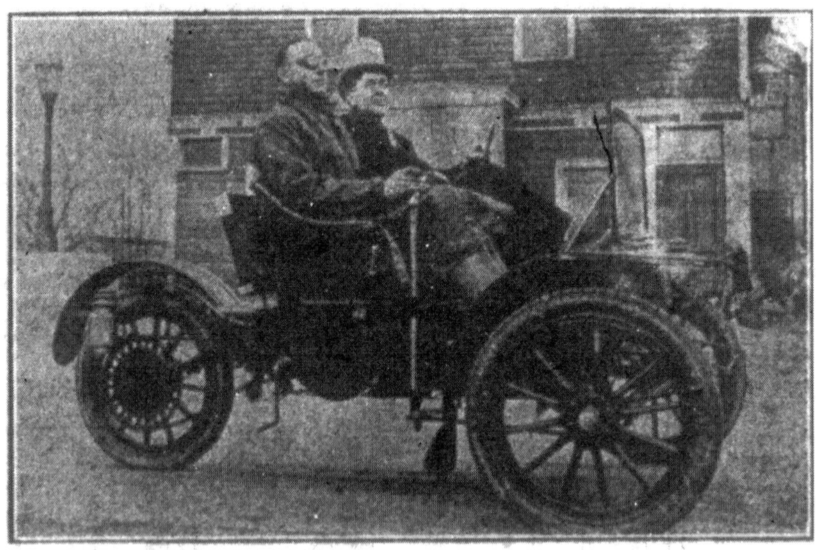

Figure 1.1. Clarence Wemett (wearing a hat) and Carl Seutt in Wemett's "Motor-ette," a 1901 vehicle manufactured by C. W. Kelsey Co. First published March 29, 1929 in the *Livonia Gazette*, republished May 3, 1929 and July 17, 1947. Photograph courtesy of the Livingston County Historian. Public domain.

In 1929, just a few years after Route 20 received federal highway status, and the same year that ushered in the Great Depression, Clarence Wemett launched a bold new version of an old idea at a place where one might not expect to find it: an old-fashioned shop, modeled on those found in the South, where "hand-made fancy art pottery is manufactured for sale."[17] First named "Bloomfield Pottery," that moniker quickly became narrowly anachronistic as the business expanded from clay to textiles, metal, and wood. "Roadside Craftsmen" more accurately described the enterprise's ambition and breadth of inventory as well as its location (see figure 1.2).

Good Roads

Hemlock, New York, Clarence Wemett's hometown, was settled at the very end of the eighteenth century. Located at the north end of one of the smaller Finger Lakes, the village was originally known as "Slab City" for the rough-cut lumber produced there. Hemlock's economy clustered around forestry and sawmills, serving the growing building demands of Rochester, the city farther north. In warmer weather, logs were floated up

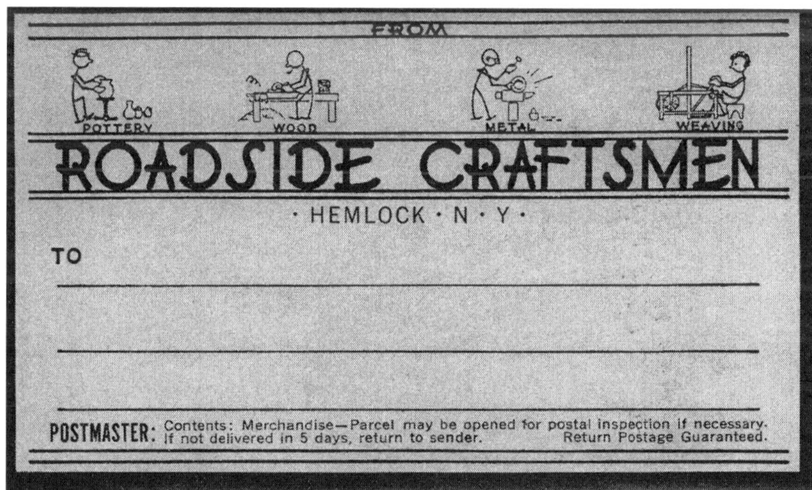

Figure 1.2. Hand-drawn stick figures depicting the four Roadside Craftsmen as presented on a shipping label. Photograph courtesy of Lee J. Wemett and http://www.wemett.net.

the natural transportation route Hemlock Lake conveniently afforded and, in the winter, tugged across the lake's ice by teams of horses. Another use for Hemlock's abundant timber was found during the brief decade around the mid-nineteenth century when "plank roads" became popular—at least until the boards twisted and warped. In 1850, the Plank Road Company "paved" twenty-five miles of what later became Route 15A, south from Rochester, installing a toll booth at the northern end of Hemlock. Wealthy Rochesterians summering at the lake's hotels and cottages, traveled there on Plank Road. In the 1930s, were Wemett to drive from Hemlock to either one of his craft businesses, he would have taken Plank Road north to Routes 5 and 20.

At the intersection is the village of Lima, with East Avon five miles to the west and East Bloomfield ten miles at the east. Lima is an interruption of the briefest kind—little more than a hiccup—between the villages on either side. Even today, a 30-mph drive through its business district might take two minutes, with or without hitting the single traffic signal at the four corners. On the southeast corner sits the American Hotel. Local lore holds that John Hill, an early Hemlock toll road developer, was murdered there by a mid-nineteenth-century traveler angry about the usury of Hill's toll. Built at a cost of either $500 or $5,000, depending on the source consulted, Hill's 1853 route, running along the east shore of Hemlock Lake, offered a gentler incline than nearby alternatives for northbound foresters and travelers. A good story, it illustrates as much the (pun aside) steep price of progress as the conflicting details of tall tales. The less dramatic scenario is that the toll-averse traveler's 1854 argument took place in Hemlock, not Lima, and that instead of being a victim of a felony, Hill suffered a heart attack after he "became greatly excited" and died. Hill's toll road, like other such privately commissioned roads, was an enterprise from which he never profited. Some reports, doubtless as apocryphal as the murder scenario, say Hill earned precisely one nickel.[18]

East Avon and East Bloomfield, New York, are sandwiched between Rochester, Batavia, and Buffalo. They are at once in the middle of nowhere but at the center of everywhere. Both villages are located along the only stretch of highway where Routes 5 and 20 are conjoined, from Avon to Auburn.[20] Each highway is a major east-west thoroughfare traversing the upper portion of the state, running roughly parallel to much of Lake Ontario's shoreline. Both Routes 5 and 20 followed Native American trails, later privately developed as turnpikes beginning in the colonial era. Route 5, earlier the more freight-bound route, contrasted with 20, which

CROSSROADS

Drive north from Hemlock, New York, on Route 15A—Plank Road—and a container of coffee will not cool to sipping temperature by the time one intersects with conjoined NY 5 and US 20. There, at the American Hotel (1840), across the street from the Mason's Hall (1866), 1930s travelers, including Art Cole, the Avon Coppersmith, who scouted locations in Lima before settling on Avon, stopped to rest, eat, and sleep. Today, a short walk east or west from the hotel is like flipping through a 1920s vest pocket guide to American residential architecture. Noticeably absent, though, are homes in the International Style—commonly called "Art Deco"—that never found purchase.

To the west of the hotel, a grand, federal-style home perches majestically atop a gently sloping hill. Next door is a cobblestone house of the same style, though more rustic in appearance.[19] Greek and Gothic Revival structures sit side by side with Italianate and American Four-Square homes. Victorian Painted Ladies, brassy, unapologetic symbols of an emerging nouveau riche class of conspicuous consumers, appeared by the third quarter of the nineteenth century. Their garish colors contrast sharply with the somber, muted palette of "modern" design Craftsman-style bungalows built at the turn of the twentieth century. The oldest Lima homes are stately and conservative, self-assured and confident. They evoke the mindfulness associated with polite, formal society; they have been there longer than most and long enough to have earned their place. The gussied-up Victorians seem perfectly unaware of the juxtaposition between their appearance and the prudish connotations later associated with their name. The wealth required to build them suggests that style and taste, like status and refinement, were commodities to be purchased and the houses ostentatiously announce their ability to do so: Bright, multicolor-painted fish-scale siding on pointed gables with tall, narrow windows seductively admit narrow shafts of light into darkly paneled interiors. The tall, sharp rooflines of the Victorians lift the eye upward, while the low-slung, horizontal lines of the bungalows draw the eye outward, as though to a fictional prairie horizon nowhere near the hilly, glacial-carved Finger Lakes region. The Craftsman homes a bit too eagerly telegraph their earnestness, expressing it with exposed construction elements. Broad, generously overhanging eves with shaped rafters rest above ganged windows that open to dark stained-chestnut interiors; the glazing that brings the outdoors inside forbids homeowners the interior wall space on which to park a bookcase.

Across from the American Hotel and up a slight hill, is one of the nation's first coeducational schools: Genesee Wesleyan Seminary. Founded in 1832 by the Genesee Conference of the Methodist Episcopal Church, Genesee College was added in 1850. "Looming" sounds too ominous for a campus with neoclassical temple architectural grandness and a religion-infused, educational mission. Its topographic location, though, undeniably positions the campus a bit above all else, even if any town-gown separation in Lima would seem preposterous, as there were so few of either cohort—total 1930 population was just under nine hundred. Genesee College moved to Syracuse in 1870, despite protests by villagers, forming the basis of today's Syracuse University. The seminary briefly hosted an experimental New Deal vocational school to train underprivileged students, closing in 1941. Since 1951, the seventy-five-acre campus is home to the Elim Bible Institute and College, an organization that figures late in the Roadside Craftsmen story.

skirted major population centers except Albany on the east and Buffalo on the west. The majority of Route 20 is two lane and connects the state's smaller communities, avoiding traffic congestion, while providing access to larger ones. A significant New York agricultural artery, Route 20 is part of America's longest federal highway. Just under four hundred miles compose New York State's leg of the highway's 3,300 coast-to-coast miles; Route 20 terminates in Boston, Massachusetts, on the Atlantic Ocean and Newport, Oregon, on the Pacific.

By the 1920s, Route 20 became known as "the Yellowstone Highway," identifying one of its western scenic destinations. Earlier, it was known as the Genesee Turnpike in western New York and the Great Western Turnpike in the east. Across the Finger Lakes, Route 20 was promoted as the "Great Broadway" for the tourist appeal of its resort virtues.[21] Well before the New York State Thruway made cross-state travel not quite an afternoon drive, Route 20 served the same purpose, though at a much slower pace. Then, drivers motored through towns, villages, and hamlets, stopping only for infrequently placed traffic control devices and, more often, errant cattle. Like many highways, Route 20 was as much a means for transportation as it was a method for diffusing commerce into the spaces between settlements. Bloomfield and Avon's locations on Routes 5 and 20 placed Roadside Craftsmen and Avon Coppersmith on a historically well-traveled road, one commercially familiar as much to farmers as entertainers. Among the latter, the upstate New York vaudeville circuit prospered thanks to numerous stops along Route 20. Besides being close and convenient to home, both villages were near Wemett's already established petroleum businesses. His oil business experience no doubt taught him what all successful capitalists know, guiding his decision for locating the craft enterprises: go where the most customers are who most want your product.[22]

BOOKENDS

Civil War monuments set in public parks are the bookends that bracket the Route 20 highway connecting Avon and East Bloomfield. Identical in height (forty-five feet) and guarded on four sides by cannon, each monument is capped with a statue of a soldier. In Elton Park, once known as the Village Square, Bloomfield's sandstone monument was erected following a $6,000 fund-raising campaign. Reportedly, its October 14, 1868 dedication was attended by three thousand people.[23] Avon's granite monument cost $4,300, was supported by a fund-raising campaign begun by citizens in 1865, and completed with taxes levied in 1874. The monument, finally dedicated on Memorial Day, 1877, was installed at what today is named Circle Park. Originally, the park was a square where cattle and sheep grazed. When Clarence Wemett developed his craft businesses, earlier-settled Avon's 1930 population (3,566) was slightly more than double that of East Bloomfield's (1,631). A significant commercial strip, including an opera hall (1876), abuts Avon's Park while Bloomfield's is commercially nearly vacant, instead surrounded by churches, an academy (1838), and a tavern (1808).

Clarence Wemett could have quickly driven the seventeen-mile distance between the two monuments, assuming good weather, moderate traffic, and few cattle crossings. Speed limits for 1930 country roads, if posted at all, were widely ignored. In contrast to densely packed urban areas where cars competed with pedestrians, horses, and trolleys, there seemed little need for such regulation in the sparsely populated country. Clipping along at thirty-five miles an hour, he would have required no navigation; it is a straight shot on Routes 5 and 20. Mostly, Wemett needed only to hold the wheels straight and the accelerator steady, as curves are few and the hills gentle.

Between the monuments were once dozens and dozens of cobblestone houses situated on farmland, like books on the highway shelf; the houses marked the road's path as much as the growth of population and the local economy. After the American Revolution, settlers migrating westward to central and western New York were slowed by the absence of natural transportation routes. Significant population growth occurred only once construction of the Erie Canal was completed in 1825. The canal carried people who began farming and established population centers, accompanied by businesses and industries conducting commerce affiliated with the crops raised. Much earlier, the Ice Age's redesign of the region's topography carved out valleys and hills. In that process, nature's bullies shoved, rolled, and twice polished stones with grinding friction and melting water. Sharp edges were rounded, rough surfaces smoothed, and the cobbles, as they became known, were liberally distributed over what later became farmers' fields. Ecological litter, they were a problem only among those who insisted upon plowing and cultivating the field that the cobbles were strewn across. Industrious frontier settlers, all requiring shelter, harvested and transformed the locally sourced (long before that phrase became a bumper sticker) materials for an architectural solution to home-building. Combined with crushed limestone for mortar, the cobbles gave rise to a new form of construction. Adapting techniques used in building the Erie Canal, craftsmen erected cobblestone homes, most in the Greek Revival style, with tapering walls of massive thickness.

Typically built between 1825 and 1860, the cobblestone structures are a nineteenth-century form of folk art, "the last generation of completely hand-built houses," and examples of sustainable architecture "created from the materials of its own site" developed well ahead of today's popular expression.[24] While estimates vary, the region once hosted more than a thousand such buildings:[25] the largest collection and perhaps greatest density of cobblestone structures in the United States. A century before Wemett launched his roadside craft enterprises, craftsmen found commercial opportunities for their craft, erecting the buildings on the farmers' fields bordering the highway connecting Avon and Bloomfield. Today, cobblestone homes are noticeable mostly by their absence; no more than a half-dozen are visibly extant in 2022 on the same stretch of highway Wemett traveled between his craft shops. Except during those months when plantings shed their foliage: only then do dwelling foundations' reveal their cobbles to attentive passersby and the early form of commercial craft. The cobblestones, once more visible than the Civil War commemorations, were the monuments documenting less destructive and more creative impulses of civilization.

Commercialism, initially serving indigenous agrarian interests, had driven development of most transportation routes. Land speculators sought to maximize profits, and farmers envisioned expanded markets. Covering distances less well accommodated by hoof or foot, transportation occurred first on natural waterways, such as Hemlock Lake, followed by man-made ones. In New York, Governor DeWitt Clinton's idea for the Erie Canal—linking the natural bodies of the Great Lakes to the Hudson River and Atlantic Ocean by means of a man-made ditch—was widely derided as a preposterous "folly" and its $7 million cost viewed as incredible. Its (and his) redemption was the extraordinarily cost-effective service to the interests of commerce beginning in 1825, and the Canal's rapid return on the state's investment. The Erie Canal irrevocably changed Clinton's "state and America's economic destiny."[26] Within a quarter century, though, traffic on the waterway began to be siphoned off by the New York Central Railroad, installed nearly parallel to it. A consolidation of nine separate lines, the New York Central was completed in 1853. Freight shifted first from turnpike roadways to the Canal; and, later, rails effectively eliminated stagecoach firms.[27] By the 1870s, railroads were the dominant, foreseeable future's established form of long-distance transportation for commercial freight as much as for human cargo. They moved merchandise farther, more efficiently, more rapidly, and less expensively than older options. One good idea yielded to a better one, and the new supplanted the old.

In their heyday, alternatives to the tracks were nearly as unthinkable as the rails had previously been to waterway transportation boosters. In addition to commercial enhancements to water routes, railroads helped foster a leisure revolution by contributing "to the expansion and democratization of vacationing";[28] Fred Harvey's chain of trackside tourist accommodations in the Southwest, begun in 1876, were among the earliest examples. The nation's westward expansion across the frontier was abetted thanks to parallel tracks that spider-webbed across the continent. History repeated itself when public allegiance shifted from tracks to pavement once highways and cars proved to be even better drivers for the leisure revolution. By 1890, the CLOSED sign was hung out on the American frontier, Frederick Jackson Turner observed. No sooner had that door swung shut, largely putting to an end what Alexis de Tocqueville earlier described as restless American westward mobility, than the advent of the modern, twentieth-century highway began prying it back open. The fingers throttling chaotic wilderness into civilized rationality belong as much to the automobile's highways as the railroad's tracks.

Railroads, coupled with the postal system, facilitated a business innovation that allowed manufacturers to expand from a provincial to a national customer base. Mail-order catalogue sales, where businesses and buyers were not simultaneously tied to proximate physical locations and where retailers were circumvented, was an initiative launched during the golden age of railroads and solidified by rural free delivery (RFD)[29] and, later, parcel post. Marketers, including Elbert Hubbard at Buffalo, New York's Larkin Soap Company, in the early 1880s recognized the economic efficiency, lower customer cost, and enhanced profitability gained through cutting out "middle" (sales) men.[30] "From factory to farm" served as one Larkin selling slogan, at once implying both an economy and a relationship between manufacturer and customer.[31] Merchandise could be sold directly to retail catalogue customers and their selections delivered by rail. The first Sears, Roebuck watch and jewelry mail-order catalogue was issued in 1887.[32]

While railroads were the first long-distance commercial shipping mechanism to begin satisfying retail customers' mail orders, postal roads made the practice practical. They provided the means for "last mile" delivery to recipient homes. Initially an appealing idea lacking the empirical means for its implementation, RFD could not be fully operational without roadways to deliver mail. Roads connected extant natural and man-made routes. RFD's 1896 inauguration was one impetus hastening the demand for semimaintained if not paved roadways for personalized transportation. Both the number of routes and miles RFD covered grew steadily.[33] Railroads and postal authorities found their interests aligned with a growing Good Roads movement. Despite the nation's transition from a rural, agrarian economy to an urban, industrial one by the turn of the century, most road construction took place outside the cities. Better roads, railroaders thought, were a way to attract more business[34] by bringing freight to their tracks; rural roadways also ensured the post office's ability to deliver mail to its final destination.

Post-hoc stories about the "logic" behind the evolution of roads crisscrossing the countryside are easily invented. Typically, they feature four-legged critters yielding their worn-smooth paths to two-leggers much the same way two-wheelers later relented to an onslaught by four-wheelers—quietly. As though the former acquiesced to an inevitable manifest destiny of the latter. Foot-worn trails later made road planning a little less difficult, as a popular path of least resistance was already mapped.

Pre-twentieth-century road building was largely conducted by private enterprise—such as John Hill's Hemlock toll road—for personal profit and convenience and largely without interference or intrusion by local, state, or federal authorities. While the "mania" that produced plank roads lasted longer than the one encouraging paving with sawdust, most roadways remained "in miserable condition" at the end of the nineteenth century.[35]

Emerging in the late nineteenth century was an organization with a colorful name interlaced with an advocacy movement carrying a self-explanatory one—the League of American Wheelmen and "Good Roads": both would have a significant impact on modern transportation history. "Good Roads" was popularized beginning in 1878 by Albert Augustus Pope, a shoe form manufacturer who introduced a "safety bicycle," one of several alternatives to high-wheel bikes. And Pope's enlightened self-interest in conjunction with cycling clubs organized under the umbrella of the League of American Wheelmen advanced their Good Roads movement to legislative agendas. Founded in 1880, the League's advocacy for road improvement made little legislative progress during its first fifteen years, in large part because bicycles were a luxury product (costing $150 to $200), and the benefit would go to so few.[36] With an increasingly sizeable cohort of automobile drivers, and broader appreciation for the benefits accruing to farmers, after the turn of the century that began to change. By 1913, there were "more than fifty large [sized] 'Good Roads' associations and at least five hundred smaller ones" advocating their singular cause.[37] Good Roads proponents were not restricted to the wealthy membership of the League of American Wheelmen. Construction firms and their suppliers; real estate speculators and land developers; and, as the market for automobiles expanded, auto manufacturers and their suppliers—including the petroleum industry—all held self-serving interest in improving and improved roadways.[38] Unsurprisingly, if not ironically, railroads were complicit in the Good Roads movement that later led to their insolvency. In 1901, railroads cooperatively supplied the Good Roads trains that crisscrossed the nation advocating for improved and federalized roadways under the sponsorship of the National Good Roads Association.[39]

Spurred as much by military needs to transport men and materiel for the World War I effort as by commercial interests to connect sparsely settled farming communities to one another, Woodrow Wilson signed the first Federal-Aid Road Act into law in 1916. The Act arrived eight years after Henry Ford introduced the Model T. A sturdy, "democratic machine . . . for the great multitude," the Model T was designed to travel over the pervasively difficult terrain of contemporary roads.[40] At the time, little more than 10 percent of American roads could be even charitably described as "surfaced."[41] The Act, signaling the emergence of "highway federalism,"[42] established a new federal Bureau of Public Roads. The Bureau's initial $75 million budget, spread over five years, funded state-initiated road construction and improvement projects; states would share the construction costs and maintain the completed roads.[43]

Progress, though, was not always rapid; indeed, some thought it almost glacial. Municipalities seeking redress to transportation problems had managed improvements with gravel, shell, or oil to only 7 percent of roadway surfaces by 1904.[44] By 1920, only 13 percent of nonurban highways were hard surfaced. The figure rose to 23 percent by 1930, but most highways remained "untreated dirt roads or overgrown two-tracks."[45] The 1916 Act succeeded insofar as all states had some form of sponsored road construction, and the 1921 Highway Act helped promote a construction boom.[46] Still, by 1925, "travel by auto, at best, could be an adventure and, at worst, a harrowing experience."[47] Nonetheless, the number of US highway miles increased by 60 percent from two million miles of "rural roads" in 1904 to more than three million in 1930, along with a whopping 330 percent increase in loosely (sometimes generously) defined surfaced roads.[48] Fifteen million Model T's were sold by the time their production ended in the late 1920s; comparatively, ten million bicycles were sold in the 1890s. Once good roads were built, the high-riding Model T became an anachronism. Twentieth-century legislation married to nineteenth-century advocacy by bicyclists did for personal mobility and (unintentionally for) commerce in the consumption of Crafts what the communications revolution beginning in the third quarter of the twentieth century did for information: a transformation in behaviors and habits, ways of viewing the world, and understanding how things should "work."

As several writers note, travel routes anticipate their use rather than answer to some current articulated need: roadways were built "in advance of, not in response to, the areas they served."[49] Road building of nearly any sort, and especially early twentieth-century highway building, was a gamble on the future rather than satisfaction for the present. Well before "If you build it, they will come" found its way into a Hollywood script, whether toll road or free, highways were built, drivers later appeared, and utility was found. While much has justifiably been made of the profoundly broad effects of the introduction of automobiles,[50] "the miracle," Susan Croce Kelly wrote, "was not the automobile." It was the highway "that gave automobiles someplace to go"[51] and, we add, the path to get there.

The advent of the highway and the automobile broke the tyranny of railroads. Perhaps this is too strong a metaphor, as few may have felt oppressed at a time when there were few alternatives to railroads. But undeniably, railroads prescribed "the same restrictions on the enterprise of travel as [the rigid efficiency of assembly line] Taylorism imposed on the process of work."[52] The flexibility and freedom of autonomous auto-mobility delivered emancipation from trackside crowds and the myriad conformities demanded by railroading: predetermined departure times to fixed destinations, Pullman reservations, and "standard time." If train travel encouraged cocooned, quiet meditation and reflection, automobility animated deliberation through interaction and appreciation for diversity (above variety) of experience. The highway was a form of firsthand empir-icism, actively engaging all the senses. Being untethered from the tracks meant being unscheduled and spontaneous, allowing one to follow natural rhythms instead of those artificially imposed.

Twentieth-century highways quickly proved their hyperlocal superi-ority to nineteenth-century railroads and canals for some kinds of travel and commerce. There, on the open road, auto-gypsies were free to set their own pace, determine their own destinations, and individually chart their preferred route to deliver themselves—including their self-delivery to such retail shops as Roadside Craftsmen and Avon Coppersmith. The roadside, Wemett recognized, was perfect for exploiting and capitalizing on the consistent traffic flows delivering customers to his shops. Connecting present to past, the federal highway system, more efficient than the nine-teenth-century canals and railroads before them, were the early twentieth century's World Wide Web. Wemett anticipated what internet pioneers later recognized: a medium for delivering customers to businesses. Highways knit together citizens, communities, and commerce, simultaneously compressing time and space. A more flawless system for bringing customers to sellers had not been invented. In fact, not until commercial broadcasting—first radio and a quarter century later, television—were customers as efficiently delivered to advertisers.[53]

❦

There was no imaginable worse time than 1929 to launch a business selling "tchotchkes" to tourists. Or, for that matter, *any* business. The

Depression plunged the United States into a deep pool of unparalleled economic calamity. But Clarence Wemett saw prosperity and profit despite the shrinking income of the not-yet-dispossessed. His Depression-era retail craft venture was an extension of his well-established business as petroleum merchant: Both catered to cars and, more precisely, their drivers and passengers. The petroleum business, though, serves a demonstrable need: automobiles require fuel. Otherwise, Wemett's craft shop initiative was counterintuitive, illogical, and, in the vernacular of a slightly later period, just plain cockamamie. His new business would satisfy the unmeasured, impetuous desires of transient drivers with the ambitiously optimistic, long-range intention of building a customer base for trinkets and travel mementos. And although local customers would not be shunned, little effort would be expended seducing them. Moreover, and every bit as ridiculous, customer recidivism and brand loyalty were neither expected nor sought: mostly, theirs would be a one-and-done relationship. Topping off the carnival of absurdity was the sales venue to house his craft shop: a derelict, hundred-year-old church located in a remote, out-of-the-way town that he had painstakingly disassembled and trucked forty miles to reconstruct in another.

If all this was not contrarian enough, as the design industry simultaneously gazed nostalgically backward to agrarian colonial times and raced imaginatively forward toward streamlined, urban-energized modernism, Wemett's business vehicle looked affectionately into its rearview mirror for inspiration. Manufacturing would involve inefficient, labor-intensive handcraftsmanship to produce discretionary merchandise in a decorative style more than a decade out of fashion. Completing the irreverent picture, his business goal was modestly grand: capture the tiniest sliver of the many, many people literally driving by the business. The key to success, apparently, was the punchline to the vaudeville joke: volume. In short, Wemett's unconventional business would offer handmade, out-of-style, discretionary goods to a small fraction of those who still had squanderable cash and sufficient leisure time to blithely automobile down a country road. The business's customers, "auto-gypsies," would be carefree, unencumbered by what that 25 percent of the desperately unemployed population simultaneously experienced. And if one such business was a good idea, then two would be better. Clearly, this was either unbridled optimism or full-on nuttiness.

COMMON CARRIERS

Twentieth-century roadway developments parallel elements of an emerging communications technology: broadcasting. Nearly as often in conversation as in policy, transportation and communications were used interchangeably through the first third of the century. Like the canals and railroads before them, highways and broadcasting were common carriers, and information was treated much like freight. The impulse to regulate each was similarly derived, and broadcasters as much as drivers chafed at restrictions on their presumed inherent freedoms: expression and trade. Regulation meant freedom was more conditional than absolute.

At first privately initiated as well as privately owned enterprises, some highways were federalized beginning in 1916. Broadcasting—more precisely, the electromagnetic spectrum—was federally regulated beginning in 1912, defined as a public resource in 1927 but privately operated under license. In each case, the need for governmental intervention was nearly identical: achieving order. The chaos across the ether mirrored that on the road. Signal interference, frequency jumping, and power boosting, in one instance, were analogous to right-of-way collisions at street intersections, vehicular-pedestrian (and horse) accidents, and failures to stay in assigned lanes, in the other. The paired symptoms had a nearly identical solution: a traffic cop to maintain orderliness, enforce turn-taking, and mete out punishment to violators.

The Radio Act of 1912 was prompted by the *Titanic*'s spectacular disaster on another transportation route: the sea. The loss of lives might have been averted by an awake radio operator. The federal government exerted its authority over, especially, technical aspects of the medium. The Act's implementation and enforcement were assigned to the Secretary of Commerce and Labor. The 1916 Federal-Aid Road Act mandated states to administer federal grants "in accordance with technical regulations and congressionally legislated formulas" for road planning and construction.[54] Another parallel between federalizing highways and broadcasting is geographic coverage. Roadways connected the nation well before broadcasting. Beginning with the Radio Act of 1927, some broadcasters were licensed with signal power capable of (more or less) national or regional service, and others served more localized geographic areas. Tying the two transportation threads together was Herbert Hoover, who began his stint as secretary of commerce in 1920, overseeing radio and hosting two national conferences on street traffic.

Like highways, media innovations had a profound and widespread social impact.[55] One further parallel between highways and communications technologies is especially resonant: liberation, personalization, autonomy. Roads and cars did for citizens' travel at the beginning of the twentieth century what the VCR and later the internet did for communication content seekers at century end: what, where, when, and how were steered by the individual instead of some external entity such as the content's distributor. With all this freedom, the problem roadside entrepreneurs had to solve was how to arrest consumers' independent forward motion and persuade them to stop at the place the entrepreneur built specifically for the entrepreneur's own benefit. "See-it-made" was the hook Wemett dangled before drivers, luring them to halt their journey and discover his shops. Anticipating late twentieth-century innovations in digital communications, his two craft businesses relied on large numbers of potential customers in order to find financial satisfaction by persuading a small fraction to become buyers. The tyranny of the railroad or boat schedule—where it determines when and where passengers go—was overturned by the autonomy of the auto. Public liberation in the century's first quarter is replicated in the third.

2

See-It-Made

Accompanying settlers' westward push across New York State were those whose interest was as much in cultivating the soul as the soil. Mac Nelson's history of Route 20[1] documents an extraordinary collection of religious, quasi-religious, and utopian-socialist colonies that formed alongside and nearby the road in New York. Among them the earliest and today perhaps best known were the Shakers. The United Society of Believers in Christ's Second Coming was formed in the late eighteenth century with locations in such Albany-area towns as Watervliet, Niskayuna, and Mount Lebanon. These communal farmers generated revenue with sales of their seeds and herbs. More closely affiliated with Bloomfield Pottery's product, though distantly located at the other end of the state near Woodstock, was Jane Byrd McCall and Ralph Radcliffe Whitehead's Byrdcliffe Colony and founded in 1902. There, unlike in Bloomfield, handcraftsmanship was viewed as salvation from the uniformity and standardization introduced by industrialization. As though anticipating both Wemett's Roadside Craftsmen and the spirit of the 1969 music festival, the artists in residence at Byrdcliffe produced and sold art and handcrafted metalwork, ceramics, and furniture.[2]

Though devout, Wemett appears to have had no interest in proselytizing. Nor is there evidence to suggest he possessed any particular talent for any craft,[3] left-leaning politics, or the sometimes-squishy romanticism associated with either. Instead, Wemett saw craft as a business amenable to being profitably monetized. Also, significantly, craft business could be made symbiotic with his growing gasoline network. Craft shops would exploit opportunities to reach into travelers' pockets as they drove by or, better still, stopped to refill their tanks. Breaking with most preindustrialist businessmen's sensible and conventional prejudice toward localism, Wemett recognized the endlessly replenishing virtue associated with capturing over and over a fraction of the steady and increasingly deep stream of potential one-time customers flowing past his businesses. Of course, motorists stopped at gas stations because they had to; gift shop stops were purely discretionary.

Migration South to North

Inspiration for Wemett's new industry, enthusiastic reporters indicated, came from his 1929 motor trip to Florida. As highways to southern states opened in the second decade of the twentieth century, "tin can tourists" from the north began making their way to exotic, palm-populated Florida.[4] No details of his trip are known. We have to imagine it. It would not have been a short journey, probably no fewer than eleven hundred miles. That would have been four or maybe five days' travel assuming diligent driving; longer, of course, if taken at a more leisurely pace. Plans for sophisticated, modern highways such as the Skyline Drive and Blue Ridge Parkway through the Appalachians were formulated in 1925 though were not realized until the early 1930s. Cruising south at thirty-five miles an hour on irregularly, unpredictably maintained highways, he would have had to climb and descend fairly steep hills and a few mountains. Neither roads nor vehicles possessed the comforts, conveniences, and necessities we today expect. Accommodations and services—as much for man as machine—would have been spotty.

While on the road, Wemett became "possessed with the idea of 'See-it-made'" when he observed potter Guy Daugherty at the kick wheel demonstrating hand-thrown pottery making,[5] probably in Bethune, South Carolina. Wemett acted quickly on the inspiration, forming his own Bloomfield Pottery the very same year.[6] He not only poached the idea but also its leading actor.[7] Early reports about the Bloomfield Pottery pridefully assert the backward, almost antimodern nature of the operation—along with the "see-it-made" appeal—as the magnet for visitors.[8] Amy H. Croughton, columnist for Rochester's afternoon newspaper, *Times-Union*, described it this way: "The burning of the Bloomfield pottery is done in a primitive brick kiln in which two-foot logs are burned. Both the kiln and the primitive clay-mixer, which is operated by a horse attached to the end of a long beam, are built in the open and their operation add to the interest of a visit to the pottery."[9]

Either nostalgia for days gone by remained reporters' selling point to their editors, or little improvement and modernization at Bloomfield had occurred by 1935. Then, Eleanor Chester's article, for the Rochester morning newspaper, the *Democrat and Chronicle*, echoes the rustic theme earlier expressed by Croughton and is titled, "Turning Back History to the Day When Horsepower Was Just That."[10] The largest of the four photographs accompanying Chester's story depicts "the power of the flesh and blood horse" that the image's caption describes as pulling "the shaft that operates machinery to grind clay for pottery works." The article underscored the contrast between modern and ancient: "Even though high powered cars stream past the roadside shop all day long and electricity does the work of the villagers, as in cities, the craft shop spurns modern machinery for primitive methods." Chester concludes her description of the Roadside "co-operative" and her thumbnail biographies of its artists by explicitly calling out mythic, preindustrial virtues: "These are students and craftsmen who take all the time with the work that guild craftsmen of medieval times devoted to making things before power machinery was dreamed of."

The youngest son of Roadside's woodworker remembers the pottery operation similarly to Croughton and Chester, though less dramatically.[11] However, his record of the clay preparation and firing location places it behind the building and out of the view of passing motorists:

> In the rear (north) of the building was a horse-powered clay pug mixer. Special clay, shipped in from somewhere, and water were put in the barrel of the mixer and the mixer blades were turned by a horse going in a circle. After the clay was mixed it was cut into appropriate chunks for making whatever the potter was doing that day [beneath a covered pavilion at the south westside-front of the building]. After the piece was turned on the potter's wheel and dried, the pieces were dipped into a bath of glaze, let dry and put into the kiln. The gas fired kiln was on the west side of the building. As I recall the kiln was about eight feet by ten feet and about six feet tall [and] was protected by a roof.

The appeal to "see-it-made" that first drew Wemett's attention was implemented at Roadside from the start. Though records do not exist, Bloomfield

Pottery probably operated only seasonally, from 1929 to 1934. Wintry weather would have curtailed the outdoor demonstrations, of course, not to mention traffic in front of the buildings. And the Roadside Craftsmen's preferences, especially Guy Daugherty's, could have been accommodated by an understanding owner. The pottery's original venue was two small, one-story houses next door to Wemett's gas station and under makeshift structural shelters later described as pavilions. Not until 1935, when Roadside Craftsmen had its permanent structure in place and expanded its offerings to include wood and textiles did the enterprise take on the trappings of a tourist attraction: "The building was about thirty feet from Routes 5 & 20 with a gravel parking area between. The potter's and the woodworker's gazebos were [at] either end of the parking lot about fifteen feet from the road. During the summer, especially on Saturday[s] and Sundays, Homer [Bullock, woodworker] and Guy [Daugherty, potter] would do their work in the gazebos with potential customers and the merely curious watching. Hopefully they would then find their way into the sales room."[12]

Tin Can Gypsying

Automobility's introduction at the beginning of the twentieth century coincided with broadening interests in out-of-home leisure pursuits, including tourism and family vacations.[13] By the time Wemett introduced Roadside Craftsmen in 1929, forty-five million Americans—more than a third of the population—took auto vacation trips.[14] Although Wemett's onset-of-the-Depression timing for launching his craft enterprise was less than propitious, his idea was prescient. This was later documented by a massive study commissioned in 1929 by President Herbert Hoover, tracking changing social trends in the United States during the first three decades of the twentieth century.[15] Wemett could not have known the study's results when he initiated Roadside Craftsmen, as they were not reported until 1933. But he would have read journalistic reports on the broad topics under study by the president's researchers.

The press stories were contemporaneously but separately published in newspapers and popular magazines and in such specialty periodicals as *National Petroleum News*, a trade publication targeted to petroleum vendors, including Wemett. The social trends studies would later confirm scientifically many of the earlier anecdotal, impressionistic journalistic reports. Both corroborated the soundness of Wemett's business idea. So rapid was diffusion of the newfound pleasure of auto touring that covering it became a journalistic "beat" across a range of automobile-interest (*Motor Camper and Tourist*) as well as general circulation magazines including *Sunset, Outlook, Outing, Munsey's, Popular Science*, and *Popular Mechanics*. Among the stories percolating in mass circulation publications was an innovation named "autocamping": A first-quarter twentieth-century version of the early twenty-first century's "glamping," but without the "glam."

Almost immediately following popular adoption of the car and developing organically, autocamps served the overnight lodging needs of "gypsying" tourists. Distant predecessors to the motel, which did not reach maturity until after World War II, these less-than-formal rest stops for auto tourists were thrifty substitutes for city hotels and a (short) step up in sheltered convenience from pitching a tent in a farmer's field next to the highway. As early as 1921, *Petroleum News* reported service stations offering free camping "to show their appreciation of the patronage of the overland tourists."[16] Peoples Oil Company did exactly that at four of its Georgia stations located along the Dixie Highway, a road stretching from northern Michigan to Miami. Thanks to the symbiosis of gas station and campground, Peoples Oil experienced financial success with enhanced sales to autocampers at their gas pumps. By decade's end, and no longer a novelty, oil companies overtly urged their retailers to build up-to-date overnight cottages adjacent to their service stations.[17] Travel writer Elon Jessup's *The Motor Camping Book*, published in 1921, was followed within two years by two related titles.[18] The travails of cross-country motor trips, including overnight accommodations, often little more than diaries, were published by Gladding as a Lincoln Highway adventure and, less cheerfully, by Massey as "it might have been worse."[19]

Ingenuity has few boundaries and many imitators. Municipalities saw a local economic benefit to accommodating—often without a fee—the increasing number of travelers on their public grounds. Tourists who stopped and stayed at municipal auto-campgrounds were likely to leave money behind at the town's restaurants and shops. The Denver, Colorado Tourist Bureau placed a sizeable display ad in the April 1921 *Chicago Daily Tribune* touting its "FREE AutoCamp" [*sic*] for motorists and boasting about its $250,000 cost.[20] By the end of the 1920s, roadside cottages renting on a daily (and weekly) basis began to encroach upon free or modest-fee municipal autocamps. Operated by private entrepreneurs, tourist cabin courts were little more than wood frame shacks. Free-standing and clustered together, each was not much wider than the cars parked before them. Cabins afforded a single sleeping room; toilets and showers were usually shared facilities. In Avon, the Twin Swans Motel began as nineteen cottages located next door to Avon Coppersmith. In Canandaigua, farther east, Dibble's Lake Shore Station and Cabins and Birx Motor Court were both located on Routes 5 and 20. In between, on the same highway in East Bloomfield, Culver's Cabins featured steam-heated rooms with private baths and a Mrs. Morton also operated a tourist cabin court.[21] What began as a "squatter encampment," autocamps became a public institution and evolved into a private business.[22]

Between 1900 and 1931, the number of horseless carriages grew from 8,000 to almost twenty-six million.[23] By the mid-1920s, prices for new autos had dropped, installment purchasing became common, and a secondhand market for them emerged. Tourism grew as both discretionary income and the number of leisure hours increased dramatically between 1900 and the late 1920s. Together, these factors prompted an "American wanderlust" that produced more than $3.3 billion in tourist business to roadside communities by 1927, up from $2.5 billion just two years earlier.[24] Statistical findings in the social trends studies were as formidable and authoritative as the journalists' rhetorical flourishes were colorful. As quick as they were to begin covering a new beat, and as a way to further legitimize the specialty, journalists were equally quick to give the new form of long-distance tourist and tourism with catchy, evocative, and memorable labels: auto tramp, auto gypsy, roadside gypsying, motor gypsies, motor hobo, motor hoboing, motor vagabond, auto vagabond, vagabonding. Many terms suggested a mix of something exotic and slightly risqué, occasionally bordering on the shady side of legality. Even the FBI's widely known director, J. Edgar Hoover, weighed in to affirm potential roadside dangers.[25] Plopped into a cover headline, the names functioned like billboards, drawing readers to the story and the publication carrying them.[26]

Dubbed "a vacation alternative for the relatively comfortable middle classes," autocamping released travelers from "the monopolistic rail-hotel complex."[27] Contemporaneous writers rhapsodized at length about the wonders and rewards of auto touring. Reading them today, some reports seem almost a first draft for lyrics to Roger Miller's 1964 hit song, "King of the Road."[28] Often, perhaps predictably, the car is favorably contrasted with the confining restrictions of mindless rail travel. Even such automobiling hardships as flat tires and engine repairs requiring a mechanic's knowledge were presented as romanticized opportunities for engagement with the land and friendships with invariably selfless, helpful locals. Adversity built character; train travel was a sign of softness. The "Flivverists" (Model T owners) and their auto touring, reports suggested, were exemplars of American progress.

Automobiling knit together the distant spaces, places, and people of the United States. The parallel between mythic nineteenth-century frontierism and early twentieth-century road gypsying were proclaimed by journalists' reports. Motor touring motives ranged from family reunions among the lower classes to vacationers on holiday among the middle and upper classes. Belasco's history of the auto tourist describes how the more casual trespassing, tent-pitching approach to motor-hoboing gave way to inexpensive, democratic melting pots of organized autocamps. The melting pot, though, was not without its drawbacks. For instance, a 1922 report indicated the Norwich, New York autocamp began receiving lodger complaints within one week of opening. Some campers were obliged to move after being subjected to the "vile and indecent language" of unruly, obnoxious boys at the camp's swimming hole.[29] "Motor hobo" yielded to "Tourist camper" by 1927, nearly simultaneously with the plain Model T's replacement by more luxurious sedans. "Tin Can Tourists," as they were sometimes known, was an expression at once describing what they ate from and what they drove in; over time, the expression morphed from sweetly sentimental to one of disparagement. The autocamp began losing its allure and customers at about the same time Roadside Craftsmen entered the tourist trade, when the practice and reputation of auto touring began moving upscale.

Beginning in the twentieth century, leisure took on a greater and, paradoxically, a more productively meaningful association beyond simply "time off." Since, as one wag observed, if "time off" was the only criterion, then the unemployed possessed considerable leisure—though they would not recognize it as such. Notions of leisure as both a temporal unit and a behavioral activity were subsidiary to a newer and more significant interpretation: recognition for the rejuvenating power of recreation, including its wholesome association with progressive reform that together helped further democratize the concept. Moreover, there may have been a Theodore Roosevelt–like sense that inhabiting the great outdoors—albeit above four wheels—was antidote for or respite from the corrupting, stifling influences of metropolitanism identified by the social trends studies. Densely populated urban areas were fertile ground for such commercial (and popular) recreations as movies, billiard halls, and saloons; the latter two examples were inhospitable places segregated by sex, age, and income. Travel and camping, on the other hand, were democratic and family friendly, like movies, and offered the promises of revitalization and self-renewal.

The beginning of the twentieth century also coincided with the socioeconomic emergence of a consumer culture challenging Victorian mores of abstinence and moderation. Spending became valued over thriftiness and indulgence took the place of restraint.[30] Vacations were a novelty for most at the turn of the century. Wider public adoption required the economic ability and the desire to travel, both coupled with the time to do so. By the 1920s, financial power matched psychic desire.[31] During the century's first three decades, people experienced real gains in personal time and discretionary income.[32] The US population grew by forty-seven million between 1900 and 1930, nearly two-thirds as much as it had in the 125 years prior to 1900; most of the growth occurred in urban areas.[33] "A widespread travel psychology" took hold, thanks to the automobile, accompanied by "extensive use" of public highways and a tourist business that "swelled."[34]

Even in the midst of the Depression, sociologist Robert Lynd noted, the growth of consumer culture with expenditures on radios, cars, and vacation travel led the way and was supported by installment purchasing.[35] Weinberger's 1937 report showed that 85 percent of vacation travel in 1935 was by car and that automobile touring remained stable.[36] Auto travel expenditures were greater than that of any other form of amusement and double those for motion pictures between 1929 and 1935. Roadside businesses—including Wemett's—sprouted in anticipation of an increasingly mobile group of leisure travelers. Rural retail outlets grew more than 40 percent between 1910 and 1930;[37] one writer later claimed 110,000 roadside stores were in operation by 1931.[38] The commercialization of roadsides with advertising occurred rapidly. So much so that by the end of the 1920s it was identified as a "blight." In the extreme, various highway and automobile associations took to striking protest bonfires fueled by retailers' advertising signs.[39] Despite the drawbacks, Wemett recognized and was bold enough to act for mutual advantage at the intersection of the highway, automobile, and roadside retailing.

Like members of the growing outdoor advertising industry, Wemett discerned that highway development would be followed by similar expansions alongside the roadways. Indeed, roadside commerce had commenced much earlier and in about the space of a gnat's eyelash following the introduction of roads themselves. Val Hart's early, conversational work,

The Story of American Roads, offers the example of late eighteenth-century capitalism along the Natchez Trace. Little more than a wilderness path running between Natchez, Mississippi, and Nashville, Tennessee, "rude taverns, called 'stands,'" appeared in short order.[40] Likewise, road development typically was followed by premodern versions of the gas station: stagecoach stops and blacksmiths. Twentieth-century auto tourists required service industries for their machines as much as for themselves: gas stations and restaurants for fuel, places for temporary residence, and recreation for "distraction." Filling stations located outside of urban areas, and the distribution systems necessary to support them, catered to the needs of casual motorists. Though highway business in 1920 was still a novelty, by 1930 "people had begun to find out."[41] Early twentieth-century roadside entrepreneurs were "hard-pressed farmers with highway frontage [who] found tourists a better summer crop than corn or wheat."[42] Soon, populating the highway's shoulders were businesses of every kind, or at least every kind that might serve the interests of those who passed them and could be tempted to stop.

Cafés and diners, trading posts and souvenir shops, and "museums" displaying natural and supernatural wonders cluttered the roadside. One writer characterized the 1920s roadside commercial scene as a "tawdry bazaar" another as "brazen commercialism and tacky aesthetics."[43] More gently, Gudis described businessmen such as Wemett as entrepreneurs who turned "open countryside into commercial byways and business streets."[44] Kelly reports one family sold homemade baskets and furniture from their roadside stand, but "it took the advent of the automobile, highway pavement, and the American tourist to turn [their crafts] into a way of making a living."[45] The business press reported widely on the frequently colorful, entrepreneurial strength of roadside retailing, a "highly competitive, ever-changing new industry."[46] Catering to the itinerant were "tourist trap" craft stores, purporting to offer homegrown goods. In the Southwest, along Route 66,[47] Native American craftsmen sold their pottery, jewelry, carpets, and baskets to appreciative tourists wishing to experience the "authentic" West as well as to document the experience for the benefit of their neighbors. Thanks to roadside commerce, tourists could bring a little bit of their travels home with them—mementos and souvenirs, empirical evidence of their journeys—much the way visitors attending nineteenth-century fairs and expositions did previously. MacCannell suggests modern society identifies its triumph over the premodern by transforming premodern artifacts into tourist attractions that confirm a belief in progress.[48]

The twentieth century ushered in alternatives and additions to individualized, noncommercial leisure—hunting and fishing, making music, and playing games[49]—with the emergence of such organized and mediated commercial leisure activities as movies, sound recordings, and radio. Unlike the mediated industries and their strain toward vertical integration and oligopoly, there were few such trade impulses or restrictions in the nascent travel-highway marketplace. There, mom-and-pop retailing remained dominant, and standardization by manufacturing multiples was eschewed in favor of unique, custom-crafted one-offs—precisely Wemett's business. Also, roadside commerce, unlike some media, mostly avoided the scrutiny of vice crusaders and the arched eyebrows of morality monitors. Movies, for instance, as reported by industry insider and the medium's early historian Terry Ramsaye, practically from their first appearance, ran a regulatory gauntlet ranging from civic protest to the 1915 Supreme Court decision denying them First Amendment protection and making them vulnerable to threats of federal regulation.[50] For roadside entrepreneurs, about the only comparable civic concern was murmuring suspicion about illicit behaviors by unmarried couples inside tourist cabins.

The automobile's significance persisted from boom times in the early 1920s through the hard times of the Depression. Things were so good, many reports suggested, that auto touring, like the movie industry, seemed "Depression-proof." They were not. By the mid-1930s, both industries noticeably constricted. As before with the 1929 founding of Roadside Craftsmen, just when things looked most dismal, Wemett opened his second craft shop, Avon Coppersmith. But this may not have been as contrarian as just suggested. Instead, perhaps Roadside's initial spark had been sufficiently fanned by the breeze of commercial success to sustain itself through an economic stillness that settled in later. Recreational travel rebounded somewhat in 1940–41[51] followed by curtailment of pleasure driving due to gasoline rationing for the eastern US beginning in May 1942 as part of the war effort.

3

Sheltered Space

One of the earliest and lengthiest reports about Roadside Craftsmen, published in 1932, begins: "Over on Route 20, a short distance this side of East Bloomfield, a new industry has been developed—new to this section, but generations old in the southland where it is very extensively carried on."[1] Columnist Amy Croughton, for one, thought favorably of the concept, pointing out to her *Rochester Times-Union* readers the venue's unique aspects and underscoring (without mentioning) its inspiration: "While the district about Rochester has innumerable gift shops, the Bloomfield Pottery, the Patchen [*sic*] basket studio at Patchenville [*sic*], and the wrought-iron forge of George C. Brown [on] Spring Street, Brockport, are the only places we know of where one can watch the operations of these arts going on."[2] Probably unknown to Croughton (and, likely, most others, including her readers and Wemett), was a similar, sympathetic operation running chronologically nearly parallel to Roadside Craftsmen and located downstate: Putnam County Products. Replicating a country craft market in the country might be a quaintly attractive idea, even if it is redundant. Importing the roadside-countryside craft market from the southern United States to an area where below-freezing temperatures and snowfalls occur with great regularity (and for four months a year) was a less-than-practical idea. The original physical setup for Roadside Craftsmen, modeled on the southern venues that initially inspired Wemett, transferred poorly to upstate New York. As quickly became obvious, something a bit less casual, more permanent, and preferably heated, made more sense.

DOWNSTATE AND UPSTATE

Clarence Wemett's idea for Roadside Craftsmen was not novel, as he likely would acknowledge. After all, Wemett's motor trip to Florida led to his exposure to roadside ceramist Guy Daugherty and the "see-it-made" idea that he re-created in upstate New York, importing Daugherty as his "star" craftsman. Nor was Wemett alone in transforming Craft from a personal to a public product. The Southern Mountain (later "Highland") Handicraft Guild, for instance, created in 1930, originally allied eight mission schools and craft centers, helping Appalachian craftsmen "meet the demands involved in producing items for the consumer public."[3] The Berea (Kentucky) Student Craft Industries helped transform objects made for family use or barter into commercial goods more widely available.

Downstate, and near Garrison, New York, an effort similar to Wemett's but with philanthropic intentions coincidentally also began in 1929, the same year as Roadside Craftsmen. Putnam County Products was initiated as a market outlet and source of income for the poor: a way to help "people of small means and capital," its founder, Aileen Osborn Vanderbilt Webb wrote.[4] Aileen Webb (1892–1979) was from a wealthy family of art patrons who rubbed shoulders with similarly positioned "Hudson River Families." In 1912, she married Vanderbilt Webb, great-grandson of railroad and shipping baron Cornelius "Commodore" Vanderbilt. Thanks to a tireless lifetime effort, Webb's name is virtually synonymous with the professional-ization of Craft, raising its and the craftsman's profile and status. The "Cliff Notes" version of her resume is best expressed by Braznell: On behalf of Craft, Webb "founded an organization [American Craftsman's Cooperative Council, 1939; World Crafts Council, 1964], a magazine [*Craft Horizons*, 1941], a school [School for American Craftsmen, 1943], and a museum [Museum of Contemporary Crafts, 1956]."[5]

Bearing a somewhat less-evocative and magnetic name than Roadside Craftsmen, Putnam County Products facilitated the sale of "whatever a per-son living in Putnam County would make or produce."[6] With her friends, Nancy Campbell and Ernestine Baker, Webb began Putnam County Products with low expectations about their enterprise's inventory: "We expected to be asked to sell string beans and eggs, but on the contrary there poured in objects people had made themselves. This was especially true of the women who brought their home crafts of needle and stove. Some men brought articles made in wood," Webb recalled.[7] The similarity between Webb's and Wemett's initiatives is the consumer market each was directed at. In a 1935 letter to her eldest son, Webb identified Putnam County Products as "catering to the tourist trade and the summer trade."[8] There is no evidence of any connection between Wemett and Webb or, for that matter, even awareness of one another's enterprise. In each instance, the initiative was localized and, likely, word of it pretty much remained local.

PATCHIN STUDIO

Described as an artist, painter, and teacher, Sally Nutall Patchin (1874–1958) gained regional fame for her hand-painted baskets. The "cottage industry"[9] she founded attracted the attention of celebrities such as Eleanor Roosevelt, Lily Ponds, Lowell Thomas, George Eastman, and New York Governor Herbert Lehman, who traveled to her studio to purchase them. Patchin claimed to have "stumbled onto" the work for which she became known. She and her husband wintered in Stuart, Florida. While there, in the early twentieth century, she painted and sold bamboo fans to help raise money for a public library. "As this was successful," one retrospective article, published in 1956, reported, Patchin "tried the same idea on baskets and china. She has been doing this for more than 40 years."[10]

Born in Philadelphia, Patchin studied portrait painting in Paris. After her 1902 marriage to Bert Patchin, owner of an indoor racetrack, she moved to Patchinville, just south of Wayland in Steuben County, New York. Bert built a studio for her opposite their brick home. A 1937 report bluntly notes: "One day she took stock of herself and decided that she was wasting time and money and would never become a great artist, but her hunger for color and urge to use her clever fingers soon conquered, and before many months she began to express herself through the medium of hand-painted basketry."[11]

Baskets were acquired from a Chinese vendor and shipped to Patchin twice a year.[12] Typically, her oil paintings on baskets took the form of floral arrangements accompanied by one of two birds: something like a bluebird or robin and what Patchin called a "Filly-Filloo," parrotlike and featuring a long tail, this creature was her invention.[13] To help fill customer orders, Patchin employed and taught young women to paint in her style.[14] Baskets were signed with a blue, oval paper label with silver lettering: "Patchin Studio/ Baskets/Wayland, N.Y." Today, unsigned baskets are attributed to her by the black circle or dot at the center of flowers. The interruption of World War II meant the end to Chinese imports, including baskets, and Patchin adopted new media for her art: tin, wood, and ceramics.[15] Although the spigot supplying raw materials from Asian factories was shut off and pinched Patchin's business, for domestic craftsmen—such as those at Roadside and Coppersmith—the same phenomenon reduced competition from foreign sources.[16]

The twenty-year Wayland town historian and the first member of the Steuben Historical Society, Patchin regularly corresponded with *Rochester Democrat and Chronicle* columnist Arch Merrill, who called her "Sally of the gay heart and the merry laugh" and "vivacious" when he profiled her in the newspaper's magazine section.[17] Patchin had a relationship with the furniture-manufacturing Plail family of Wayland and Woodcroftery, successor to Roadside Craftsmen. The Plails rented Patchin's Conesus Lake cottage, according to a 1910 issue of the *Wayland Register*. And many Woodcroftery products featured tole-style painting as a result of Patchin's professional relationship with John Plail Coley[18] and his mother, Honnie Plail Coley. Sally Patchin's obituary recounts a lengthy list of civic engagements from public libraries to scouting and from parent-teacher associations to a forty-two-year membership on the board of education.[19] Like many populating the present book, Patchin was a bit quirky. Her obituary reports: "A determined woman, she decided to donate the tower clock [now] on the front of the Wayland Central School building after plans for the clock were turned down by officials in Albany. She said that after her death the clock would still be there to say, 'Sally, you're still ticking.'"

Making Formal the Informal

Almost exactly one hundred years after it was erected, the Branchport, New York Baptist Church was razed, moved, and repurposed in Bloomfield. Branchport is at the tip of the shorter of the two arms (or branches) forming the Y-like shape of Keuka Lake—the "west branch," as it is known. Depending upon the route taken, Branchport is thirty to forty miles southeast of East Bloomfield. Contemporary newspaper reports indicate significant portions of the church, including the front of the building and its frame, were sold as a unit for $500 with the remainder of the structure sold as salvage.[20]

When originally built, the church was not inexpensive. Nor, of course, was the church vacant, as it had been for the three years prior to its 1934 demolition. In the late eighteenth century, the area's earliest settlers in Bluff Point and Jerusalem were without a place of worship until about 1812. Parishioners met in a log house near the Elder Elnathan Finch's home until 1822. Membership grew, and when it approached sixty, they resolved on January 29, 1834, "to build a meeting house in Branchport, said house to be 40 x 50 feet, the posts to be twenty-four feet long, and the house to have a belfry and steeple." Clarence Wemett later described in heroic language the church's construction: "Hardy pioneer workmen hewed from virgin forest the timbers . . . exercising their skill in the erection of a house of worship, . . . fashioning out of the unspoiled materials of the Creator a tangible expression of their aspirations and ideals, they must have felt not only that they were building a house in which to worship, but that their labor was in itself an act of devotion."[21] A cost ceiling of $2,000 for the structure was set. Once completed, Branchport Baptist membership rose to eighty-three, with thirty-nine people "baptized into the fellowship of the society."

A far cry from the original log structure, and now with many more members, the church's proud steeple was topped with a handsome, fish-shaped weathervane. But throughout its history, the church experienced considerable pastoral churn. Its nineteenth-century ministers "received but small salaries and were obliged to engage in manual labor to supply their wants," explained one source. The anonymous 1873 author of the church's nearly fifty-year history concludes by alluding to the ongoing problem of retaining preachers: "Branchport is a pleasant little village. The Baptists have a neat, commodious house of worship, remodeled in 1870 at an expense of over $1,800. They are a small but excellent band of brethren possessing considerable financial means and ought to have a good pastor."[22] Pastoral attrition persisted as a lamentable problem for the church into the twentieth century. A 1910 story, for instance, reports on yet another clergy change but concludes optimistically that "the Branchport Baptist church is beginning to live anew, and plans are being laid ahead that the church may take her rightful place in the community."[23]

Local newspapers covered the structure's razing. The "finishing touches" to the building's demolition occurred on September 26, 1934. The stories' predictable ledes emphasized as much (and mostly without irony) the building's centennial as its landmark status.[24] The church had disbanded in 1931 and the building sat unused. News stories dutifully identified Hemlock gasoline and hardware dealer C. E. Wemett as the buyer for the building's major parts, and Stanley McCaul of Branchport as the broker who sold the salvage lumber to a Binghamton firm. Wemett's plan, the newspapers reported, was to use the structure "for the manufacture and display of pottery." And, the stories read, "There is now an outdoor pottery plant on the same place." As though to comfort local residents and mollify past congregants, the *Elmira*

Star-Gazette wistfully noted, "The old church tower, reassembled, will be set up near the plant. The old weather vane will top it and inside will be a museum called 'The Life and History of the Branchport Church.' "[25]

The disassembled building was trucked to East Bloomfield, just east of the location where Wemett's gas station was already established. There, the old church was reerected. The reassembly was conscientious, Wemett reverently reported: "In restoring, great care has been used to replace each timber to its former position. The size and form of the building has not been altered, and original wood pins are used in fastening framework together. All the timbers were hewn and several of the beams in the structure are more than one foot square and from 40 to 50 feet in length. The doors are also from the former building, two of them being used originally in the vestibule part of the church."[26] The "museum" referenced by stories of the church's razing, though, apparently did not amount to much. The same Wemett report notes: "A few items belonging to the Baptist Society and dating back to the establishing of the church have been loaned for display there." Later reports, following a "stubborn" 1940 fire at the Roadside building, fought in a "stiff two hour battle" by local volunteers, suggest the casual informality of the "museum" by noting unspecified church records, a pewter communion set, a few pews, and long-handled collection boxes as among the artifacts of the original church.[27]

More significant and prominent was the retail display space that now occupied what was once the church parishioners' pews, "22 feet in height, with a balcony on three sides." It was "fitting," Wemett loftily remarked, "that the product of [the original craftsmen's] skill should now be used as a place where worthy craftsmen carry on the tradition of cooperation and fellowship with the Creator as they put into tangible and enduring form their ideals and dreams of beauty."[28] Roadside Craftsmen's new home offered a different form of worship for a different kind of deity for a very different congregation.

The emplacement of the Branchport structure transformed Roadside Craftsmen from an informal, outdoor venue suitable only for seasonal, fair-weather trade to one exuding permanence and presence: "There was to be a resident potter and woodworker who would prepare items for sale; they would do most of their work in the basement. In the summer, to draw in potential customers, the potter and woodworker would perform outside under gazebos along the road in front of the building. There would also be a weaver who would perform inside the display and sales room."[29] On the building's exterior, in large, block letters easily visible to drivers, its (old) name was painted: Bloomfield Pottery.

As was the case a short distance west, at Wemett's other craft shop, Avon Coppersmith, Roadside took its place alongside the heavily traveled Routes 5 and 20 and welcomed those passing by with a professional sales room displaying its products. The Roadside woodworker's son describes it:

Above the basement was the display/sales room that filled that floor except for a couple of offices. The room was well lit with several windows on both the east and west sides. The walls were plastered and painted white and the roof trusses were in view. The oak floor was highly polished. A beautiful sight, too bad I wasn't allowed to spend any time there. The wares were spread out on tables throughout the area except for one corner where the weaver had her loom and other equipment set up. The double doors on the southern end of the room lead out and down a flight of about ten steps to the parking lot in front of the building.[30]

The Roadside Craftsmen had its formal opening May 30, 1935. For many years, a sign reading OLD MEETING HOUSE hung above the entrance (see figure 3.1).[31]

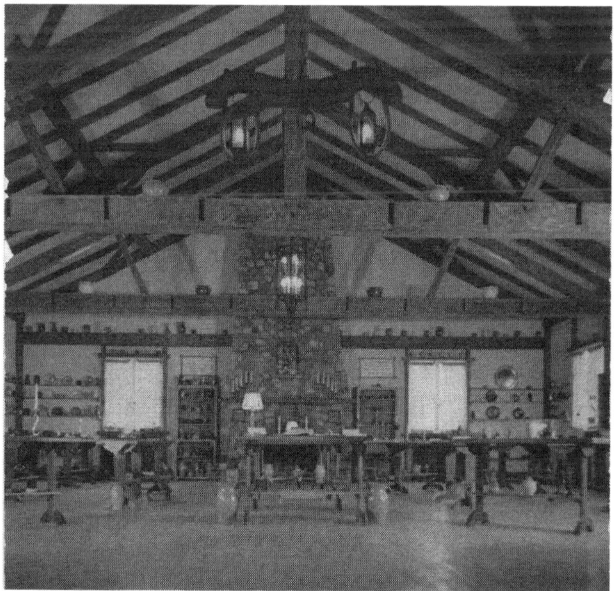

Figure 3.1. Roadside Craftsmen's interior display room. Photograph courtesy of the East Bloomfield Historical Society. Public domain.

Arts and Crafts

America's affair with highway automobiling coincided with peak interest in the Arts and Crafts movement. A form of decorative arts design popular in the United States beginning at the end of the nineteenth century, the style's boastful simplicity contrasted with the exuberant decorative excesses of the earlier Victorian period. Arguably, the greatest virtue of the Arts and Crafts aesthetic was its emphasis on restraint over flamboyance. But, in fact, the Arts and Crafts style was a logical evolution of a design trajectory set previously by the more restrained Victorian design styles of the Aesthetic and Eastlake periods beginning in the 1880s.[32]

Arts and Crafts affected a softer voice, as though objects awaited discovery rather than shouting their presence. Embellishments were displaced by plainness and surfaces were intentionally dulled instead of shined. "Harmony in color" was its more palatable way of phrasing "monochromatic." Sympathetically indebted to Shaker forms produced much earlier, Arts and Crafts furniture was compatible with rustic, hyper-natural, often bark-encased Adirondack-styled furniture. Frequently referred to—then as now—as "Mission" style,[33] furniture was most often made from abundantly available American white oak and typically was boxy and rectilinear, heavy and dark in appearance. Period ceramics were of traditional shapes, often featuring stylized and conventionalized decoration retaining sufficient representational qualities as to evoke familiarity among observers. Metalware, most often formed from base metals—commonly copper—retained the coppersmith's pronounced, bumpy hammer marks on their usually darkly colored, artificially "aged" surfaces. The evidence for hand and hammer was on the object's surface, instead of planishing it to glasslike smoothness as colonial silversmiths would have.[34]

Prominent Arts and Crafts personalities and manufacturing firms were located throughout the American Northeast as well as in such geographically dispersed places as Chicago and San Francisco. A bit of a conceit, some Arts and Crafts makers replicated the industrial factory's efficiencies on a garage-style scale. Although public and manufacturers' interest in the Arts and Crafts style and its products had faded by 1920, the movement influenced Clarence Wemett in several ways. The clearest and most direct impact of the movement was on how the products were made at his two craft enterprises and their aesthetics. A portion of the work produced at Roadside Craftsmen and much of that created at Avon Coppersmith was informed and inspired by the media, craft techniques, and design aesthetics introduced, and preferred a quarter century earlier.

BACKWARD AND FORWARD

Avon Coppersmith and Roadside Craftsmen were as skillful negotiating or eliding contemporaneous tensions between two prevailing but aesthetically incompatible decorative arts styles as they were producing their products. Bracketed by two world wars, Colonial Revival and Modernism followed and displaced Arts and Crafts. This was a post–World War I rivalry between nationalism and internationalism played out in the decorative arts arena. Their very names assert as virtues a competition between old and new, domestic and foreign, derivation versus innovation. Hints of each filtered through, occasionally emerging in the craft product designs created by the Coppersmith and Roadside.

Differences between the two styles could not have been sharper. Modernists eagerly looked forward to the urban future while Colonials gazed fondly backward at the rural past. Modernism announced its newness by name, as Colonial Revival pridefully telegraphed the opposite. At the same time, twentieth-century Colonial Revival insisted upon copying forms (e.g., lighting) previously made while modernizing (i.e., electrification) their manufacturing and use. The Colonials built "out" while Modernists built "up" with skyscrapers. Natural materials were favored by the older and manmade synthetic innovations by the newer. Industrialism was pitted against agrarianism, speed versus a slower pace, machines against handwork, sleek minimalism versus fussy ornamentation. Progress was to be resisted or welcomed, and reformation fought revolution.[35] The contrast between the two was evident as readily in the arts (painting, sculpture, film, music) as in the decorative arts.

Prompted by the Philadelphia Centennial International Exposition (1876) celebrating the nation's founding, popularization for Colonial Revival may be exemplified best by widely owned, color-tinted photographs of invented pastoral scenes and domestic interiors. Produced by Wallace Nutting, his "Colonials" depicted eighteenth-century people in period attire situated amid interior spaces populated with period furniture and decorative accessories. Furnishings originally used as props for the photographs led to their later reproduction and manufacture by Nutting himself, as well as by such other well-known manufacturers as Kittinger (Buffalo, New York), Berkey and Gay (Grand Rapids, Michigan), and even the L. & J.G. Stickley Company (Fayetteville, New York), once one of the premier Arts and Crafts furniture manufacturers. Rhoads reports ironwork in the Colonial style grew in popularity beginning in the late 1920s.[36] Several Colonial Revival iron forges were, for instance, located in New York State, including a Kingston operation named "Paul Revere Forge," after the Massachusetts patriot. The products often were in a manner compatible with at least some of those created at Roadside's Hemlock Forge.

Large-scale historical re-creations, including Henry Ford's Greenfield Village (1933, Dearborn, Michigan), the Rockefellers' Colonial Williamsburg (1935, Virginia) and, later, Electra Havemeyer Webb's Shelburne Museum (1947, Vermont),[37] added to public excitement for and access to the style. Other initiatives enhancing the Revival's prominence ranged from Eleanor Roosevelt's 1927 Val-Kill Industries (Hyde Park, New York), producing metal, weaving, and furniture, to the federal government's mid-1930s response to the persistence of the Depression's grip with the Works Progress Administration's Federal Art Project. Further spurring interest in Colonial Revival was antiques collecting, especially Americana, coupled with the "invention of antiques as aesthetic objects and their enshrinement as museum artifacts."[38] Often, collecting involved automobile drives to beat the country bushes for "discoveries." Antiques collecting took root at the turn of the century, accelerating as magazines such as *Antiques* (1922, and beginning in 1928 *The Magazine Antiques*) began publication. The Philadelphia Exposition resurrected and galvanized interest in America's past at a time of great transformation. The Daughters of the American Revolution, for instance, was founded in 1890. Fascination was expressed by restoration of structures and sites, distribution of historical records, and revival of colonial architecture. By 1909, the Walpole Society in Boston, an exclusive men's club devoted to Americana, was established.[39]

Modernism was not just foreign (albeit principally European) in origin, it was an aesthetic distinct and largely unfamiliar to Americans. Differences in the creative impulse, manufacturing methods, and aesthetic interface between Crafts and Modernism meant that integration or accommodation was more difficult than the Craft-Colonial pairing. The exacting precision and efficient duplicative qualities of Modernism's machine age were the very antithesis of idiosyncratic handcraftsmanship. Also, unlike previously fashionable decorative trends that captured the imaginations of some—Orientalism, Egyptianism, and other exotically foreign cultures—Colonial Revival and the work produced at Roadside and Coppersmith was unambiguously *home*made and *hand*made. The evidence for both was captured by their slogan: "See-it-made." There was no better, clearer, or more persuasive appeal to honesty than that. Unlike factory assembly lines, there could be no greater assurance the work produced was entirely that of a single skilled craftsman. "See-it-made" implied "judge for yourself." That Arts and Crafts remained the touchstone upon which Coppersmith and Roadside were built is testament to the style's robustness. Colonial Revival, like Arts and Crafts, appealed to a nostalgic, idealized, preindustrial domestic past: one that had largely disappeared from view only to be seen through a gauzy filter selectively omitting the labor, inconvenience, and other personal hardships dictated by the absence of the industrial machine age.

The dominant design style during Wemett's professional maturation, Arts and Crafts made its presence felt locally. Architect Frank Lloyd Wright, for instance, was active in Buffalo (Larkin Building, Darwin Martin House Complex) and, in 1908, designed his easternmost prairie-style residence for lantern merchant Edward Boynton in Rochester. Upstate New York was a magnet for Arts and Crafts enterprises, thanks to its sophisticated, modern transportation system (railroads and canals); proximity and access to the important New York City business market; and, a bit more amorphously, the "fertile environment for utopian craftsmen as evidenced by its Shaker communities and by the Oneida Community."[40] Close to Wemett's home were Mission-style furniture manufacturers, including Hubbard, Eldredge & Miller (Rochester), Honeoye Falls Furniture Company (Honeoye Falls, New York), Miller Cabinet Co. (Rochester), Plail Brothers (Wayland, New York), Majestic Furniture Company (Mexico, New York), and many others.

OLD IS NEW

Arts and Crafts scholarship, beginning with the 1972 Princeton exhibition, has now accumulated over more years than the Movement was originally favored. Often, it somberly intones Arts and Crafts as a "response" to the industrial revolution.[41] "Reform," "rejection" and "revolution" are other terms used to characterize the movement's genesis. In each case, the unmentioned referent is to something that previously existed. Gustav Stickley's first (1900) promotional brochure for his line of Arts and Crafts furniture was unimaginatively entitled "New Furniture"; the ambiguous reference pertained as much to the catalogue's temporal appearance as the novelty of the forms presented within. Describing Arts and Crafts as an "innovation" or a "novelty" insists upon uniqueness when, in fact, a kind of regressive and at least occasionally mushy pining for what previously transpired is more apt—colloquially, the "good old days."

> The aesthetic compatibility between furniture produced by Arts and Crafts proponents and those by earlier Shaker communities is exemplified by a sparseness that anticipates the twentieth-century modernist expression "less is more." The Shakers turned wood to form round structural elements, and their rigid angularity was matched by Arts and Crafts manufacturers that squared off the wood.[42] Roadside Craftsmen and Avon Coppersmith's "plagiarism" of the past was openly acknowledged, and derivation was treated as their virtue. Both Wemett craft shops footnoted what had been extracted from previous craftsmen, celebrating and promoting their strong ties to the past. Their homage to the past suggested an air of exclusivity, asserting contemporary proprietorship for it. Roadside Craftsmen overtly positioned itself as an old-fashioned Southern pottery, and the Avon Coppersmith's intimate involvement with one of the Arts and Crafts movement's high-profile craft shops, Roycroft, was likewise widely known.[43]

As a petroleum distributor, Wemett had an appreciation for nationalized products with localized distribution and retailing. Reversing the process, a more subtle source of the Arts and Crafts influence was Wemett's intention to nationalize the customer base for his locally produced craft products. Here, lessons were drawn from the intersection of manufacturing, publishing, and the persuasive industries and applied to transient groups of potential customers. Coincidentally, three of the movement's most significant manufacturing figures were clustered near Wemett and were also periodical publishers. To the east, furniture-maker Gustav Stickley (*The Craftsman*) and studio ceramist Adelaide Alsop Robineau (*Keramic Studio*) were both in Syracuse; to the west, in East Aurora, Elbert Hubbard's Roycroft began as a printing and publishing initiative (*The Philistine*, *The Fra*) and soon thereafter, a furniture and decorative arts copper manufacturer. As with mail order retailers before them, the manufacturers sought broad dissemination for their products. Their nationally distributed magazines were the vehicles for promoting the Arts and Crafts ethos as much as their work.

Concurrent with the emergence of the movement and its publications was that of the mediated persuasive professions: marketing, public relations, and advertising. At the end of the nineteenth century, publishers pioneered modern media economics: profit for periodicals was derived from advertising, rather than subscriptions or single-copy purchases. Advertising was also significant insofar as the ads, in tandem with transportation, helped liberate the marketplace from one bounded by geography; for consumers, magazines were economically accessible, thanks to advertising's underwriting. Under the promotional professionals' guidance, print media ads became less text heavy than those in the nineteenth century, and some ads incorporated photography, including those using elaborately staged settings.[44]

Persuasion professionals also became clever about positioning their advertising messages. Ward's study reveals how *The Craftsman*'s "utilization of innovative branding and product placement techniques" quietly integrated Stickley's products into otherwise advertising-free articles. A subtle form of persuasion that was "uncharacteristic of its time," product placements made shilling more palatable (or at least less objectionable) to readers when embedded in information.[45] Among the most frequently used, overtly persuasive tactics employed by advertising appearing in *The Craftsman* and *The Fra* were testimonials, emotional appeals, and coupons.[46] In fact, each publication was often a long-form advertisement for their publishers' products nested within journalistic narrative. During the Arts and Crafts period, then, transportation, communications media, and the agents of persuasion converged in the interest of commerce and the ways in which business would be conducted. These factors together served Wemett's ambition to develop craft shops catering to a mobile consumer base without expectation of recurring purchasing and largely independent of local patronage. Wemett's application, though, also leveraged the emerging wisdom of a nascent theory of media effects as limited by the persuasively more significant "power" of personal influence. His shops' products and the theory were applied to a population taking to newly paved roads in their recently purchased automobiles.

The Arts and Crafts movement's influence on Wemett's two shops was filtered through the successful businessman's pragmatic experience and without articulation. Having lived through the decorative art form's entire lifespan, his adoption of movement elements was selective, ignoring some while adapting and customizing others to fit the Colonial Revival and Modernist decorative styles discordantly favored during the post–Arts and Crafts period. Wemett conspicuously skirted embroilment in the movement's ideological didacticism and many inconsistencies. The two shops' products drew liberally from aesthetic elements of the movement: media and construction, shapes and forms, and finishes and appearances. As well, Wemett adopted a retail price structure for his products more closely aligned with the rarely achieved idealistic intentions of the movement. Although the price points for Roadside Craftsmen and Avon Coppersmith goods may not have been so low as to prompt so-called impulse purchases, the cost of most objects was reasonably accommodated by the budgets of vacationing motor tourists. Wemett capitalized on and exploited the movement's virtues while simultaneously avoiding its more obvious conceits. Rather than try to convince customers with the movement's squishy "philosophy," Roadside and Coppersmith drew customer attention to that which stood before them—the products. At each shop, the magnet to attract the public was Wemett's "see-it-made" appeal. Customers were encouraged to observe for themselves the products being made by the craftsmen making them. Originality, authenticity, and honesty were inherent to and assured by the Western New York demonstrations, even if the products created seemed familiar. There, at the shops and before their very eyes, the goods were unambiguously on display for customers' inspection, approval, and purchase consideration.

ARTS AND CRAFTS PARADOXES

Though a design movement, Arts and Crafts was also an ideology and lifestyle. There were guilds and societies, workshops, and a phalanstery. Writers drew connections between the art and the artisan and discriminated between work and labor. Manufacturers called their factories "shops" and their shops "studios." Industrial mass manufacturing and consumerism, on the one hand, existed alongside social moralism and progressive reform on the other. Ostensibly, the movement extended an Everyman appeal; but with product pricing as a proxy for understanding their anticipated customers, many products were decidedly upscale and well out of reach for most.[47] Since principles were not always practiced, the movement's self-proclaimed virtues sometimes seemed little more than slogans encasing a labyrinth of inconsistencies. Pithy but operationally murky terms intended to resonate widely, extolling its attributes: honesty, nature, and originality. The movement's honesty was often somewhat less than that: as with today's food labeling, the movement's adherence to "nature" did not mean "natural." Oak was fumed with ammonia, to which color dyes were introduced; chemically induced patinas darkened copper to present an appearance of age.

Honesty of construction, materials, and manufacture of movement objects was a widely touted feature espoused by period writers. Honesty distinguished them from factory-made goods. To unambiguously telegraph this feature to consumers, the hand of the craftsmen was evident on the products produced. Metalware exemplified this by the ball-peen hammer marks made by the metalsmith's planishing; ridges dug into the clay revealed the ceramist's fingers that shaped the medium; and exposed joinery on furniture demonstrated the cabinetmaker's skillful abilities. Such features were immodestly billboarded—on the objects themselves as well as in the frequently politicized, preachy-teachy editorial and advertising texts promoting them. The transformative, uplifting moral and social power associated with handwork's rewards accrued, first, to the craftsman and, second, were transferable to the object's purchaser. But only a small fraction of everything produced was a one-off, and few products were entirely handmade. Machines mimicked hand-hammering at Old Mission Kopperkraft, ceramics were made (and readily remade) at Teco using molds, and furniture was produced on assembly lines rivaling those of Henry Ford.

The significance of handcraftsmanship was such that some manufacturers took care to include it in their shop signatures. L. & J. G. Stickley in Fayetteville, New York, for instance, emblazoned the word "handcraft" inside the red decal depicting a cabinetmaker's wood clamp that the firm affixed to their furniture. Both Charles Limbert's (Holland and Grand Rapids, Michigan) furniture brand and Fulper Pottery's (Flemington, New Jersey) ink stamp "Vasekraft" mark show handcraftsmanship as part of each manufacturer's graphic mark. In all three instances, the products on which the marks appeared were produced at factories employing production-line processes for serial manufacturing. Edwards, among the sharpest contemporary critics, argued that affected, ostentatious displays were not always genuine indicators of handcraftsmanship. Equating "simplicity of design with handcraftsmanship and ignor[ing] its source in mechanical efficiency" reveals "a mastery of advertising copywriting [more] than a commitment to movement principles."[48] See figure 3.2.

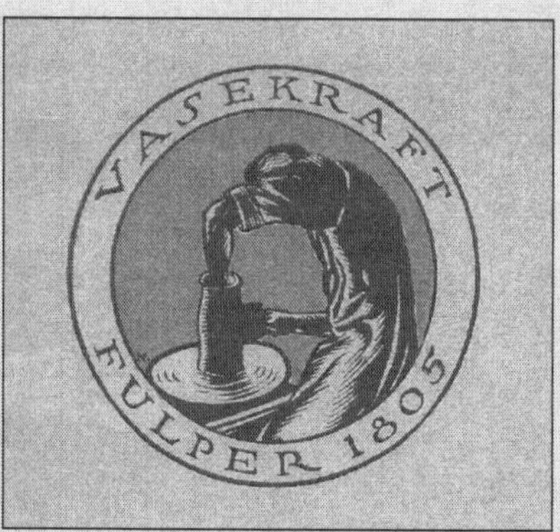

Figure 3.2. The Fulper Pottery Company's Vasekraft "Potter and His Wheel" logo used between 1909 and 1916, from the cover of the 1916 catalogue (see Kornacki, "Fulper's Marking System"). Photograph courtesy of Jon A. Kornacki. Public domain.

Interestingly, today's best-known proponent of Arts and Crafts, Gustav Stickley, did not reject the machine: "The mere question of hand work as opposed to machine work is largely superficial."[49] He anticipated an argument articulated nearly a century later. The perfection produced by machines is inspired and driven by the model first set by human craftsmen: "We set up machine technology to achieve more efficiently that which we can nevertheless and with great effort achieve without machine technology."[50] Handwork would not produce uniformity and instead yielded unpredictability for appreciation: colors, textures, and light-reflecting surfaces to prompt delightful surprise among their beholders—precisely the attributes and qualities expected of art and exactly opposite those demanded by mass manufacturing. Such irregular qualities could not be replicated by machines since they are intended to eschew such qualities in favor of uniformity and predictability. Wemett's enterprises, on the other hand, assured customers of the genuineness of his shops' handcraftsmanship with the invitation to "see-it-made."

Coy Ludwig's 1983 exhibit focused on the Arts and Crafts movement's New York State presence, including a cluster of "craft colonies" such as Byrdcliffe and Roycroft. Differentiated from the roadside enterprises later launched by Wemett, these colonies not only occupied more real estate but also typically involved more people in their operations and were sometimes infused by quasi-religious, political, and often utopian inspiration that ostensibly eschewed if not criticized the motives of capitalists. Wemett's enterprises are perhaps most closely aligned with selective elements of Elbert Hubbard's Roycroft. Today we would call Avon and Bloomfield bedroom communities of the larger city, Rochester. Beginning in 1895, East Aurora, New York was home to Roycroft. East Aurora is about the same distance from Buffalo as Avon and East Bloomfield are from Rochester. The clearest connection between the two is Avon's coppersmith, Arthur Cole, a former Roycroft metalsmith. Roadside Craftsmen began as a pottery and, likewise, Roycroft experimented with pottery. The latter exercise, however, was short-lived and its output modest.[51] But unlike Roycroft, which Hubbard grew into a sizeable, highly centralized physical community with hundreds of employees, Wemett's enterprises were spread across three small-sized locations (including the Hemlock forge), each one distant from the others, and with, at best, a dozen craftsmen. And unlike Roycroft, neither Roadside nor Coppersmith was personified by a singular, charismatic leader given as much to self-effacing humor as ponderous pronouncements. Wemett's role was decidedly offstage.

The extent to which Wemett consciously nested his enterprises in the context of (New York State) Arts and Crafts history at the time of their formation is remote. Wemett's cultivation of Arts and Crafts movement tenets for his craft operations is most accurately described as cherry-picking. Rather than harvesting, the extractions were nearly surgical in precision. Wemett's exploitation of some movement elements and his elision of others yielded the benefit of avoiding the tensions present when the movement flourished while serving modern means for merchandising.

4

Tap, Tap, Tap

Firefighters were on-site at 6:18 a.m., three minutes after the alarm sounded but too late to save the structure embodying more than a half century of history. Deliberately set, the conflagration consumed the mostly one-story building at 5480 Avon Road on Sunday, March 22, 1998. Set back one hundred feet or so from Routes 5 and 20, it was "well ablaze" and nearly fully engulfed by the time they arrived according to East Avon Fire Chief Steve Werth. Propelled by an inventory that included a substantial quantity of combustible lamp oil fuel, the fire at the Avon Coppersmith and Joy's Lamplight Shoppe had an insurmountable head start. Nonetheless, thanks to seventy-five first responders from the Henrietta, Caledonia, York, Lima, and Geneseo fire departments, "the blaze [was] under control in about 90 minutes," Chief Werth continued, though the building was a total loss. Another ninety minutes later, at about 9:30 a.m., the Livingston County coroner was called in.[1]

For almost four decades, a skilled set of hands at the Avon Coppersmith gripped, guided, and swung hammers, forming and shaping vases, bowls, and trays out of copper, brass, and pewter. Experienced, calloused hands knowledgably selected from among dozens of different hammers to carefully planish and chase objects destined for marking and celebrating happy occasions: births, weddings, and anniversaries, personal mementos and souvenirs of leisurely automobiling road trips, and prizes for yet-to-be-named winners of local art shows and charity raffles. On the cusp of the new millennium, a different set of hands, maybe with nervous or anxiety tremors, scratched a safety match across the grit held by a second. The arson was an ignominious ending to an enterprise that, for most of its life, held a singular focus: artistic craftsmanship in metal. While Avon Coppersmith's name was retained, the shop's mission for creating handcrafted metal had long been absent. A quarter century after ownership passed from craftsman to businessman, it was as though the unseemly intrusion of cutesy, mass-manufactured tchotchkes at the Coppersmith foretold their own ending.

The fire was intentional, and the lamp fuel promoted and accelerated combustion, a later news story indicated, practically guaranteeing the structure's complete destruction, despite the proximity of the fire station and the promptness of responders. When East Avon's firefighters arrived, "The owner's van was parked out front, and there was a light on in his office," Chief Werth reported. That "clued emergency personnel to expect the likelihood of a fatality," he said. Once the fire had been subdued, a firefighter on an aerial ladder looking down into the smoldering wreckage spotted a body, later identified as the building's owner, Donald E. Parker.[2] A shotgun was found nearby and arson-suicide was speculated.[3] A week after the fire, Livingston County Sheriff John M. York stated that the fire "was not the result of outside influence."[4] Death notices for Parker were unsurprisingly discreet, indicating the sixty-eight-year-old "died suddenly."[5] One journalist reported all that remained of the Coppersmith shop was the building's chimney. "Looming black and charred in the midst of the wreckage," Mark Porter wrote, "the brick chimney raises a grim, admonitory finger to passers by on Avon Road, and forms a potent symbol of the destruction of a well-loved local institution, and the passing of its owner."[6] Four years later, the vacant property on which the Avon Coppersmith once stood was purchased by the Avon American Legion and Veterans of Foreign Wars who, fittingly, built Veteran's Hall; Art Cole, the eponymous Coppersmith and original occupant from 1933 to 1970, was a World War I veteran.

Though the word "prodigy" never appears in contemporaneous accounts, characterizing Cole as such is accurate. Arthur Harold Cole was born July 20, 1898, in Colden, New York, about twenty-five miles southeast of Buffalo and ten miles southwest of East Aurora. While still a teenager, his artistic capacity was enabled by mentoring from two pairs of only somewhat more experienced but very talented hands. Cole's robust biography and, especially, his "public face," could not be fully captured by the daily press's obituaries following his death at seventy-four on January 14, 1973. Obituaries are formulaic—prestructured stories, assignments handed to cub reporters (at least in the old days) as a way to hone their writing skills. Art Cole's dutifully written obit noted all that should be noted in such texts. He died in Mercy Hospital "after a long illness" and was buried in East Aurora's Oakwood Cemetery.[7] Obits usually make mention of the deceased's selective achievements—diplomas and other distinctions. Obligingly, the *East Aurora Advertiser*[8] reported Cole's civic engagement and membership in fraternal, church, and military organizations. His role as a Roycrofter is almost invariably mentioned. But only some obits noted Cole's ownership of Avon Coppersmith—the craft, his craftsmanship, profession, and business for which he was best known during his life—without details and unintentionally assigning it equal "weight" with other life activities.[9]

Though its ending was tragic, Avon Coppersmith's beginning was hailed as a celebratory rebirth and renewal, as much for the craftsman as the craft. A brief notice in the June 22, 1933 "Local News" column of the *Livingston Republican* said as much: "Through the ages there have always been craftsmen in copper who have formed by simple hammering methods, articles of distinctive grace and beauty. There are still artisans in copper, and you will find a modern apostle of the art on Route 5 near East Avon—'The Avon Coppersmith.'" A longer version of the story, published a day earlier in the *Mount Morris Enterprise*, expands the explanation, editorializing for Depression-era readers: "Passing by, you may hear the tap, tap, tap of the hammer as this craftsman makes his forms, shapes his tools and transforms copper sheets, rod and tube into truly hand-hammered articles of use and beauty. A little more time for the joy of hand accomplishment might perhaps be a solution for some of our economic problems."[10]

Newspapers in the Genesee Valley region welcomed the Avon Coppersmith, offering prominent mention of its mid-1933 opening, though assigning its founding to the local go-getter, Clarence Wemett. The *Livonia Gazette* and the *Lima Recorder*, for instance, headlined their identical stories Clarence Wemett of Hemlock Presents 'The Avon Coppersmith' to the Public.[11] Only below does a subhead read: Arthur Cole, Craftsman in Charge, Is Experienced Artisan. A vertical photograph shows Cole posing at work with hammer in hand. The press's regional partisanship is understandable; standards such as detached, dispassionate objectivity did not become mainstream journalistic practice until after World War II. But the Coppersmith's story is almost as much an East Aurora[12] story as it is an Avon, New York story. About twenty miles southeast of Buffalo, East Aurora is bisected by US Route 20 (today 20A) and was where Art

Cole learned the lessons forming his professional life: the craft and its merchandising. Separated from Avon by fifty country miles, he and the highway link the two western New York villages (see figure 4.1).

In contrast to Avon-area newspapers, two weeks later the *East Aurora Advertiser*'s brief June 29, 1933 story is headlined, "Arthur Cole is Now 'Avon Coppersmith.'" The headline suggests reader familiarity with Cole and the story's text confirms this, beginning: "'The Avon Coppersmith,' who is none other than East Aurora's own Arthur Cole, is hammering out hand made [*sic*] copper pieces just west of the East Avon four corners, in

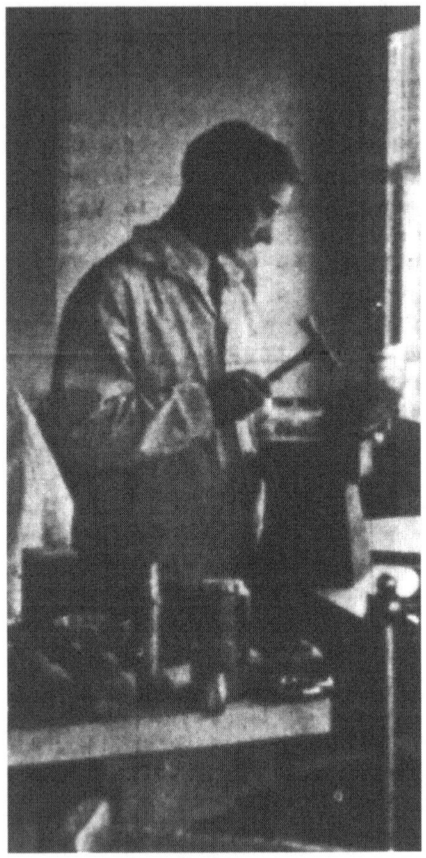

Figure 4.1. Arthur Cole, the Avon Coppersmith, pictured in "Clarence Wemett of Hemlock Presents 'The Avon Coppersmith' to the Public," *Livonia Gazette* and *Lima Record*. Photograph courtesy of the Livingston County Historian. Public domain.

a little shop right alongside the road where all who wish may come and see." Then, apparently lifting or referencing the *Livonia Gazette*'s story and photo, but reversing the order of emphasis, the *Advertiser* reports that Cole "is associated with Clarence Wemmett [*sic*] of Hemlock and plies the trade at which he has worked for some 20 years." *Advertiser* readers would have appreciated the significance of the story's lede. Some villagers were personally familiar with Cole; all residents understood the reference to "hammering out hand made copper pieces." East Aurora's most prominent enterprise since 1895 was Roycroft, led by its flamboyant entrepreneur, relentless self-promoter, and weekend socialist, Elbert Hubbard. Among Roycroft's products was an extensive line of decorative and functional hammered copper objects.

Begun in the late nineteenth century as a printing and publishing enterprise, shortly after the turn of the century Roycroft became equally well known for its artistic, hammered copper products. Bookends, unsurprisingly given their association with book publishing, were heavily featured; more than two dozen different sizes and styles were offered. From the start, Hubbard knew the enterprise could not be sustained solely by the local market. As with most publishers, Roycroft's publications—books, serials, and pamphlets—were intended for a wide, national audience, albeit one within the narrow, shallow market of the literate and bibliophiles. As well, a geographically heterogeneous consumer market was required, since some of Roycroft's pricing functioned as further market discrimination: Tooled leather-covered books, for instance, started at $10 to $30, and a price of $100 was not unusual.[13]

To transcend local boundaries, Hubbard drew on his considerable and successful marketing experience with the Larkin Soap Company, where he had been a junior partner. In charge of sales and advertising, he promoted the Buffalo firm's products through direct mail catalogue sales and premiums, thereby preserving revenue otherwise siphoned off by middlemen distributors and salesmen. Hubbard's promotional work for Larkin in the 1880s was innovative, occurring well before the emergence of the persuasive industries in the early twentieth century.[14] The monthly East Aurora publications, *The Philistine* (1895–1915), *Little Journeys* (1900–1909), and *The Fra* (1908–1917), available singly or by subscription, included inside synergistic advertisements for Roycroft's nonprint products. Periodically issued product catalogues for Roycroft's wares used subscriber addresses to form mailing lists. The sales model established at Roycroft was one the Avon Coppersmith loosely followed, adapting it for the more mobile, travel- and leisure-based economy of the second quarter of the twentieth century. But by 1933, when Avon Coppersmith opened, the once prosperous Roycroft was circling the drain for most to see.[15] As much a victim of out-of-fashion merchandise as of the Great Depression, Roycroft had struggled with viability since 1920, when the Arts and Crafts movement's drawn-out demise began. Also, in 1933, considering it had been nearly twenty years since the death of its charismatic founder, the enterprise was at best a shell of its former self: a distant if fond memory a generation removed. The grim economic reality of the Depression, though, stands in contrast to the exuberant optimism and popular embrace Roycroft enjoyed earlier.

The Anvil Chorus

"We make neither horseshoes nor coffin-nails, nor characters in Baldini's Shop," the 1910 *Roycroft Catalog* of books, leather, copper, and mottos advised readers, "but we can give you something just as good." The references therein are twofold: first, to the early, crude blacksmithing once produced by Roycroft's generically named Arts & Crafts Department—andirons, for instance. The second reference was to the follicly challenged Karl Kipp, "Fra 'Baldini,'" as Hubbard referred to him. Prior to Kipp's arrival in East Aurora, little of artistic merit was produced at Roycroft's metal shop. Now, though, the *Catalog* text continues, "So many people have been along here this Summer and have liked the Fra's bowls and lights and trays and desk-sets so well that we had to say, 'Now, don't sell that until we take its picture.'" Ever a promoter, Hubbard had little aversion to advertising puffery. But puffery aside, the *Catalog*'s following pages offer attractive photographs of Baldini's "family jewels": hammered copper objects made at Roycroft's newly named Copper Shop. "No two pieces of copper look exactly alike," readers were told, and, moreover, "therein lies the charm of the work and the beauty of the article."

In 1909, two men who began by working in Roycroft's book bindery—Karl Kipp, originally of Saratoga Springs, and Walter U. Jennings, from Weston, Massachusetts—were transferred to the Copper Shop; each would serve as a mentor to Cole. A year later, Kipp was placed in charge. A talented craftsman, his colorful background included banking as a profession, gambling as an avocation, a criminal conviction for embezzlement, federal incarceration for more than three years, and a correspondence school education in mechanical drawing. Arguably, Kipp became Roycroft's most influential metal designer and craftsman.[16] Biographically less sensational, Jennings had worked in the Boston textile industry, later becoming superintendent of finishing at a Troy, New York knitting mill. One report indicates that in 1906, "while in a bookshop, he discovered a copy of Elbert Hubbard's *Philistine*." Inspired by what he read, Jennings left the textile industry in 1908, moving with his wife Margie to East Aurora and joining the Roycrofters.[17]

Photographs in the 1910 Roycroft *Catalog* reveal considerable range and sophistication in the copper goods offered to customers. The desk sets can only be described as crude, amateurish, and homely; the Secessionist-style vases are refined, artistic, and elegant. The very heterogeneity of Roycroft's 1910 copper products prompted researchers eighty-five years later to observe this "the greatest puzzle of all." How did "the Roycroft metal workers acquire their hammering skills," they wondered. The puzzle remains unassembled, as the received history does not reveal the metalsmiths' evolution "from the home-made to the hand-crafted."[18]

Within a couple of years, Kipp left Roycroft and, with Jennings in tow, struck out on his own, moving to 636 Main Street, a few blocks east of the Roycroft campus. Advertisements for his Tookay Shop ("Two Ks," Karl Kipp), appear as early as March 1912 in *The Craftsman* and *House Beautiful* magazines. Copy below a photograph in the latter reads: "Karl Kipp at the Tookay Shop makes hand-wrought things of beauty and lasting worth for a few discriminating people." Interestingly, and likely intentionally, Kipp's *House* ad is placed amid other advertisements for "rare and genuine antiques" and art galleries. Taking after his former boss, Kipp did not shun puffery or publicity. Tookay was spotlighted in a lengthy article profiling East Aurora. Published in the *Christian Science Monitor*, the article's sub-headline describes East Aurora as a Residential Place with Industries Devoted to Home Arts and Beautifying the Household.[19] Historical significance is acknowledged in the first paragraph: the village is the birthplace of the nation's thirteenth president, Millard Fillmore. Tookay, the story made clear, was where the beautifying in East Aurora took place: "The work shop [*sic*], beautifully clean, well equipped with every convenience, well ventilated and well lighted, [is] where Karl Kipp and a few skilled helpers make—with their hands and without the aid of machinery—things of beauty and lasting worth in silver, gold, copper and leaded glass for home adornment." Plainly, the story's writer had read Kipp's advertising copy. The December 1914 issue of

Gustav Stickley's *Craftsman* magazine presented five photographs of Kipp's Tookay work in an article advising readers about holiday celebrations and the gift custom.[20] Like Roycroft, though on a far less grand scale, Kipp's shop issued at least two product catalogues.[21]

Also in 1914, and while still a high school student, sixteen-year-old Art Cole began working alongside Kipp and Jennings. The Arts and Crafts movement positioned itself in a preindustrial context. One element was the medieval guild system involving apprenticeship in service to mastering a craft. Cole's apprenticeship to Kipp and Jennings proved him an able and skilled learner (and them good masters), raising him to the level of professional coppersmith. Short and slight (five feet, five inches and no more than 150 pounds), Cole was a hard worker, eager to learn. Previously, his only other work experience had been driving the horse for a road crew's water wagon, beginning at age fourteen.[22] East Aurora High School was located practically across the street from the Roycroft Copper Shop and just a few blocks from Tookay. Cole is pictured in the 1914 Tookay Shop catalogue.

His apprenticeship with the two metal masters, first at Tookay and later, when they returned to the din of the Roycroft Copper Shop, proved doubly beneficial. Working with Kipp and Jennings, Cole absorbed the technical craft of metalwork and the aesthetics of the visible hammering on the copper. In addition to the "yield strength" imparted on the medium, the tangible hammer marks were intended to telegraph to holders and viewers clear evidence for the presence of the craftsman's hand and an assurance that the products—the art "for discriminating people" as Kipp's advertising copy read—were not machine-made, mass-produced work. Whether customers were capable of discriminating between hand- and machine-hammering is debatable. Cole was exposed to the decorative, geometric designs of Roycrofter Dard Hunter, who was inspired by Secessionist and Glasgow School sources. The article introducing Avon Coppersmith prominently references Cole's training: he is "a man who for the past twenty years has been working with metals such as copper, brass, pewter and silver, while learning, studying and executing in the art of pounding copper—all of this time in East Aurora."[23] So good was young Cole's work that he designed and made gold rings for his 1918 high school graduating class.[24] Selling crafts, though, requires a different skill set. A second "curricular" benefit to the Kipp-Jennings tutorial pertained to business. At Tookay and once Kipp and Jennings returned to Roycroft, working with them there afforded Cole an over-the-shoulder education about marketing the copper products.

Elbert Hubbard perished aboard the RMS *Lusitania*, sunk by a German submarine on May 7, 1915. His son and successor, Elbert II, or "Bert" as he was called, promptly began recruiting the return of Roycrofters who had left the campus. By December, the *Buffalo Evening News* reported, a number had, including Jennings and Kipp: "the artistic craftsman, is once more 'in the fold' [at Roycroft's Copper Shop] after four years in business for himself."[25] *The Saratogian*, Kipp's hometown newspaper, later indicated he was "superintendent of the Art Metal Department" at Roycroft.[26] Following his June 1918 high school graduation, Cole enlisted in and left for US Marine training camp in August.[27] He was one of ninety-eight original members of Company O (as was Kipp), formed in 1917 as part of the Home Defense Corps,[28] about the time the United States declared war on Germany. US troops had arrived at the front in March 1918. Almost concurrent with Cole's graduation, more than a thousand Marines were killed in the nearly monthlong battle of Belleau Wood. Cole, fortunately, was stationed in Santo Domingo, avoiding combat.[29] Mustering out September 10, 1919, Cole spent two months studying at Pratt Institute in Brooklyn, New York,[30] enrolling in a course that encompassed carving, jewelry, silversmithing, and casting.[31] Cole rejoined Kipp and Jennings at Roycroft in 1920; the East Aurora census lists him as a designer in the Roycroft Copper Shop,[32] while the 1927 telephone directory identifies him as assistant superintendent at Roycroft.[33] For several years the Copper Shop may have remained profitable. But by the late 1920s, both public fascination with and Roycroft's own leadership's interest in hammered copper goods waned.

Under both Elbert's and Bert's command, Roycroft's noble aspirations to foster, proselytize, and uphold the virtues professed by the Arts and Crafts movement were tempered by the motivation for generating revenues in excess of costs; philosophy would not stand in the way of profit. In perhaps a last-ditch effort, Roycroft's enduring interest in appealing to geographically far-flung customers' gift-giving motives is exemplified by a brief notice in the *Buffalo News*:[34] "Ernest Simmons and Karl Kipp are in Chicago, where they have charge of the display of Roycroft products at the Chicago gift show being held from February 6–20 in the Palmer house [sic]. The whole line of Roycroft copper will be shown." Two months later, in April 1928 and at Bert Hubbard's direction, Kipp began laying off Copper Shop employees. Jennings was transferred to Roycroft's Bindery where, twenty years earlier, he began his Roycroft career. A year later, well ahead of the October stock market crash, Bert demanded that Kipp either purchase the Copper Shop or be let go. Layoffs had cut the shop's staff by half, and a month later, in May 1929, Kipp resigned. Cole is placed in charge of the Copper Shop and, three weeks afterward, in June 1929, he resigned,[35] leaving the shop without its two most skilled and experienced craftsmen.

In hindsight, it was not the most propitious time to quit one's job. Cole's letter of resignation to Bert, though businesslike and formal in tone, is more accusatory than it is matter of fact in its directness. By omission, he expressed displeasure with Bert's management of Roycroft's direction. Cole began by acknowledging appreciation for the "one-hun-dred-per-cent" encouragement he received from Copper Shop workers for his role as shop foreman. Because of this, he wrote Bert, "It is not easy for me to say this which follows but I have arrived at this decision after considering the future of the Copper Shop." Cole enumerated two reasons for his decision to resign: his belief that Bert lacks interest in "continuing the Copper business except as a little shop supplying the local needs and perhaps a little mail order business" and his perception that Hubbard's interest lies "in the Book and Publishing game and not in the Copper or Gift game." Gifts and mail order to nonlocal customers would form the foundation for Cole's Avon shop.

Cole's presentation contrasts his empirical enjoyment working with "the boys and girls of the Copper shop" to Hubbard's perceived disengagement, if not neglect. Cole concludes the letter's preamble asserting his belief that Hubbard "would like to get out of the [copper and gift game] entirely or tapering it off as much and as quickly as possible." His resignation would take effect in two weeks, June 15, 1929, allowing Cole time to mentor his successor at the Copper Shop and complete sales orders and inventory currently underway.[36] The *East Aurora Advertiser* reports on this June 29, 1929: "Arthur Cole who has been associated with the Roycroft Copper Shop during the past fourteen years has resigned. After June 15, his new business connection will be as part owner with Karl Kipp in a new shop known as The Karl Kipp Shop, Inc. and located here in East Aurora." No record of what Cole did or how long he worked post-Roycroft at the Kipp Shop was located. Two sources[37] indicate Cole is presented as a "craftsman" in the 1930 East Aurora census, though by year's end, he may not have been living full-time in the village.

Though Roycroft persisted in name until the late 1930s, the work produced at the Copper Shop never regained its earlier quality, never mind its popularity. Art Deco–style designs appear in the 1928 Roycroft catalog, "The Book of the Copper Shop." The work produced by the thin, inexperienced copper staff bore little resemblance to that previously created. Objects were often smooth and unhammered and lacked the distinctive, rich chocolate brown patina Roycroft had been known for. The hammering, when it appeared, is often perfunctory, distracting, and amateurish—of a manner better appreciated by the parents of juvenile summer camp-crafters.

In contrast to the otherwise unconfirmed *East Aurora Advertiser*'s report of Cole's partnership with Kipp, Cole's son, Tom, indicates Art moved to Avon in 1930 and began his coppersmith shop working out of a residential home on Main Street.[38] By the time the Coppersmith's shop opened, a few miles east, near the intersection of NY Route 15 and outside of the residential neighborhood, he was a widower with a young son, Don. Mostly, though, what transpired for Cole between 1929 and 1933 is murky. There is not so much as a hint as to what or why the Avon area was a magnet for Cole's interests, drawing him fifty miles east from his home of thirty years. The June 1933 public announcement of the opening for Avon Coppersmith provides no information. Likewise, the extant historical record offers no clues as to the precise business connections Cole (and Walter Jennings) had with Clarence Wemett,[39] including who approached who with the idea for the Avon Coppersmith enterprise. Undoubtedly, correspondence and perhaps travel and conversations between Cole and Wemett about Avon Coppersmith took place. Perhaps cross-pollination of inventory with Wemett's earlier-established Roadside Craftsmen and the new Coppersmith was discussed. And Cole would have needed time to create inventory for the Avon shop's eventual opening. Cole's granddaughter, Jennifer, reports he considered locations in Lima and Bloomfield, New York, before settling on Avon.[40]

A secondhand report from Jennings's son, Rixford, indicates it was Walter Jennings who "was asked to come to Avon by a Texaco distributor [presumably a reference to Wemett and confusing Texaco with Shell] to help lure tourists to the area" and that Jennings brought Cole with him.[41] Only the most roundabout and circumstantial support for the claim can be located. At the time, community newspapers regularly presented fragmentary social notes about their citizens' comings and goings. In one such note, the *Buffalo Courier Express* (July 14, 1929) reported, "Mr. and

Mrs. Walter Jennings and family returned from a motor trip through the Finger Lakes region and a week-end visit to Mrs. Jenning's [*sic*] brother in Rochester."[42] Tying this note to the present question suggests only the coincidence of timing and that Walter Jennings had reason and opportunity to visit the Avon-Bloomfield area.

But the timing of Cole's 1930 move to Avon coincides with Clarence Wemett's recently launched, if rudimentarily formed, Roadside Craftsmen, a short distance away. Wemett also owned a gas station, restaurant, and tourist cabins in Avon.[43] And, by 1933 when Coppersmith opened, Wemett's plans for moving the Branchport church and a grander vision for Roadside must have been formed. The rhetoric introducing Coppersmith follows a narrative already established for Roadside: "Now that the tourist season has opened, the Avon Coppersmith is hard at work turning out a great variety of pieces. He [Cole] wants people to come in and look around, see the displays, watch him at work, ask questions. A visit to him will interest you—a man of modesty, whose innate ability and long years of experience enable him to do that of which only a few are capable."[44] A "cooperative marketing arrangement"[45] between the two shops would have appealed as much to Wemett as Cole, since each was accustomed to partnering with others.

5

The Business Plan

Travelers so distracted by roadside beguilements that they never reach their destinations were satirized in Sinclair Lewis's 1928 novel *The Man Who Knew Coolidge*. A year later, Clarence Wemett made the distractions his business. Wemett's shops were intentional forms of interruption to a traveler's goal-oriented activity—ordinarily, what psychologists call "frustration"—and the foundation of their businesses. Pre-twentieth-century handcraft businesses relied on customers strictly bound by geography and personal mobility. The customer base was tied to how far the distance and how able the walker. The adoption of motorized vehicles on paved, interconnected highways further widened the consumer circle begun by mail-order companies: from the close and settled to the distant and transient. Among roadside merchants, passersby became the most important consumer group because there were so many more of them, and fresh replenishment was constant. The significance of an individual customer's loyalty ebbed in favor of multiple customers' frequency—how many different ones passed by and how often. Perhaps especially among itinerant customers, and as handcrafted objects morphed from necessity to indulgence, the Craft product's appeal relied less on functionality and more on its emotional attraction. Utility as a driver for purchase dropped in favor of the (selfish) memento or souvenir for oneself or was altruistically imbued with emotion for gift-giving. The Wemett craft shops also held a discriminating product feature of exclusivity: a candle holder can be purchased almost anywhere, but the handcrafted candle holder only here. *How* the object was made was as important as *what* the object was. And unlike mail-order catalogue retailers of mass manufactured goods, for whom uniformity was a production, shipping, and customer expectation/satisfaction necessity, the variations and irregularities of handcraft were virtues for which customers could reasonably expect to pay more.

Because Wemett envisioned the primary customer base for his enterprises as one-timers, most costs for local promotion and advertising could be avoided. Route 20 drivers on their way to someplace else needed no "grand opening" announcements nor "sales" as inducements. Since the drivers were not from "there," everything they drove by was new to them. What the drivers required was clear signage convincing them to stop at Roadside Craftsmen; its placement next door to Wemett's gas station afforded just that. The inducement for stopping was twofold: satisfaction for an ordinary need (fuel) coupled with the convenient, voluntary reward of shopping for homegrown, handcrafted, attractively presented objects that would meet other interests. Roadside Craftsmen's and Avon Coppersmith's target market, tourists and gift-givers, shared an essential characteristic despite the Depression: discretionary funds. Together with a readiness to buy, fiscal flexibility was what made possible both the travel and the trinket purchase. The seismic commercial changes the automobile and highway enabled in the first quarter of the twentieth century reverberated for business in a similar way digital media disrupted commerce in the last quarter century: consumer mobility meant both economic opportunity and threat.

Wemett had to manufacture two intertwined concepts before producing a single product: a *reason* for travelers to interrupt their journeys and a *place* for the interruption to occur. The place, and what was inside and on offer to travelers who otherwise had no reason to stop, satisfies the reason. Though none in written form is known, the East Bloomfield-Avon business plan seemed a bundle of incongruities. The plan was at once forward- and backward-looking, promiscuously mixing the two. The crafts enterprises jumbled nostalgia with armchair "museumology," as though considering "crafts and the people who produced them as windows on the past, or specimens and curiosities to be nurtured and preserved."[1] MacCannell argues that the "artificial preservation and reconstruction" of the nonmodern world within modern society produces the museumization of the premodern, fetishizing the work of others and "transforming it into an 'amusement' . . . a spectacle . . . or an attraction."[2]

Wemett's commercial retail future was one literally driven by private, automobiling customers, to exploit their imagined past. Publicly maintained roadways, intended for taking drivers virtually anywhere other than the private retail outlets increasingly crowding their shoulders, brought four-wheeling buyers to the doors of his businesses. While commerce would be conducted on a personal level, customers were "delivered" thanks to large-scale roadway infrastructure. In its rearview mirror, the business plan evoked a mythic narrative. A time when old-fashioned handcraftsmanship was performed by artisans creating before the traveler-customer's eyes products offered for their purchase. "Occupational sightseeing," in MacCannell's term, "incorporates fragments of the primitive social life . . . elevat[ing] modernity over the past."[3] Traditional, one-off product creation at Roadside and Coppersmith was juxtaposed with the modern, industrial context; Wemett's shops lacked both the scale and monotonous, serial homogeneity of anonymously produced industrial goods. Customers were to be enticed by an appeal that they could see "their" craft purchases made by the craftsmen creating them. Authenticity was assured instead of promised, as was the case during the Arts and Crafts period. The magnetism produced a (commercial) bond between the elements involved in the process: craftsmen and object, travelers and their money.

Ostensibly, the business plan was fairly simple and straightforward. And bold. But especially in the gloom of the onset of the Great Depression, it was risky. Something few predicted, and even fewer were prepared for, the Depression's duration was unforeseeable. Wemett's business model demanded enormous optimism and faith coupled with an equally sizeable and long-term financial commitment to perseverance. Overnight profitability was as unlikely as the business's ongoing sunk costs were a certainty. While the "ROI" acronym—"return on investment"—had yet to enter common conversation, its sentiment would not have escaped Wemett. No one, after all, goes into business to lose money or, for that matter, to break even. Wemett's business plan required considerable tactical juggling.

Before launching Roadside, Wemett knew some important commercial facts. Historically, the development of and enhancements to transportation systems (canals, railroads) served to lengthen the "road" of businesses. Thanks to such systems, manufacturers became less reliant on the customers literally in their backyards. Among roadside businesses, not only was the producer's reach improved, but the frequency with which customers made purchases increased, even if it was not the same customer making the purchase. Wemett developed and grew his petroleum businesses, and they prospered along with the automobile market, though of course he could not take credit for the latter. But the federally sponsored, ever-increasing number of paved highway miles must have seemed a godsend to all automobile service providers. And Wemett would have had to go out of his way to ignore the many roadside industries that began flourishing alongside the highways. From such necessities as his own chain of filling stations to sympathetic, compatible conveniences (including restaurants), the roadside businesses fueled vehicles as much as their occupants. None of this went unnoticed. Belasco's study[4] reports the press's attention and interest in the entrepreneurial strength of roadside retailers even as the Depression's misery deepened and spread.

The pleasures associated with leisure driving were abundantly documented in popular culture, including general circulation magazines. Not the least of which was how democratic automobiling was and how small and accessible the world became with a car.[5] In 1911, the Boy Scouts offered a merit badge—one of its original fifty-seven—in "automobiling," when less than 1 percent of the US population owned a car. The badge recognized achievement for learning to drive—not for being a passenger. Parker Brothers' "Touring" card game (1926) underscored automobiling's wide popularity, taking the skill from the road and into the parlor, or backseat. One Ohio pottery, Roseville, lampooned auto tourists and their experiences in a transfer-decorated Creamware line introduced in 1916.[6] The most casual, personal reconnaissance of the pleasure derived from driving revealed a landscape cornucopia of other people's good and presumably profitable roadside merchandising ideas. Which features and attributes did the successful businesses share, and how could Wemett exploit them for his own advantage? What did the automobiling public want, need, or be persuaded to indulge in that was not already presented by the menu of roadside businesses? What passion, desire, or felt need could Wemett's roadside business identify, ignite, and satisfy? See figure 5.1.

The highway on which Wemett located Roadside Craftsmen was heavily traveled. Between 1930 and 1950, traffic volume on Route 20 increased dramatically and annually.[7] He situated Roadside's East Bloomfield building almost immediately next door to one of his gas stations. The village of Avon, meanwhile, already had established its own "draw." Since the mid-nineteenth century, health-seekers sought out the pungent mineral springs at Avon, the "Saratoga of Western New York." Just east of Bloomfield, Canandaigua—its name derived from the Native American word "kanandarque," which means "chosen spot"—was popular among vacationing tourists even before paved roads existed. The geographic setup was ideal, and the proximity to Hemlock, Wemett's hometown, was

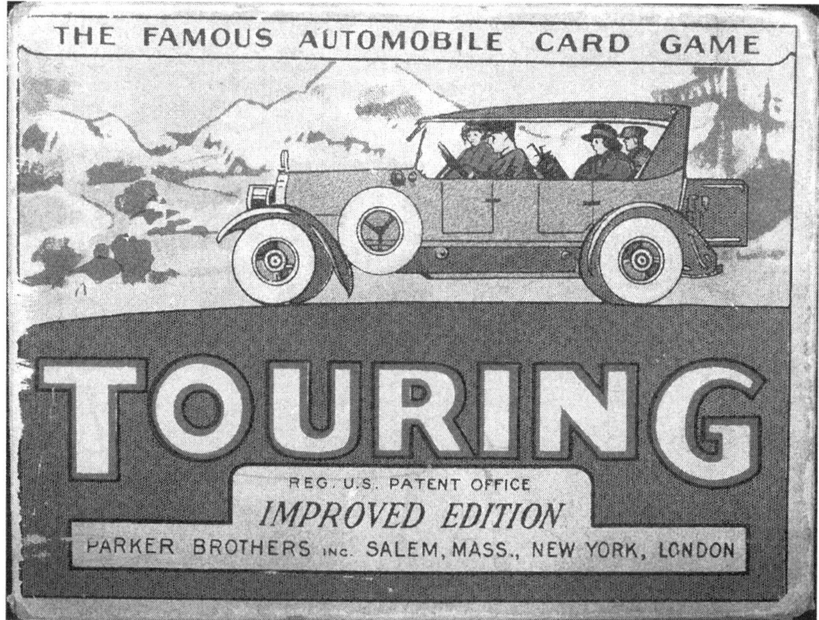

Figure 5.1. "Touring" card game released in 1926 by Parker Bros. Players race 50 or 100 miles, within city or country speed limits, trying to avoid such penalties as collision, out of gasoline, and puncture. Photograph by A. Sue Weisler.

convenient. Wemett assembled scattered puzzle pieces, bringing them together to form a singular focus for his craft enterprises.

Roadside Craftsmen and Avon Coppersmith deinstitutionalized and scaled down the business model previously followed by Arts and Crafts manufacturers. The large-sized factory and workforce employed by such makers as Stickley churned out product sold by distributors to such traditional retail venues as department and furniture stores. Direct contact—never mind sales—between manufacturer and the consumer public was occasional at best and more often than not restricted to custom orders placed by well-to-do clients or their decorators. Supporting manufacturing were printed publications. Coupled with the message-shaping persuasive industries, the magazines transcended local boundaries, extending the sales market for locally manufactured products to geographically distant, dispersed customers. Media delivered manufacturers' messages, including product images; interconnected national railway systems and the postal service delivered the products. Some serials, including those published by Stickley and Hubbard, at once served the manufacturers' own commercial interests by nesting them in a noncommercial context of articles tutoring readers about the Arts and Crafts (and publisher's) philosophy.

Recognizing the dramatically increasing number of automobiles and miles of paved roadways, and the autonomy afforded by automobility, Wemett abandoned—or rejected—the older business model. In place of the factory, Wemett substituted small-scale manufacturing by a few workers. Wemett offered direct sales to customers rather than distributors and retailers. Both functions would take place at the manufacturing site. Better than Larkin and Sears earlier, Wemett simplified by two-thirds the manufacturing-distribution-retailing model, cutting out distributors and bypassing retail middlemen.[8] The Wemett business plan ran against the contemporary grain by considering ways to mass market one-offs produced by handcraftsmanship and largely without employing mediated advertising. The point of purchase became its own advertising medium: initially as written (quite large) on the side of a building (Roadside) or displayed on signs in front of and on top of the structure (Coppersmith). Beyond that, Wemett's strategy anticipated by at least a decade the predictions of a sociological-communication theory to advance the success of his businesses: the role of opinion leaders and the two step flow of influence or old-fashioned word of mouth. Satisfied customers, especially those whose purchases ended up in the hands of grateful gift recipients, became endorsement and testimonial for the enterprises and their products. Wemett literally mobilized the yet-to-be-formalized theory for a growing population taking to newly paved roads in their recently purchased automobiles.

To be sure, his model was folksy, retrospective, and familiar to customers; one matching perfectly and sympathetically the product being sold, the Roadside building's ambience, and the customer's sales experience. The plan had appeal beyond nostalgia; it was fiscally sound insofar as Wemett's model eliminated the markup added by distributors and retailers. Pricing was more affordable for customers and more profitable for him. Moreover, and more practically, contracting with distributors for an unknown and unproven product line to sell to already well-stocked retailers would have proven challenging. (Still, both Roadside and Coppersmith offered wholesale pricing to interested vendors at 50 percent of retail.) Compared to Arts and Crafts manufacturers-publishers, additional cost savings accrued since Wemett's enterprises would not act as publishers, and his shops' work would not be marketed that way. Roadside Craftsmen and Avon Coppersmith issued no ponderous pronouncements, nor would they publish high-minded pretentions. Without a political agenda, both shops presented themselves as genuine, simple (in the best sense) craft-makers who hewed to the Arts and Crafts aesthetic using authentic, traditional handcraftsmanship. The Wemett enterprises mimicked movement craftsmen dedicated as much to the craft as to their livelihood.

Craftsmanship—"the skill of making things well"[9]—was the center-piece for each Wemett operation. "Craftsmanship" carries the justifiably lofty reputation of quality and honesty, historicized by centuries of product creation and its admiration. All were attributes manufacturers could not replicate. More than merely echoing a nonspecific past, craftsmanship evoked virtues of skillful construction, style, and design so scarce, costly, and coveted that only the elite were able to attain it. Craftsmen were invested in their work and "dedicated to good work for its own sake."[10] Craftsmen do not labor, as do hourly *employees*. Gustav Stickley recognized and exploited this, if only for promotional purposes. He first named his firm United Crafts. Perhaps fearing its socialist undertone, and the par-adox that his, undeniably, was a capitalist enterprise engaged in factory manufacturing, within two years he changed it to Craftsman Workshops. Launching a monthly magazine, he identified himself as "Gustav Stickley: The Craftsman." Craftsmanship accrues only after years of supervised training, practice, and correction experienced under widely varying circum-stances. Its twentieth-century renaissance in the industrial era—with the Arts and Crafts movement and, later, with Wemett's enterprises—presented an interesting contrast: "Age correlated with experience on the job and had been an asset for the craftsman; but it became a liability for the assembly line worker."[11] The craftsman's earned pride in his work was transferred by purchase to the customer. "Craftsmanship," Shell summarized, "cements a relationship of trust between buyer and seller, worker and employer, and expects something of both. . . . It is what distinguishes the work of humans from the work of machines."[12] Craftsmanship, coupled with the evidence of the "see-it-made" slogan, were the promotional hallmarks for Avon Coppersmith and the Roadside Craftsmen.

Identical to the earlier Arts and Crafts manufacturers, Wemett rec-ognized that, unlike such retail establishments as grocery or department stores, his craft operations would not thrive if solely dependent upon indigenous customers. Local buying publics can be relatively static in size and economically inelastic. Wemett's shops sold discretionary products, further limiting the breadth and depth of the localized market. Since there were so many highway passersby, he forecast that repeatedly drawing in one-time customers would be financially more significant than relying on repeat purchases among those living in close proximity. Capturing just a few percent of the sizeable daily traffic flow would ensure a steady revenue stream.

Conveniently, most Roadside and Coppersmith products were small in size. They were easily transported by customers in their cars or could be inexpensively shipped by parcel post. Market expansion for Wemett's roadside businesses was possible by reaching this heterogeneous, substantially larger, growing and ever-changing customer base motoring by their doors daily. An additional benefit to catering to transients: there was no such thing as "stale" inventory since everything in stock would be new to them. Dusting the inventory displays would maintain the appearance of "freshness." The trade-off, though, was to largely forgo much of any expectation of building brand loyalty or repetitive consumerism: tourist travelers cruising by the two craft operations were on their way to someplace else. Goal direction and satisfaction rested with the travelers' destination, not wayside stops such as Roadside Craftsmen or Avon Coppersmith. Wemett's model, like most other roadside enterprises, sought to generate profit through multiple, albeit modest, one-time sales.

As a form of localism, Wemett's plan cemented the physical manufacturing-retailing facility to its revenue stream. But Wemett intended to nationalize the market for Roadside Craftsmen's and Avon Coppersmith's products well beyond their physical locations. His plan for this was unique insofar as media were not employed, as was the case for Arts and Crafts manufacturers. (However, Roadside Craftsmen and Avon Coppersmith sporadically issued product catalogues and brochures to support mail-order retail business and wholesale sales of their products to other retailers.) The plan was novel insofar as, paradoxically, the two operations sought ways to mass market merchandise by personalizing relationships with customers, recognizing the superior persuasive power of personal influence over impersonal mediated messages.[13] Instead of dependency on such interventions as magazines, the Wemett enterprises leveraged and married leisure travel via personal transportation to satisfaction of travelers' interest in capturing their evanescent travel experience by selling an empirical form of permanence in the form of mementos and souvenirs.

The Roadside and Coppersmith enterprises simultaneously took the Arts and Crafts movement out of the print media age, transported it into the automotive age, and then returned it to a preindustrial era of personalized sales of handcraftsmanship. The unknown variable, of course, was the extent to which, in the midst of the Depression, people had the nonworking leisure time and discretionary capital to enable tourism and the purchase of mementos. Two persuasive tactics worked hand in glove to enhance sales, especially to geographically distant customers who never set foot in—never mind drove by—the shops: ambassadorship and altruism. A subtle, personal, and personally invested form of persuasion, the tactics would nationalize the shops' products. Traveling tourists were unwittingly recruited as Roadside Craftsmen's and Avon Coppersmith's goodwill ambassadors and product endorsers. Drivers and passengers who made purchases became an unconscripted army of salespeople carrying *their* endorsement for the Western New York craft enterprises' products to distant locations. The unenlisted salesforce possessed two enviable and persuasively potent virtues no business could manipulate. First was the customers' implicit or explicit endorsement for the products they had purchased. It was a form of credibility completely absent any self-serving interest. The latter was especially significant, as it signifies goodwill—having the other's best interests at heart—a virtue not accessible to any manufacturer. The testimonial endorsement fits neatly into what later, in the 1940s,[14] social scientists identified as "opinion leadership" and its superior significance above mediated sources in the persuasion process. Less scientific but every bit as reasonable, the Wemett enterprises' reliance on word-of-mouth fits what Belasco[15] identified in another context as "a cardinal rule of motoring to 'pass it on.'" Credibility and goodwill are elements of persuasion as old as Aristotle.

The second persuasive tactic employed by the two craft operations was their appeal to customer motives for product purchases. One motive, the most obvious, was selfish, personal satisfaction. Creating and marketing products catering to leisure travelers was not a new idea when Wemett began his businesses. Tourists and tourism developed as roles and activities for more than the wealthy and were woven into the growth in leisure beginning by the third quarter of the nineteenth century. World Fairs and Expositions successfully commercialized products memorializing the patron's experience and documenting their attendance at such events. Moving from such large-scale public occasions as an Exposition to an individual's private experience on the roadway required only modest "translation," primarily one of scale. At Roadside and Coppersmith, personal satisfaction was achieved by the shops' product discrimination from what became stereotypical mass-produced tourist trinkets and their presentation in the context of fine handcrafted objects. Travelers purchasing objects from the shop for self-satisfying reasons were buying more than an object: they bought a tangible memorial to a trip *and* an example of handcrafted art. To this emotionally compelling mix, Roadside and Coppersmith added functional utility of their objects as a further product benefit to the owner: the vase that held flowers, or the tray from which one might serve house guests, etc. More significant was the second persuasive tactic's appeal to unselfish gifting motivations for purchases.

Both Roadside and Coppersmith positioned themselves as *gift* shops. As a noun, "gift shop" describes a place; used as a verb, it describes an action with a specific intention and directional purpose. Gifts and gifting were used as a business tactic, not as part of a friendly relationship.[16] Gifts and gifting are objects and actions that at once speak to the status and regard held as much by the giver as the recipient. Purchasing something for oneself is an action motivated by and reputationally distinct from the identical action (purchase) intended on behalf of another. Gifts acknowledging special events are "indicators of what one human being thinks of another."[17] Gifting is an act of generosity rather than indulgence, altruism instead of selfishness. It is other-oriented.[18] At Roadside and Coppersmith, articulating and highlighting the gifting motive was at once an incentive and a way for customers to justify purchasing.

Customer purchases benefitted the creators and, presumably, the gifts' destination. By positioning their products as gifts, the craft operations elevated their own status as well as that of the buyers and, presumably, appreciative recipients. Theirs was a gift shop stressing timeless artistry, careful craftsmanship, and the enduring beauty of the object, all qualities that underscore the object's appropriateness and fit with the consumer's motive for giving. Handcraftsmanship, as evidenced by how the object was created, and witnessed by the gift's giver, enhances the specialness of the object as gift. Wemett's implied emotional appeal was later overtly articulated (1944) by Hallmark's slogan, "When you care enough to send the very best." It is a mixed persuasive message: appealing to the buyer's better, unselfish motives on behalf of the gift recipient's anticipated appreciation for the giver's thoughtfulness, which in turn economically benefits the seller. A thinly disguised subtext to the gifting paradigm is the philanthropic moral uplift conveyed by the purchase, qualities that are transferable in gifting to the recipient. These multiple and sometimes mixed persuasive appeals were not new when Wemett launched his craft enterprises. Roycroft metalworker Karl Kipp made nearly identical appeals in 1913 as did Gustav Stickley's *Craftsman* magazine a year later.[19] Each stressed the artistry, craftsmanship, beauty, and utility of the work. These virtues were all wrapped in a none-to-subtle subtext of the moral uplift afforded by their purchase, virtues that were as transferable when gifting as much as when owning. Positioning themselves as the agents for travelers' future acts of gifting helped move Roadside and Coppersmith away from such inward motives as acquisitions for the sake of souvenirs or novelties. Gifts reflect on the giver as much as the giver's appreciation of the recipient. And conceivably, there is no shortage of such gifting occasions: births and birthdays, promotions and retirements, anniversaries and graduations.

Clarence Wemett initiated his craft businesses in a context of high unemployment and correspondingly diminished discretionary income. The businesses were financially improbable—as much for sellers as for buyers. The all too real consequences of the Great Depression were daily reminders of "hard times": bank failures, the collapse of the stock market and the housing industry, and unemployment. For many, personal budgets were fully consumed by the necessities of day-to-day living. Frivolities such as "automobiling" were restricted to those idle by choice and well-off by position. The Wemett businesses' sunk costs, including real estate and utilities, workers' salaries, and the cost of raw materials their craftwork required, meant a steady and not insubstantial drip-drip-drip of monthly cash outflow. Employment of trained artisans demanded the businesses realize steady sales likely unattainable in the short term and (perhaps distantly) hopeful only in the future. Wemett must have also recognized several related truths: all auto gypsies need gas, and everyone needs food and a place to sleep each night; but no one needs a memento or a souvenir. Wemett had no crystal ball, and his ability to read tea leaves was no better than anyone else's. Beyond faith and intuition, what he did have as a model was his modest-sized chain of successful automobile gas stations serving an increasingly mobile, steadily growing consumer base. His craft businesses were situated along a major cross-state transportation route, one leg of a cross-continental highway, and shared promise for growth, beneficial nearly as much to craft shops as service stations. He recognized the opportunity to enhance profits driven by mutually compatible but distinctly different businesses: handcrafted one-offs and servicing a mechanized industry of multiples. And Wemett was bold enough to act on his intuition.

Each enterprise simultaneously reached far back to a heritage nested in informal craft on a localized scale and eagerly looked forward to a mobile world of itinerant consumers. Only today is the future Wemett embraced taken for granted as a normal part of a hyper-mobile and placeless digital business environment. At the beginning of the 1930s, Wemett anticipated what occurred a quarter-century later in the United States: service replaced manufacturing as the economy's driver, coinciding with the Interstate highway program's impact.[20] The Wemett enterprises' amalgamation of historical and contemporary decorative arts traditions was odd, perhaps confusing; every bit as confusing as the time in which they were set. Though their roots were grounded in Arts and Crafts movement soil, more than occasionally their products were Colonial Revival in spirit if not style, even while some of their promotional brochures flirted with Modernism. The blend of the two decorative styles, however, was not entirely surprising. Among Colonial Revival's most visible proponents, Wallace Nutting retained just enough of the Arts and Crafts ethos to resonate among those with longer memories: from exposed construction details such as pinned furniture joinery to paraphrasing William Morris in the last of Nutting's Ten Commandments for his factory workers: "Let nothing leave your hands until you are proud of the work."[21] Even Gustav Stickley, foremost among Arts and Crafts manufacturers, turned to Colonial Revival–styled furniture he named "Chromewald" in a desperate but ultimately unsuccessful attempt to thwart bankruptcy.[22]

Arts and Crafts movement manufacturers marketed and nationalized their products using print media. Consumers were alerted to design developments, philosophical ramblings, and do-it-yourself instruction through periodicals. Manufacturers' catalogues illustrated objects available directly from them or through such retail outlets as department stores. Wemett's craft enterprises retained selected elements of the Arts and Crafts aesthetic and practiced the handcraft of its philosophy while ignoring or rejecting the principal method used to market its goods: print media. By "cherry picking," Wemett's harvest yielded business longevity beyond that experienced by Arts and Crafts period stylists. With broader adoption of the automobile and the concomitant paved improvements and stretching of the highway system, even small, mom-and-pop enterprises began interacting directly with a drive-by buying public. In addition to showing consumers what they might buy, as was done in print ads and catalogues, roadside customers could handle the craft objects. Added to that mix was Roadside Craftsmen's and Avon Coppersmith's "see-it-made" pitch. In the far background was Roadside's and Coppersmith's underwriter: Clarence Wemett's public persona as presented in newspaper reports is self-effacing, occasionally self-deprecating, and avoids any sense of loftiness or self-importance. But Wemett's public modesty belies a sophisticated appreciation for publicity put in service to his enterprises rather than himself.

Wemett's craft businesses leveraged some of the advantages of "the billion-dollar smile" produced by the industrialization of amusement and entertainment that began in the late nineteenth century.[23] A form of "art for the people," industrialism in the factory was matched by that under big tents, bringing entertainment to the many instead of the few: amusement and entertainment rather than education and moral uplift; active and engaged audiences instead of passive and polite ones; appealing to diverse publics rather than largely homogenous ones. Performance—see-it-made—was as much a part of Wemett's enterprise as it was to burlesque and vaudeville. Wemett and his roadside entrepreneur craftsmen colleagues—wittingly or not—represented a break from an alarming and rapidly growing trend toward inexpensive retail chain stores. Featuring self-serve-style shopping for mass-manufactured merchandise in a "no frills" and often urban environment, chain stores nearly tripled in number from the beginning of the century to the end of the 1920s: from 50,000 to 142,000.[24] Whereas the chains offered depersonalized shopping for faceless, anonymous, and mind-numbingly mass-produced merchandise, Wemett returned retailing to familiar, comforting populist territory: community-based trade between independent, skilled craftsmen and appreciative customers.

6

Drivers

In John Ford's 1962 movie *The Man Who Shot Liberty Valance*, a long-cloaked "truth" about a well-loved frontier politician is uncovered as false. If published, it would discredit and cast shame upon him, disillusioning his admirers. A newspaper editor gruffly pulls away his reporter's notes and tears them up. "You're not going to use the story?" the politician asks. "This is the West, sir," the editor replies. "When the legend becomes fact, print the legend." So too for Roadside Craftsmen's story, albeit less dramatically.

The Roadside Craftsmen shop was built on clay. Other media followed in short order, including fiber, wood, and metal. But clay formed the nurturing environment for Roadside's incubation. A perfect medium for a solid, nearly self-leveling foundation, clay was amenable equally to utility and to art. Americans were well acquainted with the ceramic craft's robust applications, including its qualities as a form of artistic expression. In no small part this was due to late nineteenth- and early twentieth-century world's fairs and expositions where the work of such art pottery manufacturers as Rookwood (Cincinnati), Teco (Chicago), and Grueby (Boston) were on display to tourists eager to see the age's latest developments. Pottery as art had established itself by 1876 at the Philadelphia Centennial Exhibition. Composed of 250 pavilions stretched across 300 acres and visited by nine million people, the pottery decoration on view was often interchangeable in technique and style to oil on canvas paintings. By 1893, the World's Columbian Exposition in Chicago featured "one of the largest displays of contemporary ceramics."[1] At the very beginning of the twentieth century, the founding of university-level curricula in clay modeling further legitimized the medium's artistic status: first, at Alfred University (Alfred, New York), and then, a few years later and many miles closer to Bloomfield, in Rochester at the Mechanics Institute. A June 3, 1932 *Livonia Gazette* story about Wemett's "pottery factory" indicated "Guy Daugherty of Spartanburg, South Carolina, is the potter in charge of the work." The report suggested a sense of permanence: "Mr. Daugherty expects to move his family from the south to East Bloomfield some time this month."

Guy Daugherty: The Bloomfield Potter

Roadside Craftsmen was Clarence Wemett's idea for East Bloomfield, but Guy Daugherty implemented it. While Wemett was an astute businessman willing to make and "stick" with a risky investment, potter Daugherty made the idea empirical. And judging from numerous press reports in which he was featured, Daugherty personified Roadside Craftsmen. Over the course of its nearly quarter-century history, several craftsmen and at least a few women were employed at Roadside. Today we know little about any of them.

Rhapsodizing at considerable length, the 1932 article introducing Roadside Craftsmen traced the potter's art from the Egyptians and Assyrians to the Babylonians and the ancient Greeks before jumping centuries ahead to the Carolinas in the United States.[2] There, in the Carolinas, the author wrote, "Wherever there is a good deposit of clay there is pottery." To enhance the craft's credibility, the writer marshalled additional evidence: the Bible is called in to witness on behalf of the art, American Indians are acknowledged for their understanding of "the making of crude pottery of the stone age type," and industrious Carolina colonists are described as the descendants of seventeenth-century Englishmen, "from Staffordshire, the pottery center of England."

Perhaps a portion of the far-reaching historical enthusiasm presented by the article had been "planted" by or lifted from an undated Bloomfield Pottery brochure. There, potter Guy Daugherty poses at work inside a baluster-shaped vase's outline. An identifying headline below it in italics reads: "*The Potter by the Side of the Road.*" Text below the image instructs: "You might have viewed this very sight in old Athens before the Christian Era, or on the pike that leads to Jericho. It's an olden craft he plies; and yet, old as it is, it produces a type of individual beauty in pottery out of all comparison with vases and bric-a-brac turned out by Twentieth Century production methods." In addition to building genealogical credentials for the craft, the text asserts the superiority of Bloomfield Pottery's product by taking a swipe at what readers would recognize as its inferior competition: mass-manufactured "bric-a-brac."

The historical context is drawn broadly, and 1932 readers of the news report learned this "characteristic southern pottery" opened in East Bloomfield. This, the article advises, is thanks to the broadly foresighted acumen of Clarence Wemett, who saw "commercial as well as artistic interest" in the enterprise. The story's writer introduces Guy Daugherty of South Carolina, whose family background and years of personal experience at the wheel affords him craft expertise, and Elizabeth Rogers, a graduate of the Alfred State School of Ceramics. Daugherty and Rogers, readers learn, execute their pottery-making in the traditional way "combined with the modern." They were capable of producing an ambitious four to five hundred pieces a week, the article boasted. "Glazing is done in all colors," and "special designs and shapes are made to order and hand decorating is also done."[3]

The Bloomfield Pottery brochure (figure 6.1), though undated, was published earlier than the news report, as it makes no reference to Roadside Craftsmen. Also the brochure belies some of the article's assertions that may have, in fact, been accurate by the time the article was later written. The monochromatic pots pictured in the brochure, for instance, were available in one of three colors—and not "all colors," as the news story reports: blue, green, or gunmetal. The conventional shapes included bowls and jars, lamp bases, pitchers, handled vases and baskets, flower vases, jugs, and mugs. Prices ranged from forty cents to four dollars for an eighteen-inch two-handled vase. Most items cost about a dollar. The brochure closes with text that a newspaper's features writer might also have found useful: the Bloomfield Pottery "has been created with this one thought in mind,—to restore one of the greatest handicrafts this world has ever known. Thus it has been built, reproducing as nearly as possible one of our old traditional southern potteries. All the work here is done by the most primitive methods, a kick wheel, a horsepower clay mill, and a wood burning kiln being of special interest."

A brief, closing paragraph cleverly if incongruously ties the present to the past with recognition for how Bloomfield Pottery's visitors would arrive: "As next you pass this way step aside from the hurry and bustle of the age. 'Let the motor cool,' and browse around for a while." Depersonalizing

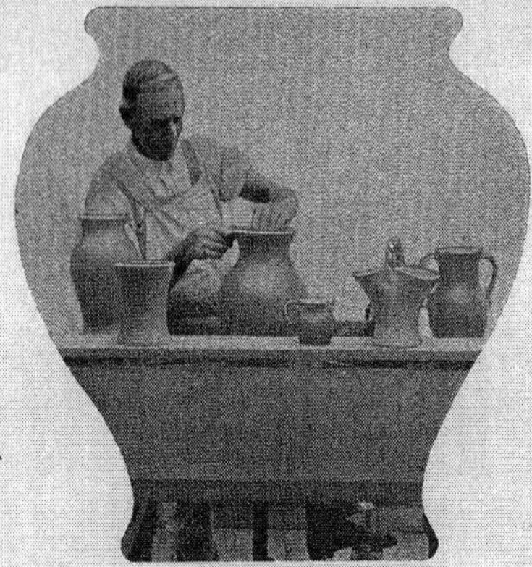

Figure 6.1. Cover for the four-page Bloomfield Pottery brochure depicting Guy Daugherty inside a baluster-shaped vase. The photograph appears in the *Livonia Gazette* (June 24, 1932) and in the *Lima Recorder* (June 29, 1932) where the caption reads: "Guy Daugherty of South Carolina as seen working at his wheel at the new Bloomfield Pottery." Photograph courtesy of the East Bloomfield Historical Society. Public domain.

its front cover, the otherwise photo-less back of the brochure concludes with a one-letter addition to the cover caption quotation "The Pottery [emphasis added] by the Side of the Road" in italics, altering the emphasis from the individual to the enterprise. Unlike many commercial potteries, Bloomfield Pottery's wares were undecorated save for color and glaze. Form and color served as the visual magnets. Vessels did not feature portraits or landscapes, abstract designs or dripping glazes, and the repertoire of shapes was limited. Appreciation, if not inspiration, occurred by holding the object or gazing at its placement within the home. The aesthetic effect is one closely aligned with Alfred University's Charles Fergus Binns, who "disdained surface decoration in his personal work, relying instead on a vessel's form and glaze."[4]

Other contemporaneous reports likewise build a mythically heroic narrative of the enterprise's founding. The received history of Wemett's recruitment of Daugherty reads like formulaic Hollywood scripts where inspiration meets serendipity. Text from a later exhibition of Daugherty Family Pottery, far removed in time and space from Bloomfield, for instance, reports that "while working at a kick-wheel turning vases . . . a well-to-do businessman offered Guy a job, to work as a potter in Bloomfield, New York."[5] Just like that.

Guy Daugherty (1878–1958) was raised in Denton, Texas, a hot, agricultural prairie area sparse in citizens but bountiful in clay-heavy soil. Today it is the thickly populated area at the northern end of the Dallas–Fort Worth metroplex. After the arrival of a railroad in 1881, Denton potters made and sold such utilitarian household wares as crocks, churns, and jugs to the substantial influx of settlers arriving without such items. Guy's father, Daniel, had two beehive kilns and produced flowerpots for a local florist and architectural elements and bricks for builders responding to the demands of Denton's growing population. Like his father, Guy operated a kiln and pottery shop in Denton. But in the 1920s he began a peripatetic journey, first moving to South Carolina. There he worked at Clayton Pottery (Spartanburg County), perhaps a couple of nearby North Carolina potteries located just over the border, and finally settled in Bethune, South Carolina.

Seemingly using information first presented in the June 24, 1932 *Livonia Gazette* article,[6] Amy Croughton's July 2 column for the *Rochester Times-Union* enhanced the original story. She describes Daugherty as "a descendant of one of the old families who brought the secrets of the pottery art from England more than two centuries ago." A few weeks later (July

30), Croughton embellishes the narrative with even more details: "Mr. Daugherty, whose father and grandfather—and his father before him—followed the trade whose rules and traditions had been brought to South Carolina by an ancestor who came out from one of the pottery centers of England."[7] In fact, Guy's grandfather, James Madison Daugherty, had moved to Texas from Cherokee Indian Territory in Missouri. Earlier still, James's father (and Guy's great-grandfather), William, came to America in 1760 from Ireland, was adopted into a Cherokee family, and married a Cherokee woman named Sally Bunch.[8]

Wemett, the early news reports indicate, was fascinated as much by the pottery process as the product. He was not alone. Columnist Croughton explained to her Rochester readers that "roadside cabins in which pottery of traditional shapes is often exhibited are familiar sights to the tourist driving through the Carolinas, but the potteries themselves are usually hidden away from the main highway and it is only the person of enquiring temperament and unlimited time who goes exploring for them." Both Wemett and Croughton thought that by putting the potter on display while at work, the "pottery will attract many interested sightseers"[9] and would be a stimulus for the business. Daugherty's daughter, Ellen, remembers her father "had a great big window in his [Bloomfield] shop, and that's where he put his kick-wheel, so that people driving by could see the potter at work."[10] Other reports make no mention of any such window and instead indicate a basement and an outdoor location where clay throwing was demonstrated and practiced.[11] As for Daugherty, he seemed "faintly amused at the astonishment expressed by visitors who watch a shapeless mass of clay expand and rise to symmetrical form under his light touch."[12] In addition to onsite demonstrations for customers and public-school shop classes, beginning in 1934 Daugherty was one of six kick-wheel potters who demonstrated their craft at the New York State Fair in Syracuse.[13] See figures 6.2, 6.3 a–d, and 6.4.

Daugherty, like those who worked with him, performed his work indoors, in half the basement of the building when outdoor conditions were prohibitive. One observer recalls two or three men working with him "during peak production." As well, the pottery workspace "consisted of a potter's wheel and many, many racks for drying the green pottery. This half [of the basement] seemed quite a bit darker than the woodworking side although there were just as many windows."[14]

At least occasionally Daugherty split his time between East Bloomfield and the south. Certainly, this was true for Roadside Craftsmen's earliest

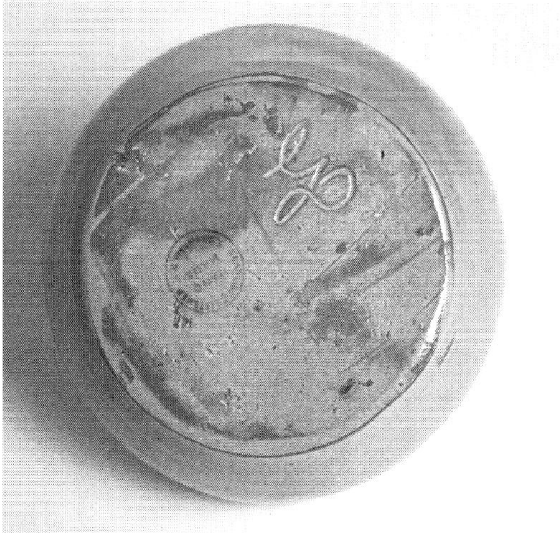

Figure 6.2. Ceramist Guy Daugherty's signature on the bottom of a Roadside Craftsmen vessel. Joseph A. DiTucci collection. Photograph by A. Sue Weisler.

years and before the church was relocated and Daugherty moved his family north. Even as late as Elliott's 1941 story, the writer notes, "Guy Daugherty has traded his potter's wheel in North [*sic*] Carolina for the one in East Bloomfield, at least for the summer months."[15] Ruth Wemett Woodruff's 1950 presentation to Rotarians indicated "Mr. Doherty [*sic*] still comes north and spends the summer months turning out a high grade of pottery."[16] Perhaps initially, Roadside's operation was seasonal, beginning, for instance, no earlier than April and running through October or November. Other reports,[17] though, suggest a year-round indoor operation, once the pottery's building was in place. Shortly after moving his family to Bloomfield, in 1935, Daugherty's wife, Neitha, died at age forty-six, leaving him a single father to five children.[18] A brief September 13, 1950 report in the *Buffalo Evening News* was one of the last local stories found about Daugherty. But an *Ithaca Journal* report[19] indicated Daugherty was still throwing pots in Bloomfield and at the state fair during the summer of 1953. Lois O'Connor wrote that he remained at Roadside Craftsmen (most likely under its successor's name, Woodcroftery) where he delights "visitors with his dexterous handling of clay"; a year later she notes his droll humor, quoting him as saying that being a good potter "takes a steady hand and a weak head."[20] This, though, was probably his last time in New York.

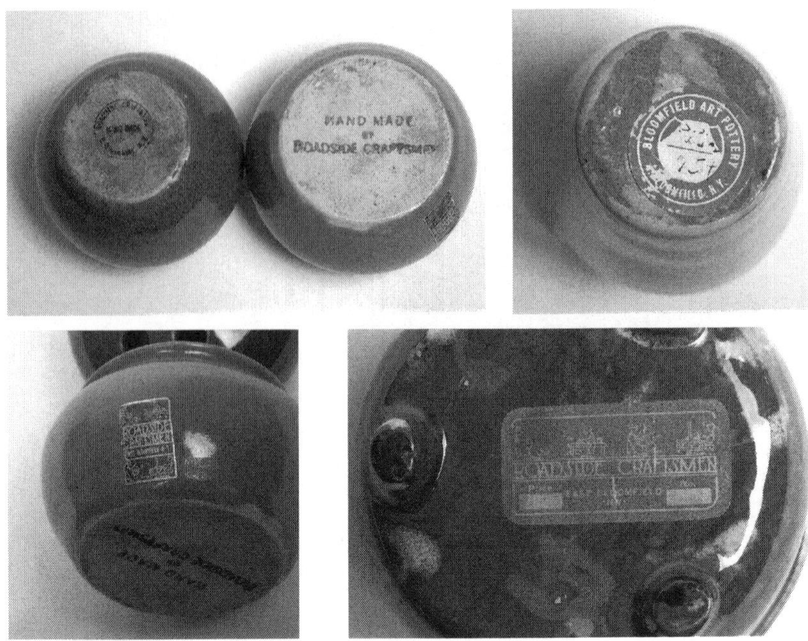

Figure 6.3a–d. Paper (or foil) labels and ink stamped signatures used on the bottoms of Roadside Craftsmen ceramic vessels by Roadside Craftsmen. Joseph A. DiTucci collection. Photograph by A. Sue Weisler.

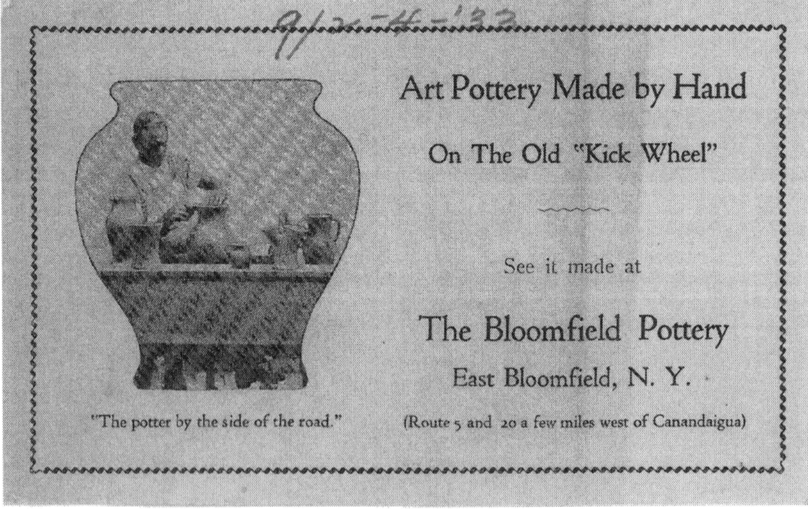

Figure 6.4. Trade card for Bloomfield Art Pottery. Photograph courtesy of the East Bloomfield Historical Society. Public domain.

A short July 1953 note in the *Livonia Gazette* states, "Rumor hath it that Mr. and Mrs. Clarence Wemett" left for North Carolina and were trying to "secure a moulder for the pottery at East Bloomfield."[21] But Roadside had closed its business in May; Daugherty had returned south to work his "Kershaw County mud." A 1952 story in the Hamlet, North Carolina *News-Messenger*, for instance, discussed the writer's apparently regular visits to Daugherty's studio and shop. In addition to throwing pots, the story notes, Daugherty "also prepares clay and ships it all over the state to high schools that teach the rudiments of this art. In one recent month, postage on such shipments amounted to over $100 . . . [and] this past year he shipped pottery to every state in the union except Oregon."[22] Guy Daugherty's headstone in the Antioch Baptist Cemetery, Kershaw County, South Carolina, memorializes him simply as "the Clay Potter."

Art Cole: The Avon Coppersmith

Clarence Wemett and Art Cole were not the only ones thinking about novel ways to capitalize on the public's fascination with automobiles for private profit. Nor were they alone at being successful. Barely four years into the Great Depression, the Avon Coppersmith's mid-1933 opening coincides with the initiation of another car-catering enterprise more than three hundred miles southeast of Avon. Each business sought to exploit the automobile for purposes other than the car's intended ones: personal travel and transportation. In Camden, New Jersey, Richard Hollingshead Jr. and Warren Smith formed a movie exhibition company, Park-In Theatres, Inc. Their company opened the nation's first drive-in movie theater in June, almost exactly the same time Coppersmith debuted. Both enterprises tapped into the growing market of people engaged in automobiling. Another similarity between the very dissimilar businesses was the period during which each thrived. The heyday for both the Coppersmith and drive-in theaters was nearly identical: Avon persisted under Cole's guidance and ownership until 1970, the same year the number of drive-in theaters began a precipitous decline. The drive-in offered moviegoers an already well-established form of entertainment at an alternative venue to the "hard-tops" to which they were accustomed. Coppersmith presented customers with a familiar, widely accepted purchasing motivation (mementos, gifting) for increasingly less common handcrafted products instead of mass manufactured ones. And both Avon Coppersmith and drive-in movie theaters were located in the country; "ozoners," as drive-ins came to be known, required ten to fifteen acres of "open air" real estate.

There were, of course, vast differences between the two. Instead of relying on loyal locals for its customer base, Avon Coppersmith appealed to the numerous itinerant travelers driving along Route 20. A steady stream of travelers formed a nearly infinite potential customer base comparing favorably to the more or less finite number of locals. Hollingshead's drive-in theater appealed exclusively to the local market and required repeat customers for profitability. The two enterprises also differed when it came to what customers purchased. Avon Coppersmith sold a physical product: one reviewed, selected, paid for, and then either taken home in a bag or shipped in a box. Drive-ins, like all movie exhibitors, sold customers something intangible and intended as a kind of surprise (how a story unfolds). An old chestnut about the theatrical movie business extols its economic virtue by explaining what is being sold: the movie exhibitor who owns the "product" still owns it after the patrons go home. Movie theaters, like amusement parks, sell experiences.[23] The link between the seemingly divergent businesses of hammering copper, on the one hand, and projecting moving image entertainment, on the other, is composed of automobiles and highways: in each case, retailing to people on the road, driving cars. And the "trick" is getting them to stop: at the shop or theater.

Situated on the south side of Routes 5 and 20, the original Coppersmith shop was tiny. Judging from photographs, it could not have been much more than five hundred square feet; Cole's son, Tom, estimates its size even more conservatively. Later, as many as eight people staffed a much larger shop, but in its earliest iteration the space would not have accommodated half that number. Granddaughter Jennifer Cole described the shop's interior: "The original small building had just enough room for a kerosene stove for heat, some room for workspace and a cot to sleep on."[24] There seemed barely enough room to turn around. To the east of the shop's slightly off-center entrance door were side-by-side double-hung windows, a single double-hung window was on the west, and a chimney perched at the roof's peak. The shop's name, printed on a sign above the door, was centered at the roofline. At some point in the early 1930s, Cole and Wemett came to some kind of a business agreement. The date and precise contours of the agreement are presently unknown. Likely, though, it involved a partnership marrying Wemett's financial support to Cole's creativity and labor.

Wemett purchased the property March 11, 1938,[25] from prominent Avon judge and attorney William A. Wheeler; presumably, the property had been rented or leased from Wheeler before that date. Ownership of the land and structure belonged to Wemett until 1947, when he sold it to Cole; the business partnership between Cole and Wemett was dissolved two months later.[26] A congratulatory display advertisement, complete with a photograph of the building and appearing in the *Livonia Gazette*[27] confirms the historical details. The text was apparently written by the newspaper, and the ad shows the Coppersmith's building accompanied by a thumbnail history: "The Avon Coppersmith was organized in 1933 by Clarence E. Wemett of Hemlock and Arthur H. Cole of East Aurora. Early in 1947 full ownership was acquired by Mr. Cole." Prosperity and profitability must have occurred relatively quickly since, by the early 1940s, an addition to the east increased the shop's size by about a third. Later the same decade, another addition, to the west, again increased the shop's extant size by another third, including a stone fireplace. Also a small, separate structure in back and on the east side was built that housed annealing and nitrous cellulose lacquer spraying; a fire hazard, it was later closed down by authorities.[28] Sometime in the 1960s, a second story was added at the center of the structure and extended south, behind the shop entrance. As Cole expanded the size of Avon Coppersmith's footprint, a sales room at front was created with living quarters at the back.[29]

Following its 1933 opening, little more about the Coppersmith shop is reported in the community press until after the war. Wartime restrictions, including the War Production Board's May 1942 copper conservation order, had wide effects, from Cole's craft enterprise to motion picture projection equipment. Cole closed the shop and went to work at Delco Products (General Motors) in Rochester as a tool and die maker.[30] Postwar, Delco tried to retain him as an employee, but Cole declined, saying, "No, I have a business to run."[31] Both the Avon Coppersmith and Roadside Craftsmen reopened in September 1945, shortly after V-J Day.[32] As though to welcome back the Coppersmith, an oddly headlined ("Little Known Industry") 1948 story in the Avon newspaper began with a question: "The Avon Coppersmith is a familiar sight along the road in East Avon but how well known is this home Industry which employs eight local men and women?" The question's answer concludes the boosterish article while also testifying to the soundness of the Coppersmith's business model: "At one time or another approximately every state in the union has been represented among the people who stop to browse in the Avon Coppersmith show room." In between, a photograph shows Arthur Cole admiring an item while standing by the Coppersmith's fireplace accompanied by several objects displayed across the mantel. Other press reports mentioning Avon Coppersmith include Wemett's May 22, 1947 sale of the property to Cole and the July 11, 1947 dissolution of their partnership.[33] But mostly the reports are more a way to indicate Wemett's enduring entrepreneurship than to report on Avon Coppersmith. In mid-1949, for instance, after the partnership dissolved, community newspapers reported that Wemett had turned his attention to creating a two-hundred-acre "vacation center" or girl's camp.[34]

Arthur Cole maintains a presence in mid-1950s newspaper reports, though not for his craftsmanship or shop ownership. Instead, his activism on behalf of Route 20 roadside commerce attracted press attention. The New York State Thruway began its encroachment on leisure travel, and especially, the economic climate of communities and businesses located parallel to the tollway in the 1950s. The Thruway's first section, running from Utica to Rochester, opened in 1954. Initially, there were moments of complacency concerning the new highway's inroads on local economies and traffic.[35] They were short-lived. Quickly, by 1955, there appeared reports of a 30 percent loss of traffic volume on Route 20 and disproportionate economic suffering in the Finger Lakes region, including Avon.[36] "The opening up of the N.Y. State Thruway has had its influence," the *Geneva Times* editorialized, "on speeding tourists right past many an interesting and beautiful spot, presumably unmindful of it."[37] Located on Route 20, Geneva is fewer than ten miles south of the Thruway. Press reports characterized the Thruway as acting as a "siphon" to local businesses and the road's relationship to Route 20 commerce characterized as "a rivalry." Only an occasional voice touted lemonade instead of lemons and suggested the Thruway represented progress and that it might even "prove a boon" to the Route 20 corridor. The Thruway, one editorial opined, perfectly accommodated fast drivers, thereby diminishing traffic and making "motoring over the old routes now much more pleasant"[38] and less-hurried for all the others.

Businesses along Route 20 responded to the Thruway's economic threat by forming the US Route 20 Freeway Association of New York State in 1955. Art Cole was an active participant. The distinctly named "Freeway" (as opposed to "toll-way") Association's leadership was composed of "men representing motor court associations and natural wonders organizations."[39] Claiming membership of more than one thousand, the group's membership drive was headed up by motel owner Walter Mintel, who made "temporary headquarters at the Crest Hill [*sic*] Motel, Avon. Working closely with him is the Freeway group's treasurer, Albert [*sic*] Cole, who is more popularly known throughout the country as 'The Avon Coppersmith.' "[40] The group unsuccessfully petitioned the state to change Route 20's name to "State Freeway"[41] and launched a campaign to lure motorists back to Route 20. Under the slogan "Save the Toll and See the State," the Association printed a half million color brochures touting the virtues of the highway.[42] Claiming distribution across the United States and Canada, the brochure extolled "the charms of scenery along the route" to travelers who picked up a copy.[43] Appearing often in news reports about the Association, Cole is sometimes mentioned as one representing business interests in the Routes 5 and 20 area or Avon, specifically. Other news stories describe Cole as an officer in or being a representative to the Association. Only rarely is his Avon Coppersmith affiliation mentioned.[44]

Despite the hopes of a few, any Thruway "novelty effect" was a better predictor for enhanced public attraction and long-term adoption than the opposite. Traffic on the Thruway increased steadily. The Association's colorful brochure may have persuaded some but not nearly enough to make up for the tremendous loss of Route 20 travelers and customers to the faster highway; the Association disbanded in 1962. In the absence of press reports to the contrary, and given the persistence of Avon Coppersmith until 1970, there must have been sufficient business for, at least, Cole's enterprise. Still, the handwriting on the 1954 Route 20 blackboard traversing New York State was clearly legible. For those businesses dependent upon casual passersby in automobiles—restaurants, motels, gift shops—that pool of customers was fast evaporating. In the late 1950s, Art Cole explored the possibility of opening a satellite location for the Avon Coppersmith. Tom Cole recalls his father taking off for Florida in the family's 1958 Chevy Biscayne with a friend; they were back in a week, Tom reported, and nothing further came of the idea.[45]

The Cole-Coppersmith public record is spotty, and there is no evidence to suggest Cole was independently wealthy, never mind that his business was an act of philanthropy. Quite the opposite. His son, Tom, confirms Cole's long work hours ("He would answer the door at any hour"), noting the family "didn't take vacations" and "we never went anywhere" because they were so tied to the shop. Opening at 8 a.m. and closing at 5 p.m. (or 8 or 9 p.m. in summer months), the shop was open

364 days a year. A small sign invited people to ring the shop's bell during off-hours, and it was not unusual for Art to switch on the lights and tour visitors through the facility at all hours. Business was strong enough for Cole to hire others to work for him at the copper shop and on the sales floor and did so throughout much of the time he operated it. William Nelligan, for instance, worked on and off as a coppersmith at Avon; briefly, he owned his own shop, in competition with Art, just down the road from the Coppersmith.[46] Several Avon women found professional fulfillment working there as salesclerks; both Ivy Loeper Gaylord's and Edna Roberts's[47] obituary make note of their Avon Coppersmith careers. We can assume some level of continuous profitability as Cole enlarged the shop multiple times during his ownership (see figure 6.5).

As its name suggests, the turn of the century Arts *and* Crafts movement accommodates an alliance and affiliation between equals. Two streams merging to form a river. A few decades forward, the Craft (or Crafts)

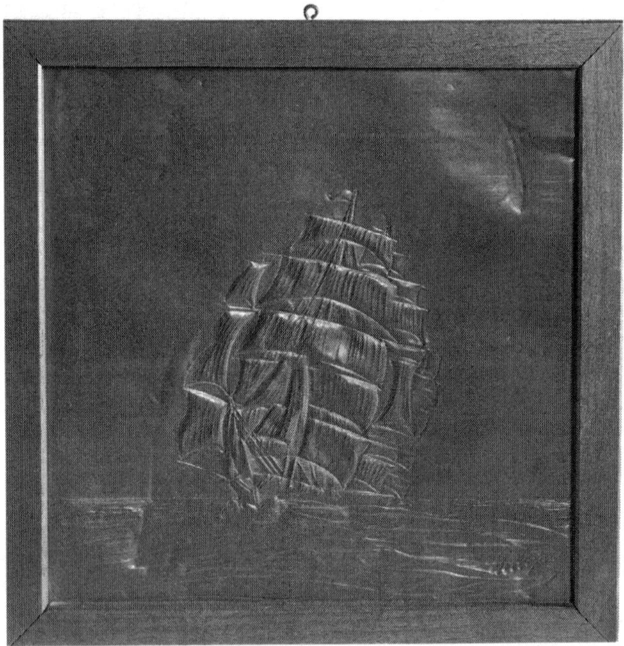

Figure 6.5. Framed hammered copper plaque by William Nelligan who occasionally worked at Avon Coppersmith. Dated 1940 in pencil on the back of the frame and with a paper foil Avon Coppersmith label. Private collection. Photograph by A. Sue Weisler.

movement asserted a singular identity, one independent of and no longer beholden to the status and legitimacy of the other. Braznell claims "the American craft revival was already brewing in the early 1940s."[48] Around the time of the Second World War, actions asserting the legitimacy and significance of uppercase Craft began to emerge. No longer to be thought of as homebound hobbies, or pursuits taught to juveniles at summer camp, Craft asserted itself. Aileen Webb, its most visible advocate, brought with her financial capital and social status. Arthur Cole's involvement in a broader Craft movement is undocumented and his likelihood of doing so seems remote. There is no evidence for this in his biography; instead, public reports suggest a modest craftsman engaged in a few civic organizations and perhaps equally involved in a businessman's self-interest group. With more than twenty years professional experience at his craft—he had, after all, earned a living at metalwork—Cole would have been self-confident about his professional legitimacy. Enlisting in an amorphous, nascent army of aspiring craftsmen might seem redundant if not superfluous to someone already abundantly self-aware of the profession's legitimacy.

Like the "drive-in" movie theater, "The Avon Coppersmith" is a perfectly descriptive name revealing where and what. Asserting professionalism and exclusivity—there is but one—it is without mystical or historical pretentions as was the case with Roycroft. The name neither invites nor promotes conversation and doesn't require explanation or lecture, as might have been Hubbard's intention at Roycroft. "Avon Coppersmith" is unambiguous about what the public would see and was being offered. The name is telegraphic in its straightforward simplicity and is complete without any implication of braggadocio. By contrast, at the East Aurora enterprise, one could purchase copper objects along with a substantial menu of other consumer items: books and magazines, printed mottos, paintings, furniture, a hotel room for the evening, and even dinner. While dining at the Roycroft Inn, one might sit below a bark-backed oak log emblazoned with the carefully carved admonishment: "Fletcherize." This was also available for sale as a printed motto (unframed or, at extra cost, framed) or on a two-foot long, smooth-sanded oak plank with a deep red-brown color suitable for hanging above one's own dining table. But Avon Coppersmith did not entirely disassociate itself from Arts and Crafts and its Roycroft "roots." The medium—copper—was the unambiguous link, at least for those customers with long memories; the handwork evident by the hammer marks was another. And it is unlikely Art Cole would have refrained from any mention of his past work and employer, even if he did not volunteer it. The shop's stylistic metalwork coupled with hand-craftsmanship evoked nostalgia as much as it did contemporary aesthetic preferences and quality standards.

7

Passengers and Passages

Roadside Craftsmen's weavers and metalsmiths received only glancing press attention, but its woodworker, Homer E. Bullock (1888–1957), is featured in several reports. As with Daugherty's biography, the facts about Bullock's as presented in contemporaneous press stories are somewhat elastic. The stories transcend national boundaries as though to better underscore their (and his) colorful glamor. One report painting an especially exotic picture indicated that "Bullock spent his boyhood on the Isle of Pines,"[1] today Isla de la Juventud, the second-largest Cuban island. Family history indicates otherwise;[2] Homer worked there with his brother from about 1919 to 1924, when he was in his thirties. Unmentioned in the news story was perhaps a motivating factor for his move to Cuba: a nonspecific *Rushville Chronicle and Gorham New Age* report of Homer's 1919 bankruptcy.[3] Eleanor Chester's 1935 article further exaggerated the Caribbean, Spanish-accented tale, describing him as "a middle-aged man, who has spent most of his life in Cuba."[4] Most of his life was spent in the United States, however: all of it in Western New York. Homer Bullock worked steadily at Roadside Craftsmen beginning in 1934 until the war interrupted the craft business, along with most everything else, in 1941.

Roadside's Costar

Born in 1888 at his parents' East Lake Road home on Keuka Lake, Yates County, Homer Bullock took to woodwork at an early age, helping his father in the sawmill business. In 1908, his parents moved to the Isle of

Pines, he married Mary Rector in 1911, and he farmed rented property in Milo, south of Penn Yan. Following the death of their first child, Homer and Mary moved to Waterloo, where he was a trolley conductor, and then they joined his parents and a brother, Edgar, in Cuba. Edgar had started a box manufacturing company, the Pine-Box Lumber Company, that supplied fruit shippers, including the West Indies Fruit Importing Company, with containers for their products. There, Homer taught himself wood turning, producing a line of "novelties" including vases and candleholders.[5]

In both the 1925 and 1935 newspaper reports, Bullock's expertise with wood is established by virtue of his residence at a distant foreign location. In the earlier report, the story simply states his familiarity with the indigenous woods. The later assessment is more detailed: "From the rare woods of Cuban jungles—satin wood, smoke wood, granadilla, yaiti, sabicu, juimiqui, roble [gallo] and Ramon d'Acosta—the woodworker [Bullock] fashions his wares." The woods are so rare, the 1925 report states, many are "found only in virgin forests where there are no roads." As though not poignant enough, "Only the trained woodman can locate them," the story continues, and the logs "have to be cut into short lengths and carried out on the backs of the workmen." So exotically foreign are the woodworker's raw materials that "even the Boy Scout troops failed to recognize any of them." Bullock's skill as a craftsman is less well articulated. The 1925 report only indicates his early love for woodcraft and that "he later learned the art of wood carving." Chester's article doesn't discuss Bullock's training and later seems to contradict her earlier assertion about the expertise required for working the raw, rare material: "The art of the wood craftsman, like that of the Potter and Weaver, lies in the simplicity and utility of the articles which can be made from inexpensive and everyday materials."

Returning to the United States, Bullock thought of a way to monetize his recently developed interest in wood novelties. The *Penn Yan Express* reported Woodcraft Products Corporation was formed at the end of 1924 with $10,000 capital stock and governed by three directors: Charles D. Willis, J. D. Rogers, and J. K. Sheridan, all of Penn Yan.[6] Bullock returned to Cuba in November the same year and shipped a substantial quantity of the exotic woods back to upstate New York.[7] A small factory near Bullock's Second Milo home was erected, and in March 1925, the *Penn Yan Democrat* reported that Woodcraft Products would "manufacture novelties such as vases, jardinieres, lamp standards, bases, etc., from choice wood imported from the Isle of Pines."[8] Bullock won prizes at local fairs for his many novelties.[9] Small display ads in community newspapers for a few Penn Yan and Elmira stores featured Woodcraft's products that were priced at fifty cents to four dollars with most items averaging two dollars. The advertisements advised readers they would "make ideal Christmas gifts." And, in early 1927, Bullock traveled to New York City on behalf of Woodcraft to drum up business for their "entirely new line of novelties."[10] The enterprise, however, was short-lived. By the end of 1927, a sheriff's sale of Woodcraft's real estate property was ordered, and it took place in February 1928. Voluntary dissolution papers for the corporation were filed in April 1928.[11]

Following the collapse of Woodcraft, and a year later, the collapse of the world economy, Bullock worked briefly at the Singer Sewing Machine Company's distribution outlet in Geneva. An irregular string of jobs followed, including delivering coal, while his wife, Mary, handled baking duties, and his sister, Ruth, sold cookies to neighbors. Clarence Wemett had heard about Homer's skills from friends familiar with Woodcraft and from newspaper reports. Wemett was also a distant cousin of Homer's wife, Mary. And, luckily, Homer still had an ample supply of the exotic Isle wood in storage along with equipment from the failed Woodcraft enterprise.[12] In 1934 Bullock became Roadside Craftsmen's woodworker, earning $18 a week.

Bullock's hiring dovetailed with the relocation of the former Branchport church. Bullock's son, Paul, remembered his father's workspace this way:

His woodshop took up the eastern half of the basement floor; the potter had the other half. The basement was at ground level on the north end and underground on the south end [where Routes 5 and 20 are located]. The southern end of his space was the finishing room where the wood products were given several coats of lacquer. The lacquer booth had a large fan to evacuate the fumes and the rest of the room was filled with racks for the drying products. [Either Paul Bullock's memory is inaccurate—as this description places the exhaust fan underground—or there is a text error in the original memoir transposing "southern" for "northern" in the finishing room's placement.] Between coats the product was lightly sanded to prepare for the next. The finishing area was separated from the rest of the space by a large cloth curtain. The balance of the woodworking space was filled with a table saw, a band saw, a small turning lathe, a large lathe, a belt sander, and other equipment. In the summer, the large lathe was moved outside in front of the building for Homer to perform his turning skills for potential customers. The space was well lit with windows on the both the north and east sides. Although there was a blower that evacuated the sawdust outside, this area was a very dusty place.[13]

In the basement or outdoors, Bullock turned bowls of various sizes, mostly from gum wood, Paul recalled. Only occasionally would Homer work with his "prized exotic woods," as they were difficult to turn. Clear or colored lacquer finished the pieces, depending upon the beauty of the wood's grain. While some of the work was displayed and sold in the building, "much was sold wholesale to department stores and the like." Homer's oldest son, Phil, worked at Roadside when needed, earning $12 a week.[14]

The start of the war prompted closures at businesses nationwide, especially among those not vital to the war effort. Both Roadside and Coppersmith felt the pinch, and many craftsmen went on furlough (as did their paychecks). To help support the family, Mary Bullock, a stay-at-home mom, babysat and cleaned house for her Bloomfield neighbor and the boss's son, Norris Wemett. During the war, Homer worked at a furniture factory and then at a plant that made parts for Army rifles. Beginning two years before the war, Homer made string instruments, violins, and violas. Described by the reporter as "a natural-born craftsman,"[15] his output was modest. Work for Roadside may have been spotty, though there is no documentation for this. A short entry in the *East Bloomfield Review*, a monthly newsletter, suggests the opposite. Amid numerous war-related reports, the October 1944 issue noted Robert Bullock, Homer's son who helped him in Roadside's shop, left for the service. "Since the importation of fancy goods from abroad has been stopped," the notice indicated, "there has been a great demand for Mr. Bullocks [*sic*] wooden articles in the best New York shops. . . . Most anything you can think of can be turned by Mr. Bullock."[16] Beginning in 1945, Bullock and his son, Phil, worked together out of the family home in Holcomb (immediately east of East Bloomfield) producing wood products similar and identical to those once made for Roadside. Named "Bullock and Son" and "Finger Lakes Woodcraft," Phil was a reluctant partner, his younger brother recalls, and the business folded in 1948, when Homer was sixty years old. A December

11, 1946 advertisement in the *Kingston Daily Freeman* featured handmade polished woodenware, products of New York's "Roadside Craftsmen." The ad listed four specific items: "Modernistic salt & pepper, $1.75"; "Glass & wood relish dish, $3.75"; "Cheese and cracker tray, $ 5.45"; and "3-pc salad set $6.65."

The public record for Bullock is a fraction—quantitatively and qualitatively—of that for Daugherty. But reporters followed a nearly identical narrative outline for each man. The Bullock script was colorful with portions of the narrative scenes foreign. Local readers would immediately apprehend the contrasts implied, even if imprecisely depicted: sandy beaches lapped by ocean waves under warm, blue skies versus the gray, snow-covered terrain and harsh weather of long western New York winters. Schoolhouse versions of the sixteenth-century explorer Ponce de León and the quest for a fountain of youth, foreign language, even palm trees and their association with a mystical internationalism would have been evoked. An embellished biography was coupled with elements of tropical exoticism of material and medium to advance a drama that together elevated the story, the craft, the man, and the enterprise. Skilled human talent captured and shaped unformed, scarce raw materials into conventional, recognizable products readers would at once find useful and beautiful. Readers may have experienced a sense of uplifting inspiration by reading the stories; admiration as much for the Roadside enterprise as for the craftsman, coupled with the potential for patronage, were the benefits derived by Roadside Craftsmen from such reports.

"Guest" Stars

Some reports about Roadside Craftsmen refer to the enterprise as a "cooperative." This may suggest, especially to contemporary readers, some kind of shared ownership or a financial and managerial responsibility for the business among those working there. Such was not the case. Roadside Craftsmen was a "cooperative" insofar as the enterprise gathered together in one place and under a single business name craft workers in different media. Those working there received modest paychecks.[17] The work produced at and sold by Roadside Craftsmen carried its name and, only rarely, the mark of the craftsman responsible for producing it.[18] Nonetheless, those working for Roadside apparently enjoyed a certain camaraderie. For instance, Roadside Craftsmen fielded a baseball team, coincidentally mirroring the baseball team and musical bands at the earlier-formed Roycroft craft community in East Aurora.

Guy Daugherty was Roadside's senior craftsman both in terms of personal chronology and as the one holding the lengthiest association with Wemett's Craftsmen enterprise. Daugherty was also the most prominently and frequently mentioned craftsman in press reports about Roadside and was first as the ceramic craft master. Bullock's presence at Roadside was made significant physically—with an outdoor demonstration and workspace and, indoors, by occupying half the basement—and, to a much lesser extent, in press reports. But neither Daugherty nor Bullock worked alone. Over the years Roadside Craftsmen was in operation, two dozen or more other people were employed there. One report suggests (but probably exaggerates) that with resumption of metal production after the war, the Roadside Craftsmen's wrought iron operation in Hemlock alone might employ about twenty craftsmen.[19]

Most likely the earliest Roadside crafter, aside from Daugherty, was Mrs. Nora Taylor. A native of Berea, Kentucky, she was involved with Roadside's weaving production for a decade.[20] Taylor introduced weaving at Roadside Craftsmen in 1930,[21] and six of her students were reported as Roadside Craftsmen weavers. Chester's 1935 article mentions Georgia native and Berea College (Kentucky) graduate Gertrude Denning as working "an old weaving loom" at Roadside Craftsmen; several 1935 *Victor Herald* reports indicate this was a summer job and other reports state Denning later moved to Elkton, Maryland, for a job as "home demonstration leader." Perhaps as many as a dozen or more students and graduates of Alfred University's ceramics program worked with Daugherty over the years. The earliest, Elizabeth Rogers, was a School of Ceramics graduate who decorated the vessels Daugherty threw and fired (and who worked beginning summer 1932 through fall 1936.[22] Richard Thomas worked with Daugherty during the 1936 and 1937 summers before graduating from Alfred.[23] Later, in 1941, Heinz Rodies, a junior studying ceramic engineering at Alfred, likely was a summertime assistant to Daugherty.[24] Former Roycroft coppersmith Walter Jennings was reported as "a part-time contributor" at Roadside Craftsmen,[25] as he was at Wemett's other craft enterprise, Avon Coppersmith; how often, if ever, Jennings was working onsite is unknown, but his role is more likely one of consignor than demonstrating craftsman. And, at the short-lived Cooperstown satellite location (see "Spreading Out," below), Deborah Sweet, a Rhode Island School of Design graduate, made sterling silver jewelry when the shop opened in November 1941.

In addition to Daugherty and Bullock, only one other craftsman enjoyed a long-term relationship with Roadside Craftsmen: Clarence N. Curtis (1900–1970) of Lakeville, New York. In fact, his Roadside career may have been among those with the longest tenure with the briefest public exposure. A cryptic note in the April 29, 1937 Lakeville Neighborhood News column of the *Geneseo Livingston Republican* indicated Curtis "accepted a position in Hemlock."[26] Variously referred to as "The Forge Wrought Iron Works," "The Forge of Roadside Craftsmen," and "The Smiths," the just-north-of Hemlock venue created ornamental iron for the Roadside enterprise. Beginning in 1937, Curtis was joined by silversmith W. Eugene Manchester until Manchester's death in 1941. A member of the Boston Arts and Crafts Society, Manchester was a summer teacher at the Chautauqua Institution;[27] and his wife, Marguerite Elwood, taught art at Rochester's Mechanics Institute and was an occupational therapist. Not much more is known about the iron works. Occasional small display ads for the iron works ran between 1949 and 1957 in local newspapers; wrought iron porch railings and house numbers by Roadside Craftsmen, the ads read, were custom-made, estimates were free and would be offered courteously, and customers were invited to visit "The Forge" in Hemlock. The iron shop business was purchased from Roadside Craftsmen in October 1959 by Mark Wemett, one story reported (probably meaning Wemett Corporation[28]). Manufacturing "continued to operate as in the past," though many items "are wholesaled through numerous gift shops." The Forge was also a dealer for an awning and canopy firm and a sales agent for Gorman-Rupp Pump Company.[29] Extant price lists for the Forge of Roadside Craftsmen, though, are dated to as late as May 1, 1962.[30] Wemett and Curtis appear, from occasional notes in local newspapers, to have had a social as well as a professional relationship; for instance, the Wemetts and the Curtises were dinner guests of the Kingsleys, the June 9, 1955 *Perry Herald* reported. Though Curtis took ill in early 1956 and required hospitalization, he was back at work by March and, a classified ad in the October 11, 1956 issue of the *Livonia Gazette* indicated he was seeking "a full-time man for a permanent job" at Roadside Craftsmen's iron shop.

Spreading Out, Briefly

Unsurprisingly, work produced at Roadside found its way onto the display shelves at Wemett's other craft operation, Avon Coppersmith, and vice versa. Wemett also saw craft and gasoline interests as intertwined and the Roadside Craftsmen building was used to host parties for the Shell operators.[31] At least two farther-flung locations for Roadside Craftsmen can be identified.

So successful was Wemett's venture initially that, at least once and for a short while, Bloomfield Pottery had a presence in nearby Rochester. Beginning in September 1932, the Pottery rented space on East Main Street, above Sibley's department store. An article about the initiative indicated that while manufacturing would continue at the Bloomfield location, the satellite location offered pottery sales through the holidays.[32] The story also reported that summer sales in Bloomfield were successful and about five thousand pieces were made and sold. No further reports about the Rochester location were found. A decade later, another retail venue for Roadside Craftsmen was established considerably east of Bloomfield: in Cooperstown, New York at 96 Lake Street, State Route 80, at the south end of Otsego Lake.[33] With unfortunate timing, it opened in November 1941, just a month before the United States entered World War II; the war's demands, as much on materials as men, rippled across businesses and the US economy. The shop was managed by Wemett's daughter, Mrs. Ruth Kenzie (later, Woodruff). Previously, Ruth had been a good ambassador on behalf of Roadside Craftsmen by, for instance, offering presentations to various civic groups on the history of pottery.[34]

The addition of Roadside Craftsmen to Cooperstown's commerce prompted a lengthy article announcing the enterprise. The feature story casts a glowing halo over the town and the manufacturer: The "village boasts a unit of one of the state's most distinctive industries," it reported. Trotting out a by-then well-thumbed script, the article emphasizes the shop's original, handmade inventory, contrasting it with factory-made goods: "This is not a workshop of machines and mass production, but one of creative self-expression and skilled handiwork." Most likely, the Cooperstown inventory was imported from Bloomfield, with the exception of jewelry, as the venue did not appear spacious enough to accommodate clay or wood crafting. Roadside's combination of traditional methods with modern techniques is noted, along with "the real purpose of the enterprise": "To renew interest in the hand crafts." Roadside Craftsmen, the article patriotically enthuses, is in the respected (but not-for-profit) company of "museums, historical and educational organizations" that together "make us conscious of the value of things from our past . . . [and] our rich American heritage." Occasional display ads emphasized the shop's gift mission: "Let us solve your Christmas Problems," a December 11, 1942 newspaper advertisement offered.[35] The duration of the Cooperstown shop was brief, though apparently considerably longer than the Rochester venue. Regardless of interest or sales, its closing was doubtlessly due to the "distraction" of the war. An October 1943 notice in the *Cooperstown Otsego Farmer* indicated the shop would close on the twentieth "for the duration."[36] Six months later, the *Penn Yan Chronicle Express* reported that Ruth Kenzie had sold the Cooperstown business and was enrolling in Columbia University to study occupational therapy (see figure 7.1).[37]

Moving On and Out

By the end of the war, Clarence Wemett's attention and interests began to turn elsewhere. But he was not ready to completely abandon his earlier projects. "A piece of sizable postwar construction is going forward rapidly

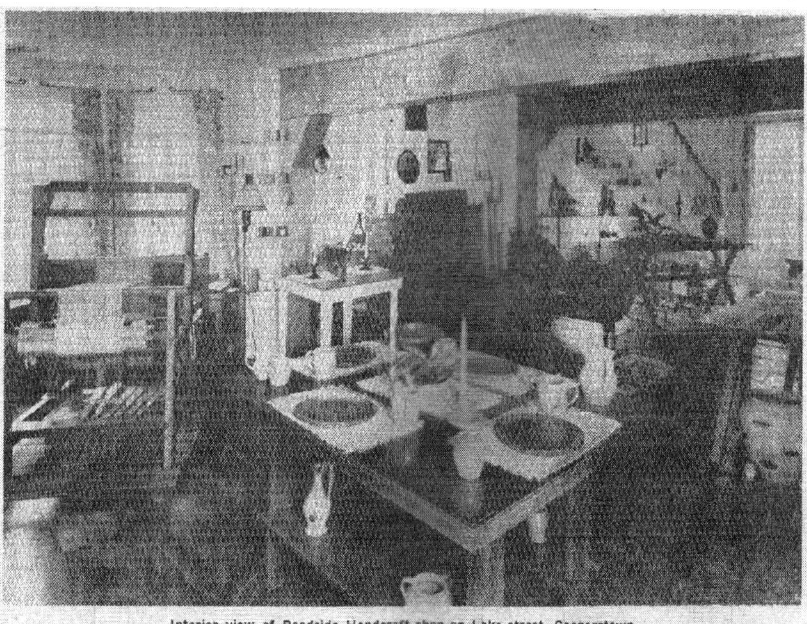

Figure 7.1. Roadside Craftsmen's satellite retail shop in Cooperstown, New York. Cooperstown *Otsego Farmer*, July 17, 1942, "Roadside Handcraft Shop Extends Hearty Welcome." Photograph courtesy of the Fenimore Art Museum Library, Cooperstown, New York. Public domain.

just north of Hemlock village," the *Lima Recorder* reported in September 1945.[38] The 42x108-foot cinderblock building being built would house Roadside Craftsmen's wrought-iron foundry, Wemett said. During the war, iron work was accomplished across the street at the Smiths "on a limited scale." Together, the effect of wartime restrictions and current demand for the foundry's product placed them "many months behind in filling wholesale orders," Wemett explained.

In 1947, Wemett relinquished his interest in Avon Coppersmith. As was true for the Hemlock iron works and the Bloomfield location, Coppersmith had also gone on hiatus during the war. At about the same time, development of Wemett's two-hundred-acre woodland vacation center, located in the Bristol Hills south of Bloomfield, must have been in the planning stages. In February 1949, a Rochester newspaper reported on the development of the "Skioscope" and "Skiland" as winter season companion to a proposed girls camp to be managed by Mary Wemett.[39] By May 1949, newspaper reports announced "Egypt Valley" as Wemett's newest initiative, and a box ad in the *Livonia Gazette*[40] and several other local newspapers identified it as a summer camp for girls. The Burby Hollow site on Route 20A is "rich in beauty," the *Livonia Gazette* reported. The grand opening took place on June 26, 1949, and within a few years it was judged as "highly successful."[41] Located not far from Clarence Wemett's summer home, the camp was described as a mix of "vacation center" and meeting-convention space with a "camp." But Egypt Valley was very much a camp (and one for girls) that included a craft house and several structures, each housing six campers. A 1955 New York State Department of Commerce booklet lists it as such, indicating a staff of twenty and its suitability for seven- to seventeen-year-old campers. Articles about it note the camp's emphasis on physical education as well as programs in music, dance, drama, photography, and crafts, suggesting at least a certain modest, albeit ambitious, relationship to Roadside Craftsmen. Most reports about the camp make mention of, if not lead with, Wemett's resume of business innovations, including Roadside and Coppersmith.[42] In the late 1950s, the camp was sold to the Ontario County, Seven Lake Girl Scouts Council.[43]

In 1950, Keuka College received a potter's wheel from Roadside Craftsmen donated by Mary Wemett.[44] The Wemett connection to Keuka may have been in part related to the Roadside church's original location but, more likely, to the fact that Clarence Wemett's daughter, Ruth, was a Keuka College alumna.[45] The donation may have been a fitting closure to an enterprise founded by faith in nostalgia but driven by modern, entrepreneurial capitalism. Also in 1950, Roadside Craftsmen's chief ceramist and the business's public "face," Guy Daugherty, was seventy-plus years old. Wemett was not far behind. Each had had long albeit very different but interwoven successful careers. Nearly simultaneously with the closing of Roadside Craftsmen in 1953, Wemett bought the White Horse Tavern in East Avon, renaming it the "White Horse Inn."

A western New York landmark, the tavern started as a hotel in 1812 and was a stagecoach stop on the Albany-Buffalo run. Located within a mile of Avon Coppersmith, on the southeast corner at the intersection of Routes 5 and 20 and Route 15, one report described it as "a landmark to thousands of motorists."[46] Wemett said a Shell gasoline station was a certain addition to the property; indeed, gas pumps and a Shell sign quickly appeared on the Route 15-facing side of the building. Projecting into the future, he said that "the most likely uses" for the building included an antique center or exchange and perhaps a country store and that he expected to reopen the inn's dining room.[47]

The historic site's acquisition proved to be another publicity generator. A few months after the purchase, during its restoration, the *Livonia Gazette* reported a dozen gems were found hidden inside one of the inn's walls.[48] A separate front-page story reported on a forthcoming antiques show to be hosted at the inn;[49] several advertisements for the antiques show followed. Those plans ended August 1, 1955, when the inn was destroyed by a fire. Eighteen fire departments responded to the blaze, and "firemen laid nearly a mile of hose lines to pump water from ponds."[50] The estimated loss was $100,000, and "only the exterior walls of the building" remained.[51] However, one year after the fire, in August 1956 and on what was announced as the fiftieth anniversary of the Wemett Corporation, Clarence Wemett opened the White Horse Shopping Plaza—what today we would call a strip mall— with the White Horse IGA Foodliner grocery store as the Plaza's anchor. The facing material for the IGA building, one newspaper story reported, "will be bricks from the old White Horse Tavern."[52]

Both the Egypt Valley and White Horse Inn initiatives suggest a change in Wemett's business orientation from those previously guiding the establishment of Roadside Craftsmen and Avon Coppersmith. The two newer venues shared with the older two operations physical locations on heavily traveled highways. As well, the two newer locations were imbued with and shared the older Roadside's significant history; the tavern's was not only longer than the original Roadside (Branchport) structure by twenty years, but arguably was more important, as it also had once served as a post office. The differences between newer and older enterprises lay with the customer base sought and the customer's reason for going to the location. Both Roadside and Coppersmith relied on the serendipitous but steady stream of passing motorists for customers. Local patronage was not ignored, but its limitations were recognized. Automobiling travelers could sustain the Roadside and Coppersmith businesses with one-time purchases because there were so many of them. However, most purchases at the Avon and Bloomfield locations occurred by chance rather than intention. By contrast, both Egypt Valley and the inn were destinations: places patrons consciously sought out and went to for identifiable reasons. The incentive motivating Wemett's entry to the new and his exit from the old, though not likely thought of in that way at the time, was the 1954 opening of the New York State Thruway. The high-speed roadway seemed certain to divert traffic—and customers—from the slower, older roadway; and, in fact, that was what happened.

When Roadside Craftsmen closed its Bloomfield location in 1953, the building was leased to a sympathetic business, The Woodcroftery Shops of Wayland,[53] located thirty or so miles southwest of East Bloomfield. The proud old building was renamed "Roadside Woodcroftery." The new name not only signaled a "merger" of the structure's previous enterprise and its new occupant but also traded on and exploited the reputations of both, including their shared and long-standing business interests, inventories, and customer motivations for purchases. The Roadside Woodcroftery, at least outwardly, very much seemed an intentional, strategic merger, even if that was not the case. The Roadside Craftsmen enterprise could proudly trace its history back nearly a quarter of a century. Likewise, certainly local residents and local history buffs, and perhaps some tourists, recognized Woodcroftery's turn-of-the-century regional roots and, since 1936, its more recent and widely recognized affiliation with crafts. In addition to Woodcroftery's East Bloomfield location, Woodcroftery operated a gift shop at one corner of Wemett's White Horse Inn, albeit briefly; period photographs show the firm's sign hanging from what was probably the northern end of the structure.[54]

Woodcroftery was formed in 1935, the same year as Roadside Craftsmen's church debut, by three Wayland family members: John Plail, Johanna "Honnie" Coley, and John P. Coley—father, daughter, and grandson, respectively. Successor to the Plail Brothers Chair Company, as press reports unfailingly noted, Woodcroftery's young president, John Plail Coley, had personal interest and skill in wood crafts. In at least that one

PLAIL BROTHERS CHAIR CO.

Clarence Wemett's craft businesses were sympathetically tied to the American Arts and Crafts movement. Roadside Craftsmen's and Avon Coppersmith's products, the craftsmanship required for making them, and, in a few cases, the craftsmen themselves were associated with the decorative style popular 1900–1920. Despite Roadside's 1953 closing, the connection to Arts and Crafts persisted with the building's subsequent occupant.

The historic church building was leased to the Woodcroftery Shops of Wayland in early 1953.[55] The building and its operation were renamed "Roadside Woodcroftery," exploiting two locally well-known names, and it was slated to open two months later in spring 1953. Woodcroftery's product line was aligned with inventory one would expect in a gift shop, as well as with Roadside Craftsmen's specific line of crafts. Local customers may not have noticed much of a difference between the two shops, if they noticed one at all; for traveling tourists without any historical context and who happened to stop, of course, it was business as usual.

The connection between Woodcroftery and American Arts and Crafts lies in the firm's history and ownership. Born in Wayland, John P. Coley (1915–2001) was the son of Richard and Johanna Plail Coley. John Coley's mother, Johanna ("Honnie," 1891–1953), was the daughter of John Plail (1868–1938), one of two brothers (with Joseph Plail, 1876–1962) who founded Plail Brothers Chair Co. in 1906. The Wayland furniture manufacturer operated out of a factory located on Second Street until 1933, employing nearly one hundred people.[56] Woodcroftery was widely reported as successor to the Plail Brothers Chair Co.[57]

John Plail worked at the Binghamton Chair Company before moving north to Wayland in 1902 with William H. Gunlocke and several other Binghamton employees. Together, they formed the W. H. Gunlocke Chair Company. Divesting their interest in the successful Gunlocke firm a few years later, John and Joseph Plail started Plail Brothers in a nearby building that once housed the American Drop Forge & Tool Co. As the local press not unhappily reported: "Wayland is to have another chair factory."[58] At Plail Brothers, John was in charge of design, Joseph was shop manager, and daughter Honnie performed accounting, office management, and sales duties. Plail Brothers manufactured a general line of mission-style furniture, as did many American furniture manufacturers during the period, and became known especially for the distinctive, slat-sided, barrel-form seating introduced about 1911. Plail barrel-back chairs featured long, narrow vertical oak slats that extended up from a horizontal floor rail to just underneath the arm rail; the chair's rear feet kicked or flared out slightly. Armchairs, arm rockers, and settees in this form could be purchased individually or as a parlor suite. The design was one appropriated as much from Frank Lloyd Wright and his furniture designs for many of his prairie-style homes, including Darwin Martin's in Buffalo, as from such European designers as Charles Rennie Macintosh or Josef Hoffman. There was also stylistic similarity between selected products produced by Plail and Majestic Furniture of Mexico, New York.[59]

Further connecting Woodcroftery to the Arts and Crafts movement was Plail daughter and Coley mother, Honnie. Described as a "disciple" of Elbert Hubbard and his East Aurora, New York Roycroft community, the Wayland firm's name is evidence for the devotion. Honnie Coley coined the name as a reference to wood crafted by hand, another reference to Roycroft's enterprise and the broader ethos of the Arts and Crafts movement. Reportedly, she made numerous trips to Hubbard's campus. Some Woodcroftery products were painted, another innovation introduced by Honnie, who learned decorative painting from a nearby neighbor, Sally Patchin.[60]

Woodcroftery advertised its products prominently, including full- and double-page placements in Buffalo newspapers. Upon leasing the Roadside Craftsmen building, Coley said the Bloomfield Roadside Woodcroftery would feature products similar and nearly identical to those already manufactured at its Wayland facility. In Wayland, Woodcroftery opened its Early American Gift Shop in 1956 inside its own former manufacturing facility on Lackawanna Street. The shop later moved to a location north of Wayland on Route 15, where it remained in business through the late 1970s.

way, his story resembles that of Roadside's Homer Bullock. The *Wayland Register* described him as "undismayed by the business reverses" of Plail Brothers and, more broadly, the Depression. Mentioning his "inability to attend college, John Plail Coley, following his graduation from Wayland High School in 1933, began in his home the production in wood of bridge sets, trays of various sizes and designs, coasters, cheese boards, candle sticks, fruit dishes, salad bowls, plates, lamps, bon-bon dishes, and other novel wood turnings. This work [was] turned out with the assistance of and under the supervision of his grandfather. Later the young man hopes to take up designing and industrial craftsmanship."[61]

With his mother as vice president and treasurer, and his grandfather as a design consultant, John Coley's Woodcroftery in 1936 opened "a roadside business" in suburban Batavia at the former Red Clover Inn and offered its inventory to the retail tourist trade.[62] Located about three miles west of Batavia, in the hamlet of Bushville, the inn was originally developed in 1923 as a tourist autocamp.[63] A newspaper report describes Woodcroftery a short while after opening in ways nearly indistinguishable from Roadside Craftsmen: "One of the newest phenomenon [*sic*] on the industry horizon is the growth of the roadside store where the American people pause to trade in their restive shopping."[64] The craftsmen were skilled artisans from local communities, one report stated, who use American materials and take pride in public enjoyment of their products. News stories characterize Woodcroftery's location as rural and isolated, its building quaint, and its ambience natural and wholesome. The same publication described Woodcroftery's inventory: "A complete line of furniture and table accessories" including "good trays, salad service of bowls, plates, book ends, candle holders, compote sets, desk and smoking accessories, magazine holders, book shelves, end and coffee tables, made in mahogany, walnut, maple and finished in natural Hazelwood. Other lines in hand-wrought products in metal, pottery and yarns will make an interesting and attractive feature of their shop."[65] See figure 7.2.

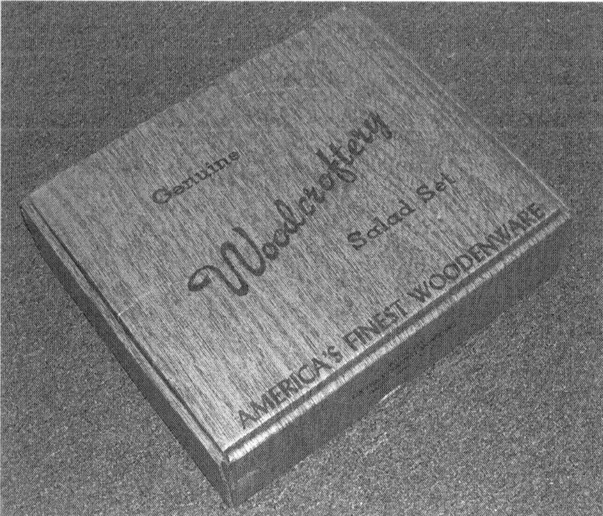

Figure 7.2. Woodcroftery box. Photograph by A. Sue Weisler.

After six years of operation in Batavia, Woodcroftery moved to a location in Wayland, not far from the Plail Brothers' original factory site, "where there is more space and facilities are available for the expanding business."[66] Woodcroftery Shops prospered, and the firm was described as having "the largest distribution of wooden bowls in the East" with "permanent display of its products in the New York gift market and also at the Merchandise Mart, Chicago."[67] Like many smaller family businesses, Woodcroftery closed during the war, and Coley served in the Naval Reserves, stationed in the South Pacific. One artist who began working at Woodcroftery toward the end of the war also painted miniature landscapes on Avon Coppersmith plates: Kitty Dennison of East Pembroke, New York. "I worked there for four years," she said, and "as a matter of fact, I believe that I was the one who started painting designs on [their] wooden bowls."[68]

The leased Roadside Craftsmen building, under its new name and management, was scheduled to open April 1, 1953. Coley said it would feature products already being manufactured at the Woodcroftery's Wayland facility. As before, two floors of the Roadside Woodcroftery would offer retail space and on the lower floor, where Homer Bullock and Guy Daugherty once worked, "light manufacturing of woodenware and pottery" would take place. Exactly how long Roadside Woodcroftery was in operation at the Bloomfield location and who was working there is not known. But its tenure could not have been lengthy. Once the Roadside Woodcroftery enterprise closed, the Bloomfield building sat idle and unoccupied for several years. But not unnoticed. The Reverend Chester Gertz of the Berean Gospel Church noticed. An undated typewritten document on Wemett Corporation letterhead outlines a "proposed sale of church property at East Bloomfield." The asking price would be $25,000. Presumably this was Clarence Wemett's proposal, and he had a buyer in mind when he composed it. The document concludes: "Mrs. Wemett and myself will pledge to missionary work $500.00 annually for a period of five years." On November 15, 1960, the Berean Church made a $25,000 purchase offer signed by Gertz for "The Wayside Craftsman [sic] Gift Shop." The mortgage for the property, between Berean Gospel Church, Inc. and The Roadside Craftsmen, Inc., in the amount of $21,700 at 4 percent interest was signed on December 20, 1960.[69] A newspaper reported the building "will again become an edifice of worship," and at least one Wemett son, Mark, worshipped there throughout his life.[70] The building's tradition of religious use continues. Since 1992, the Roadside Craftsmen structure has hosted the New Hope Fellowship, a Christian Elim Fellowship (Lima, New York) church.[71]

The Roadside Craftsmen's story is teased out from widely scattered newspaper stories. Most are brief. Neither business records nor personal diaries of the enterprise's actors are known to exist for review. Diaries would tell us a lot about a little; business records, just the reverse. Even if available, the result would remain an inexact, imperfect portrait. Invariably, some diary details are feathered and smoothed over, while others are overpainted with exaggerations, "refinements," and "improvements" made over time by different artists with different motivations and visions and using different brushes and paints.

Clarence Wemett solicited and exploited publicity in service to his craft business enterprise. Few advertisements for Roadside Craftsmen were located. As discussed in the following chapter, advertising would have helped solidify a local customer base. But the Bloomfield operation, like the one in Avon, was far more interested in attracting highway passersby as one-time clients. Although comparatively, Coppersmith virtually blitzed local papers with ads relative to Roadside's much more subdued presence. Maybe this was a function of Coppersmith's singular craft focus or its managing personality. And perhaps Wemett thought successful placement of news stories would better (or as well) serve the promotional interests of Roadside, and without the self-serving taint of paid messaging, or its costs.

Much remains unknown about the Roadside enterprise. To what extent, for instance, was Clarence Wemett a "hands-off" owner of Roadside Craftsmen, including shaping its product line and formulating its marketing? While its ceramics are often well marked to indicate the manufacturer, the same cannot be said for Roadside's other products in wood or, especially, fiber or iron. Textiles, marked with tags or labels pinned to them, long ago lost their identification. Unmarked wrought-iron objects seamlessly blend in with similarly styled pieces produced by other hands. And unmarked woodenwares are likewise nearly impossible to attribute to their makers, other than to perhaps suggest they were not the product of hobbyists or shop class pupils. Our inability to establish the origin of some currently extant objects manufactured at Roadside also means we cannot reliably estimate the operation's production output during the nearly twenty-five years it was in business. Contemporaneous reports of Roadside's pottery production volume and sales are likely invention or wishful thinking. The sources and costs of the raw materials likewise are unknown. Without business records, we do not know whether Roadside was profitable since persistence cannot be equated with profitability.

We do not know where and to whom Roadside's objects were shipped or how much of their business was driven by mail order. Nor can we estimate how much of the work was commissioned. What proportion of the total output was accounted for by sales at the whim of tourists seeking trinkets? No visitor's book—as is today common for gift shops—was located; self-reports by customers, including their addresses, are unavailable. Customer mailing lists have not been found and other promotional literature that might have been used by the enterprise was not uncovered. At the opposite end of sales and manufacturing, we know little about Roadside's employees, the creators. Were they paid hourly, with a salary, by piece work, or some combination of these permutations? Was there profit sharing? Except for a singular mention of an annual bonus and paid vacations, no further financial details about Roadside's workers were located. What were the number of hours employees worked, the number of employees (at any one time or over the course of Roadside's existence) or their employment status (full- or part-time)? As an example, one fugitive report indicates an "Ann Mattison assisting"[72] at Roadside Craftsmen in 1933 with no further reference. Aside from brief, anecdotal vignettes offered by a few workers' relatives, the workplace conditions and the equipment used by the craftsmen are nonspecific. We cannot determine with certainty its annual months of operation or who was working there, in which role, and when. Seasonal fluctuations in business operations cannot be tracked or assessed; at best, one report indicates that just before the war the business was open year-round, but only during the summer did the craftsmen offer their demonstrations.[73] Aside from contemporaneous news stories, much that remains of Roadside Craftsmen are colorful anecdotes and artifacts without context.

We do know where and for how long the enterprise existed. The extant objects in the hands of private collectors—principally the pottery—suggests a reliable, steady, and remarkably uniform output. Though handcraftsmanship was a virtue touted by Roadside, its ceramic products were stunningly similar, as though produced at a factory-like manufacturing operation rather than one-offs from a solitary potter working the clay. The early brochure for Bloomfield Pottery paradoxically suggests as much: handcraftsmanship yielding nearly perfectly identical output.

Shapes, colors, and glazes are as predictable for Roadside Craftsmen as the production pieces produced at and catalogued by such self-named "art potteries" as Rookwood in Cincinnati or the molded works created at Teco in Chicago. Truly unique one-off pots, especially those with unusual decoration and glaze (and less so their forms), from Roadside Craftsmen are so uncommon as to be surmised as "end-of-day" style pieces; what the potter threw with the clay remaining and glaze leftover before closing up for the evening.

8

Billboards

To promote the enterprise and its products, Roadside Craftsmen produced a few brief catalogues and only rarely employed paid advertising. The precise number, publication dates, and frequency with which the catalogues were issued, as well as their method and breadth of distribution, is unknown. However, a catalogue's intended audience can be inferred from its content. At least one Roadside catalogue, perhaps the earliest, is unambiguously directed at retail customers. Among the extant documents, most others seem to target wholesale distributors for Roadside Craftsmen's merchandise to other retail shop owners. An eminently portable and easily mailed sales device, printed brochures served Wemett and Roadside's ambition to achieve national reach for the East Bloomfield craft enterprise.

By contrast, Avon Coppersmith had a much more visible advertising presence. Examining a business's advertising is an unobtrusive way to understand how the business wishes to present itself to the public. Everything about the messaging, including the ad's content and description of its products or services, placement, graphics, and the selection of medium for the ad's presentation, is controlled by the advertiser; that is what they are paying for, after all. What examining ads does not allow is any assessment of the recipients' response to them. No matter how careful the scrutiny, observers will never know who saw the ads, read them, or how readers reacted to the ads' inducements. The compositional choices advertisers make indicate only how they want the public to understand their businesses.

Promoting Roadside Craftsmen

Roadside Craftsmen catalogues illustrate their products with line drawings and photographs, as had other furniture and decorative arts manufacturers previously. During the Arts and Crafts period, for instance, firms, including Gustav Stickley's Craftsman Workshops and Elbert Hubbard's Roycroft, made extensive use of regularly issued printed catalogues as trade stimulators. More than likely, Wemett was aware of such examples, perhaps even using them as models for Roadside's publications. The images present Roadside objects singly as well as in groups of like objects. Retail customers may have used the visuals to select a specific style and model—from which there may have been several—best suited for their tastes. Personalizing consumer choice by providing a menu of options helped create customer affinity for the exact object as well as, more broadly, the brand. Occasionally, Roadside's work is presented in environmental settings, helping retail customers better visualize the product in their own homes. Every bit as significant as these end-point consumers was the goal of landing Roadside's products on the shelves and in the display cases of retail stores spread out across the nation. Among wholesale buyers, the images afforded both a sample of the breadth of Roadside's inventory and an opportunity for buying agents to compare Roadside's to other manufacturers' product lines.

Among the earliest and maybe the first produced using the "Roadside Craftsmen" name is a six-page document. It was created in the 1930s, judging from the Art Deco hand lettering used for its name on the cover. In fact, Roadside's modernist typography is strikingly similar to that used on the façade for the 1931 McGraw-Hill Building in New York City (330 West Forty-Second Street), designed by Raymond Hood. The brochure's intended readers were most likely retail customers. The spare, polished design on the cover contrasts with childlike stick drawings for illustrations and hand-printed texts inside. On the cover, readers are succinctly instructed about both the booklet's contents and the contents' intended eventual destination: "Hand Made Gifts."

The cover's sparse text was a subtle but direct persuasive appeal to customers' altruism: what follows, the brochure suggests, is less for you and more for those you value, appreciate, and favor. Inside, cursive script (white lettering on a black background) individually identifies each medium and product in Roadside's inventory: hand-thrown pottery, hand-wrought copper and iron, inlaid and hand-turned wood, and hand weaving. Below, and occupying nearly half the page, black-and-white illustrations display promotional examples of the work. At the bottom third of each page, stick-figure caricatures of the personalities associated with each craft are shown, one to a page. In the case of weaving, the craftswoman is identifiable both by the presence of hair and a skirt. Each figure is accompanied by the craft's tools: the potter's foot pedal and wheel, anvil and hammer for the coppersmith, workbench and plane for the woodworker, furnace/forge for wrought iron, for wood turner a lathe, and a loom for the weaver. And at the foot of each page, hand-lettered stylized sans serif text touts the virtues of the medium and the beauty of the products produced.

The catalogue's back cover is an illustration of the shop's interior accompanied by a hand-lettered brief history of the building. The hand-drawn vignette is a reasonably accurate facsimile of the Roadside Craftsmen's interior fireplace-chimney—onsite visitors would immediately recognize the setting—and is signed in the lower right corner "RUST." The image shows a copper tray at center on the fireplace mantel with pottery vases anchoring either end and an iron candelabra in between. A log holder is on one side of the hearth with fireplace andirons and tools nearby. Copper or iron lanterns hang from the ceiling inside an oxen's yolk and a Roadside weaving lies in front of the hearth. The document's stylishly modern cover lettering is somewhat discordant with the lettering immediately below ("Hand Made Gifts") and, especially, with the interior pages that follow: images and texts best described as folksy, homey, and even backward-looking. The graphic art used for the sales brochure is nowhere near as slick or sophisticated as those used by earlier enterprises, including Craftsman Workshops and Roycroft. But the inside graphics fit the informal identity Roadside publicly expressed and its name suggested. Throughout, the booklet's design matches nearly perfectly in sentiment and tone the products being promoted: the stylistically naïve hand-lettering is congruent with the hand craftsmanship being offered (see figures 8.1–8.3).

A quarter century later, the cover for a catalogue dated February 1957 is illustrated with a woodblock-style image of a man working metal on an anvil. The image is graphically sympathetic to what one would expect from an Arts and Crafts movement publication—one temporally closer to and more aesthetically aligned with the 1930s publication. An artist's cipher, a conjoined M and W, is at the image's lower left corner. Perhaps this stands for Clarence Wemett's son, Mark, who was managerially involved with Roadside. But it might also signify Mark's twin sister, Mary Wemett, or his brother Norris's wife, also named Mary Wemett. But by

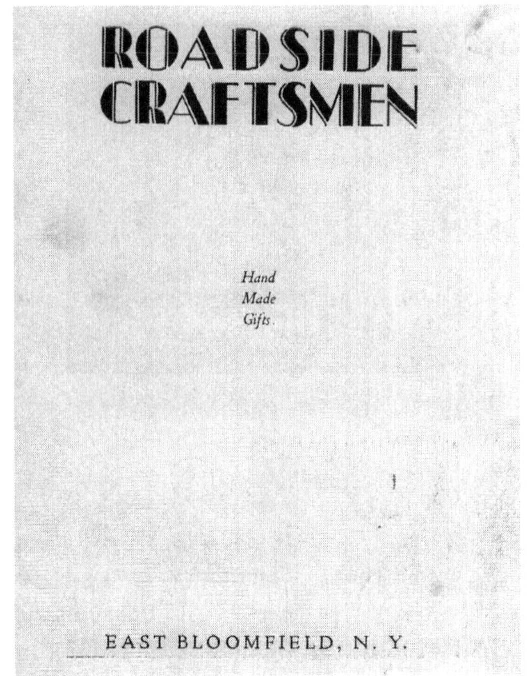

Figure 8.1. Cover for the 1930s Roadside Craftsmen retail catalogue. Photograph courtesy of Lee J. Wemett and http://www.wemett.net.

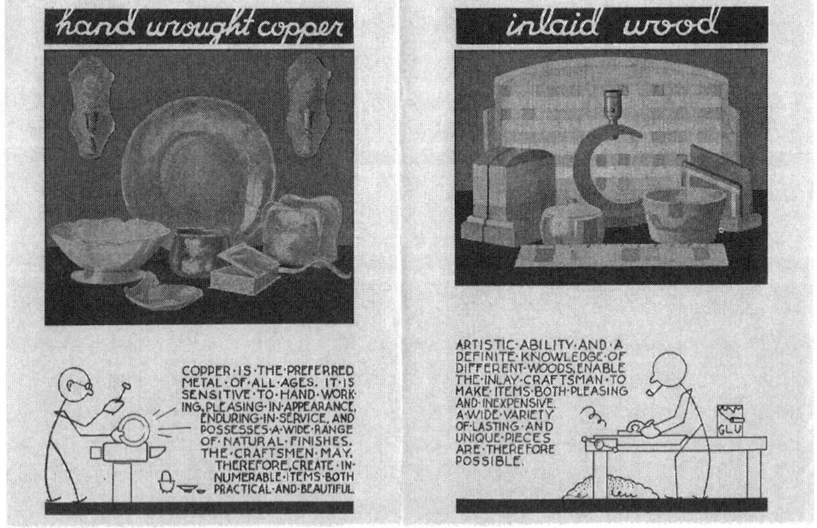

Figure 8.2. An interior spread of the 1930s Roadside Craftsmen catalogue. Photograph courtesy of Lee J. Wemett and http://www.wemett.net.

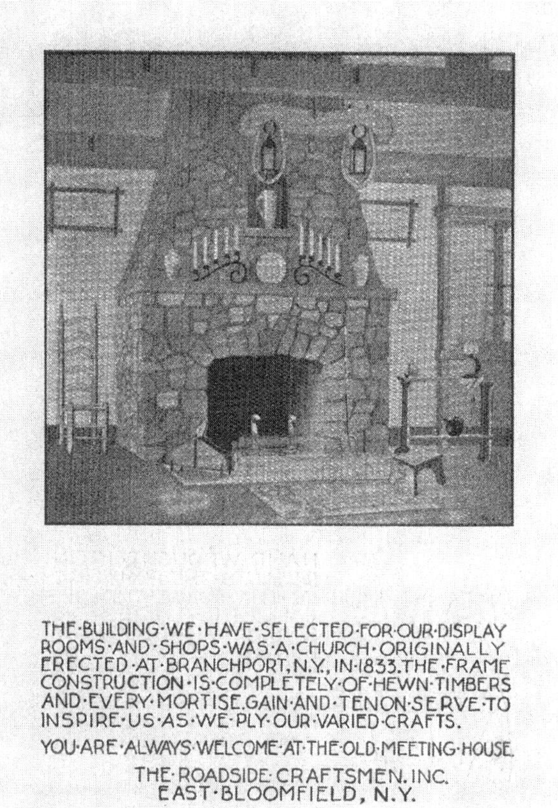

Figure 8.3. Back cover for the 1930s Roadside Craftsmen retail catalogue. Photograph courtesy of Lee J. Wemett and http://www.wemett.net.

1957, the East Bloomfield "Old Meeting House" had ceased operation as Roadside Craftsmen and the enterprise's physical presence was restricted to the Hemlock iron forge location. Roadside Craftsmen's name appears below the image in sans-serif Arts and Crafts–style lettering. Otherwise without illustrations, the catalogue offers only descriptive text for the mostly metal objects and a small selection of wooden wares, model numbers, and pricing. Pottery is not mentioned. A blue-ink rubber stamp indicates dealer prices at 50 percent of the printed retail prices. A second undated price list catalogue replicates the 1957 cover's woodblock-style print on a different color paper; perhaps, though, it is the other way around. That is, the dated 1957 cover was a reprint of a previously produced but undated catalogue. Inside, at the top of the interior back of the front cover, are the four craftsmen caricatures above Roadside Craftsmen's name printed in the now familiar rustic, stick-style lettering. The product listing appears in double column below. The presence of the caricature illustrations, the stick-style lettering, and the woodblock-style image on the cover all suggest an earlier original date than 1957 for the catalogue's publication. More persuasively, prices listed in the undated catalogue are (up to a third) less expensive than for identical items presented in the dated 1957 version (see figure 8.4).

Many professionally produced undated photographs, and line drawings of Roadside Craftsmen's products have been collected.[1] Far more product images comprise the collection than appear in any extant printed catalogue. The images may have been created for inclusion in catalogues produced by larger scale distributors who serviced retail gift and department stores and who acted as agents for and represented multiple manufacturers. Roadside's products would have been mixed among those of other craft manufacturers in, for instance, a binder. Taken together,

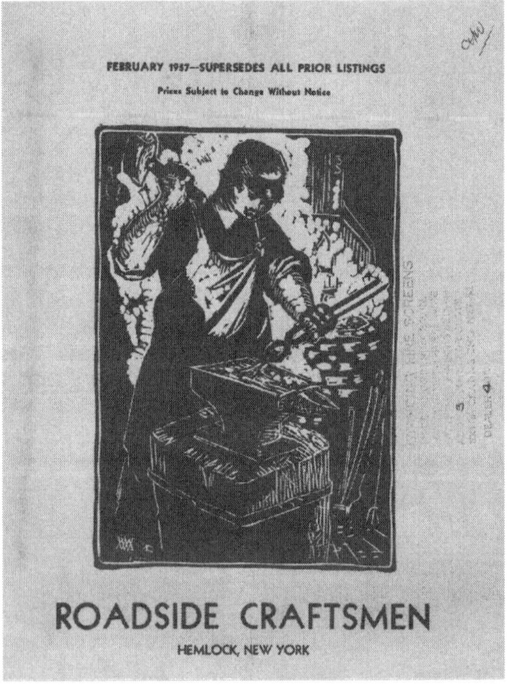

Fig. 8.4. Cover for the February 1957 Roadside Craftsmen price list for iron products. Photograph courtesy of Lee J. Wemett and http://www.wemett.net.

these images reveal a fairly extensive inventory including, among the iron products, boot scrapers, candleholders, plant stands, floor lamps, fireplace accessories, and items for picnics and barbecues. Most items are identified with a prefix letter of "I" or "R" followed by a model number. Roadside's electric lighting is strikingly similar in form to that produced decades earlier by Gustav Stickley's Craftsman Workshops in some instances. Stickley's fixtures were made of copper, brass, or iron and occasionally steel. Stickley's, like Roadside's, were suitable for both indoor and outdoor use. Individually or in groups, the fixtures hung from ceilings on linked chains or off walls from brackets. Stylistically, the Roadside metal work ranges from rustic to colonial and from Arts and Crafts (the lanterns, especially) to modernist. Occasionally, handwritten notes above or across the object image indicate the item is "out" (of stock or production). In some instances, product model numbers are typeset next to each item illustrated; in other examples, the information is handwritten or typed on a paper label glued to the image. Wooden ware, when present, is identified with the prefix "W." Notations indicate some wood products were available in gumwood, maple, walnut, or cedar; exotic woods, as discussed earlier, are not mentioned. Dates for the products' creation or entry into a catalogue or inventory compilation are not cited. Likewise, dimensions and medium are rarely noted.

Iron metalware products were especially well represented among Roadside's product drawings and photographs. This, though, may suggest only that the Hemlock Forge had a better filing system than the Bloomfield location. A double-sided vertical sales flyer, probably from the 1940s judging from stylistic elements, presents hand-drawn illustrations for interior and exterior "Artistic Railings." Indoor staircases, exterior entryways and porches, balcony railings, and decorative ironwork grilles for windows and doors are shown in seven mostly environmental vignettes. Customers are advised the work is "fabricated to your own specifications." The stick lettering for Roadside Craftsmen and craftsmen caricatures appears in one panel, and the shop location noted is Hemlock, as is the phone number, along with "Division of Wemett Corporation."

A sixteen-page catalogue for ornamental wrought iron is dated 1958. Intended for use by retailers at remote locations, it was not the Roadside Craftsmen's own publication. Noted discreetly at the bottom of the back cover, the catalogue was produced by Tennessee Fabricating Co. of Memphis for use by The Forge. On the catalogue's cover, "The Forge of Roadside Craftsmen" is printed inside a white, horizontal box below the booklet's title. The text continues, "Represented by" followed by a large blank space for retailers to handwrite or stamp their own name and contact information. Black-and-white photography throughout illustrates examples of the work individually and in environmental settings.

Many Roadside catalogues omit mention of any sale-by-mail option, do not provide shipping information, and lack any text encouraging retail customers to take advantage of such an option. Also some catalogues do not identify and price specific objects or designs within a category (e.g., lighting), and some publications do not mention the availability of custom work. The booklet format brochures would allow an opportunity for inserting a freestanding and easily updated price list, especially useful for distributors and wholesalers. Mostly, the printed documents are a very soft "sell" for Roadside products while possessing a hard brand focus. Roadside's use of the charmingly whimsical hand-drawn craftsmen caricatures, including slight variations, serve as a visual branding device appealing to the retail market. They appear on promotional materials, on stationery and shipping labels, and as outdoor signage at the Roadside Craftsmen's property. Occasionally, and irregularly, variations of "Division of Wemett Corp." appear on printed documents. Together, though, what the catalogues reveal most clearly is a reasonably extensive line of products, especially the ornamental ironwork and metal products produced at the Hemlock location referenced variously as "the Forge," "the Forge of Roadside Craftsmen," or "the Smiths."

Although we do not know the extent to which Roadside promotion efforts were successful—whether reaching individual retail customers or the so-called middle-men wholesale distributors and other retail stores—the tactic was sophisticated. The product drawings and photographs produced are profuse. Roadside's illustrated inventory was aligned with other product manufacturers' practices, including those of much larger operations. And it is indicative of Roadside's ambition to extend its reach well beyond the narrow geographic confines of Western New York. In tandem with Roadside's near complete absence of commercial advertising for itself, the form the promotional effort took suggests distributors as the target audience far more so than individual retail customers.

The Avon Product Line

The *Livonia Gazette*'s congratulatory display advertisement (November 23, 1950, 52) combines a thumbnail history of the Avon Coppersmith with a note of self-congratulation: "The Livonia Gazette gave generous space to tell of this new 'Shop by the Side of the Road.'" The ad implies the newspaper's role in popularizing the Coppersmith's product: "Many homes in this area and almost every community in the United States must have something from the Avon Coppersmith—so many pieces have been made and sold from here." In between, the copy offered a rundown of the Shop's inventory, including products from Roadside Craftsmen without mentioning that enterprise by name: "Other craft articles include Pottery, Wood, Iron and Copper and Silver Jewelry, made by associate craftsmen." The story first announcing the Coppersmith's opening said as much: "In addition to the display of the hammered copper articles, there is a variety of gift items of brass and pewter; also sterling silver bracelets, rings and pins, which are made by craftsmen with whom Mr. Cole has been associated. Many of these pieces, like much of the copper work, is hand-chased."[2]

The Coppersmith shop was stocked with consignments from other craftsmen and artists. A Cole family business road trip, for instance, might involve stops at Glidden Pottery in Alfred for ceramics, Walter Jennings's home in East Aurora for metal and, on the road back to Avon, in East Pembroke for art. At the latter was Mrs. Kitty Ann (Parker) Dennison. A painter of miniatures with a regional reputation, she had sold her art since the late 1890s. Working out of her West Main Street home, instead of canvas, her paintings for Cole were presented on sewing and powder boxes, and on unhammered, smooth-form Avon Coppersmith plates. Attractive, detailed, and representational landscape scenes adorned the center portion of the copper plaques. Her work was as carefully executed as her execution was speedy. One report, for instance, indicated she had completed 150 paintings in ten days for a Buffalo firm.[3]

Art Cole's connection to East Aurora remained strong, from the medium to his shop's signature impressed on it. The Avon Coppersmith's circular logo was designed by Rixford Jennings, Walter's son. It bears some similarities to Roycroft's signature. Avon's identifying mark entirely forms the text into a circle, and its name is fully spelled out in modern-style lettering. The hand-drawn font resembles that used at Roycroft, enough to prompt recognition without hinting at exploitation. Jennings's lettering for Avon is most closely resembles Roycroft's middle-period mark (1920–1928) featuring an "R" with a straightened right leg. Unlike Roycroft's signature with its double-barred cross above and the horizontal line within the circle, there is no other graphic flourish to the more streamlined Avon design. Jennings's design and lettering anticipates those used by Wes Wilson in some late 1960s concert posters for Bill Graham's Fillmore West. The sans serif letters tilt and bend, conforming to the circular perimeter. Unlike the Coppersmith, the first two versions of the Roycroft signature did not identify the maker by its (spelled-out) name, only a symbol. Only later, after about 1928, as any medieval mysticism about the organization had evaporated, along with the movement of which it was a part, was the Roycroft name articulated. Cole's Avon Coppersmith mark was fully complete at its outset and did not change over time; "Avon, NY" and "Solid Copper" were added, outside the logo, in the 1960s (see figure 8.5).[4]

Because of its logo's constancy over time, dating the execution of an Avon piece is inexact. But if Roycroft's evolutionary chronology is a model, heavier gauge copper was used earlier in Avon's history. Likewise, hammering is tighter and more profuse on earlier pieces. Avon's work is rarely, if ever, signed by the craftsman who executed it, as was also the case at Roycroft. Granddaughter Cole reports that Roycroft Copper Shop artist Henry Unverdorf went to Avon with Art Cole and spun the copper and that Walter Jennings "worked for Art as a jewelry maker."[5] More likely, as Clark and Thomas-Clark suggest, Jennings either sold or offered his jewelry on consignment at the Avon Coppersmith.[6] Tom Cole recalls auto trips to East Aurora to visit with Jennings and to pick up consignments;

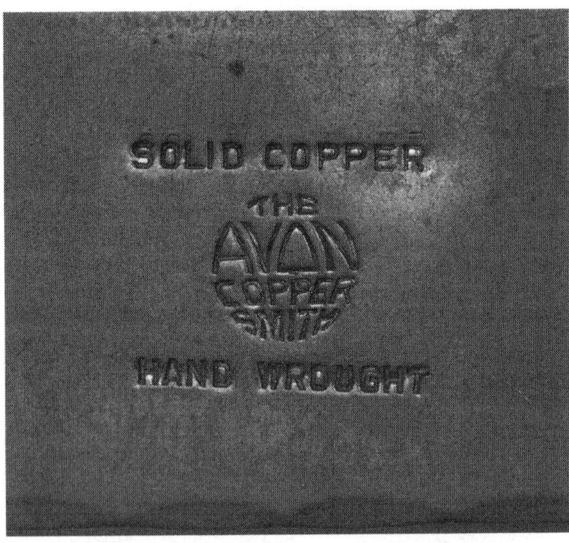

Figure 8.5. The modern-looking logo for The Avon Coppersmith designed by Rixford Jennings. Joseph A. DiTucci collection. Photograph by A. Sue Weisler.

Jennings would also occasionally visit and work at the Avon shop.[7] An Avon Coppersmith stationery holder of heavy gauge copper and featuring quatrefoil decoration suggests Jennings's hand as he used the design element at Roycroft, at Tookay, and for original work completed in his home studio and signed by him (see figure 8.6).

Avon Coppersmith's products retained elements of the Arts and Crafts aesthetic but leaned significantly and noticeably toward softer, less severe, and more colonial revival–style forms and, perhaps, its customers' tastes. Avon's somewhat fussier designs are in contrast to the more austere, architectonic, and rigid Arts and Crafts forms with their sharper angles and sometimes riveted construction. The hard edges of Arts and Crafts yielded to softer and rounder forms at Avon. Some Avon vases, for instance, feature a "ruffled" base soldered to the vertical container; the same design motif is seen at the base of a crimped fruit bowl and some candleholders. While Avon's smaller-sized chambersticks are stylistically nearly identical to the work of numerous Arts and Crafts period metal shops, Avon's candleholders veer sharply away from anything produced at Roycroft. For instance, one pair of 9.5-inch-tall Avon candlesticks feature a circular disc base with raised center, an elongated S-shaped squared-off

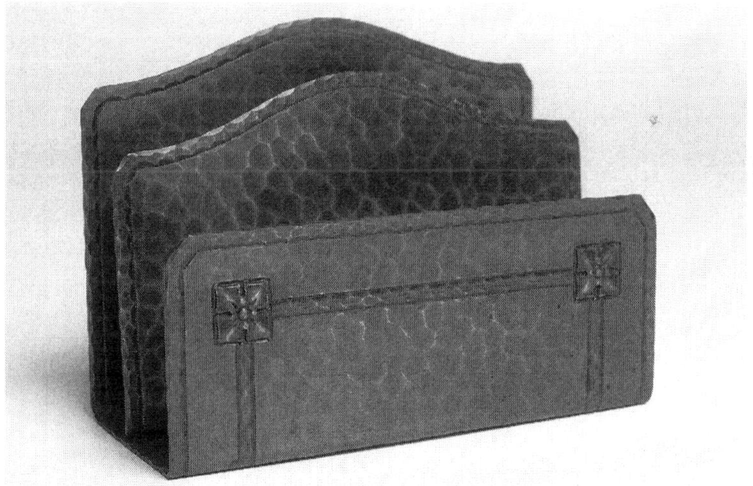

Figure 8.6. A stationery holder marked by Avon Coppersmith and probably executed by Walter Jennings who earlier used the quatrefoil design at Roycroft. Joseph A. DiTucci collection. Photograph by A. Sue Weisler.

stem riveted to the base, and a delicate candle cup and bobeche at the top. Avon's bowls, bookends, and trays retained the greatest fidelity to Roycroft's and, more broadly, the Arts and Crafts style.

Bowls, bookends, candleholders (short or tall, in a pair or singly), a candle snuffer, and trays (ash, sandwich, and serving) are crowded into a single horizontal photograph of an undated Avon Coppersmith brochure. Granddaughter Jennifer Cole's chronology of the Coppersmith structure's evolution dates the building shown on the brochure's cover to the late 1940s.[8] At four pages, one sheet, and folded once at center, it is hard to stretch a description to that of a "catalogue." In the same product display photo there are such domestic items as an ivy holder, flowerpots, vases, and, for the kitchen, a dipper, kettle, and a skillet. Prices range from $1.25 for a plain three-inch diameter coaster ($1.30 hammered) to $25 for a twenty-inch-diameter serving tray ($35 hammered). Readers are advised that an oxidized copper finish is priced the same as the plain or hammered item and that prices are adjusted annually. No street address is noted, simply the fact that the Coppersmith is in East Avon, on Routes 5 and 20, and is south of Rochester. Nor is a telephone number present.

In contrast to print advertisements (see "Advertising Avon"), Arthur Cole's name is conspicuously absent. Instead, and quite Roycroft-like, the brochure's front cover text begins: "Our Craftsmen are mighty proud of these articles, made mostly by hand, though aided by a few power tools to help keep the price down so you can buy them." The shop logo is present on either side of the photograph of the building. The brief cover text invites readers to the shop where they can "watch us at work" and browse a salesroom where "there are many useful items of Copper, Brass, Copper and Sterling Silver Jewelry, Wrought Iron, Wood and Pottery for sale." Unmentioned is that most of the "wrought iron, wood and pottery" were from the Coppersmith's sister enterprise, Roadside Craftsmen. Concluding, the text acknowledges, "Many of you can not [*sic*] come our way this year so inside this folder you will find a group of articles from which to select your gifts." And, wrapping back to the first sentence, "We hope that you and your friends will be proud of them too." See figure 8.7.

An earlier brochure, judging from the price list where items identical to those above are 50 percent less expensive, shows that all the objects pictured are hammered, and there is no mention of an option for a smooth, unhammered finish. This brochure's cover depicts Cole in the vertical photograph used in 1933 newspaper reports about the shop's opening. The image personifies him as the eponymous Coppersmith without saying so.

THE CARE OF AVON COPPERSMITH
COPPER AND BRASS

The polished or oxidized surface of all of our copper and brass articles is lacquered with the best clear lacquer obtainable. Dust with a soft cloth. Clean with a cloth dampened with cool water. Avoid scratching or scraping of the lacquer as the unprotected metal tarnishes very quickly.

This lacquer is not alcohol proof. Do not allow anything wet to stand on the trays, or leave water in the shallow bowls but for very short periods. Cut flowers damage the finish quickly, though none of these conditions damage the copper itself. Do not use metal polishes, acids, cleaning solutions or hot water and soap unless you want to remove all of the lacquer. This would necessitate regular polishing thereafter or you may want the metal to tarnish naturally.

Articles sold as ash trays have a harder baked lacquer finish and may be washed in a mild warm water and soap solution. The ash trays should not discolor from burning cigarettes or ashes.

Should any article of our craft or the finish become damaged, kindly return it to us for repairing and refinishing at a reasonable price.

STOP AT OUR SHOP

Your order will be sent by Insured Parcel Post unless otherwise requested. Kindly add the corresponding amount shown on the following list for packing and mailing charges.

Orders valued less than $ 3.00 add 20¢
$ 3.00 value but less than   5.00 add 30¢
$ 5.00 value but less than   10.00 add 40¢
$10.00 value but less than   25.00 add 50¢

You may enclose a gift card with mailing instructions and we shall gladly mail your gift directly.

Gift boxes or wrapping are available if requested at an extra 5% of purchase price.

The
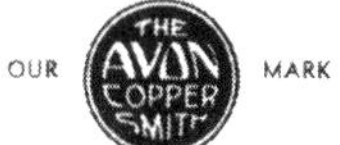

Avon, New York

OUR 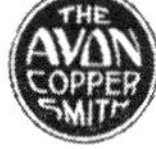 MARK

CRAFTSMEN IN
COPPER
BRASS
PEWTER
STERLING
SILVER

HAND HAMMERED
TRAYS
VASES
BOWLS
CANDLESTICKS
BOOK ENDS

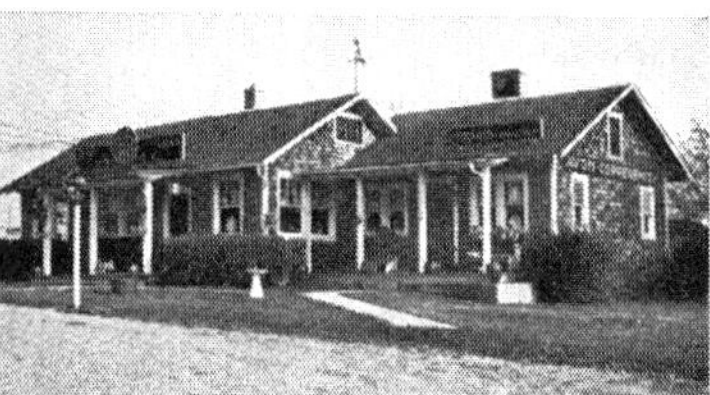

Located at East Avon, New York

Routes 5 & 20 So. of Rochester

Our Craftsmen are mighty proud of these articles, made mostly by hand, though aided by a few power tools to help keep the price down so you can buy them. We invite you to visit our shop and watch us at work; also browse around the salesroom where there are many useful items of Copper, Brass, Copper and Sterling Silver Jewelry, Wrought Iron, Wood and Pottery for sale. Many of you can not come our way this year so inside this folder you will find a group of articles from which to select your gifts. We hope that you and your friends will be proud of them too.

Figure 8.7. Sales brochure intended as a mailer for the Avon Coppersmith, circa 1945. Bryan Mead collection. Photograph by A. Sue Weisler.

Shared by both brochures is an emphasis on utilitarian products beautifully executed. There are some differences between the two brochures, as well. The caption below the photo of Cole states inside quotation marks, "The Coppersmith by the Side of the Road"—phrasing identical to that used earlier for Bloomfield Pottery—is recycled later in newspaper reports and, for readers with long memories, is evocative of Roycroft's appeal to preindustrial values. Below the caption, inside a box, is this expression: "Distinctive Gifts Worked by Hand and Offered for Sale Only at the Shop." Again, there is a similarity to the quaint, emotional, and exclusivity appeals previously used by Roycroft. Further, the Coppersmith's statement is not wholly precise: the objects shown in the brochure were, of course, also available by mail as the order form on the brochure's back afforded and the interior packing price schedule detailed. The only place the shop's logo appears is below the packing prices.

Sensibly, the earlier brochure makes a stronger inferential connection to the Arts and Crafts movement broadly and Roycroft specifically than did the later version. "Each article made as best we can," begins one text panel in the earlier brochure; it is hard not to think of Gustav Stickley's shop mark of a joiner's compass enclosing the Flemish motto, "Als ik Kan," which loosely translates "as best I can." "Priced fairly for what its [*sic*] worth in painstaking hand work and enduring material," the text block continues. And then, finally: "Offered frankly for its beauty and usefulness as an unusual gift." Mimicry of Elbert Hubbard's shop catalogues could not be more overt. The foreword to the 1910 Roycroft catalogue states, in part: "If we offer them they must be worthy of your consideration—they must have value, and the standard of value of our day is not the standard of yesterday, nor yet that of tomorrow—but it is the commercial standard, and that mooted expression means value for value received, a true noblesse oblige—and not so very wicked after all." Hubbard is wordier, more flowery, a bit humorously wry, and poetic; readers are even cued to Hubbard's poetic bent by the placement of a quote from Walt Whitman above the catalogue's foreword. Roycroft explained its workmanship to readers, as did Cole: "The shaping and hammering of copper with mallets and polished steel hammers tends to soften the outline of the articles and stiffen the metal adding greatly to its beauty and durability," the Avon Coppersmith's brochure articulates. Avon's two contrasting finishes—a polished natural copper surface and a reddish-brown oxidized surface—are explained to customers, along with how both are protected: "with the best transparent lacquer obtainable . . . to make and keep the copper most pleasing in appearance and usefulness." Both Cole and Jennings, reports say,[9] preferred a highly polished, like a new penny, surface to the darker brown patina Roycroft chemically induced to its copper goods. Roycroft also used a brass wash and a silver patina, both over copper; an acid-etched finish was introduced in later years.

The Avon Coppersmith's emphasis on gift items as inventory, including consignments by other craftsmen—and satisfaction for an implied customer motivation for purchasing—follows a sensible, well-understood persuasive tactic: one used earlier by Roycroft and by Kipp at Tookay, among many others. The *Christian Science Monitor*'s 1913 profile of East

Aurora that highlights Tookay, for instance, notes: "Among many other beautiful memories one may take away from the Tookay shop are the pastel drawings of William Morris and Robert Louis Stevenson by Raymond Nott."[10] In the same publication, a few years later, a small display ad, text only and without image or illustration, advertises the Karl Kipp Shop as "'East Aurora's Shop of Beautiful Gifts'" stocked with "hand made [*sic*] jewelry and silverware made to your special order."[11] When catering to travelers, as did Avon, the gift appeal has two targets: if not for yourself, then for someone else. Avon's emphasis on quality handcraftsmanship also anticipates the sentiment expressed by the Hallmark greeting card slogan.

Advertising Avon

It is an overstatement to describe Avon Coppersmith's advertising as understated. A classified ad announced the shop's debut in the "Miscellaneous" column of the June 28, 1933 *Lima Recorder*. Verbatim, with errors, it read: "Now Open—Visit 'The Avon Coppersmith' for copper, brass, pewter and silver gifts of unusual beauty hand-fashioned by skilled craftsmen. The shop is located ¼ mile west from the junction of routes 2 [*sic*] and 5 [*sic*] at East Avon." Not the most inviting, riveting, or persuasive appeal ever written. But the matter-of-fact tone set by the earliest advertisement persisted until the end of Cole's ownership of the Coppersmith.

During Cole's proprietorship, the Avon Coppersmith advertised regularly, if sporadically, in local community newspapers. Initially, until the early war years, brief four- to six-line classified advertisements comprised the Coppersmith's paid promotional "campaign." At first, Cole's choice to lightly advertise was sensible given the shop's appeal to highway travelers; advertising would likely go unread by this group. Even though Avon-area residents were not the shop's primary target, local advertising was a means for Coppersmith to affirm its connection to hometown consumers. Unlike travelers, local residents had motivations of convenience and perhaps "patriotism" to patronize the Coppersmith. Identical to auto-tourists, local residents' reasons for patronage included gift-giving, the other component of Avon's business model. For any one customer, weddings and other celebratory occasions are not daily or even weekly occurrences. But across the broader local community such events of course occur with great regularity and predictability. Local advertising extended Avon Coppersmith's community presence beyond its immediate physical location. Advertising placements in community newspapers gave Avon Coppersmith entrée into nearby homes and fostered goodwill. Community-based advertising was reasonably inexpensive and a nontoxic forum to remind neighbors of the service (gifting) and product (the gift) the nearby Coppersmith satisfied. By the mid-1950s, advertising locally became critically important as the New York State Thruway emerged and then flourished, siphoning off Route 20 traffic and many of Coppersmith's nonlocal customers.[12]

Visually compelling and more ambitious (and costly) than the classifieds, newspaper display advertising affords retailers an opportunity to show as well as tell. But the Coppersmith's display advertising in community newspapers was graphically simple and heavily text driven. The display ads were more informative than persuasive in tone, announcements rather than appeals. Most likely, the graphic design of the ads was created by the various publications' in-house designers for the client's approval. A December 8, 1949 display ad in the *Livingston County Leader*, for instance, is headlined "For That Particular Gift" and the copy that follows encourages readers to "Drop in and browse around our display of wrought copper, brass, silver, wood, iron and pottery."

The Christmas season ad ran in numerous small-town publications. Fifteen years later, the identical soft-sell wording appeared in a May 3, 1964 display ad placed in the Rochester morning daily newspaper, the *Democrat and Chronicle*. A decade and a half after its first appearance, there was only a bit more embellishment by copy gently admonishing customers: "Don't miss our large selection of copper, enamel & sterling jewelry [and] also [wooden] maple products and cards." A square, 1946 *Avon Herald-News* display advertisement without graphics states simply the Coppersmith's shop name and store hours. The declarative copy reads: "For the convenience of our Valued Customers of Avon and Vicinity who may be interested in a gift of lasting value made by Craftsmen of our own community. Wrought copper and brass that has been carrying the name of Avon across the country and is now sold from 225 Gift Shops and stores." The ad's text is directed to local customers and their presumed partisanship toward the local craftsman; its timing references the season's gifting tradition in conjunction with the timeless quality and durability of the merchandise; and the ad's copy at once implies the shop's role as community ambassador while suggesting a halo effect for its products' broadly endorsed prestige as certified by the 225 geographically remote stores carrying the Coppersmith's products.

Three years later, in a burst of illustrative excess tempered by textual brevity, horizontal display ads in several community newspapers featured the Coppersmith's black-and-white logo accompanied by copy again simply reading, "For That Particular Gift—drop in and browse." Even in advertising placed by other businesses selling Avon Coppersmith merchandise, text dominates. For instance, a 1949 *Nunda News* text-only display ad for Paul's (Paul Allen) Gift Shop on Oakland Street in Dalton, New York: "The Shop features copper and brass by Avon Coppersmith, pottery by Glidden and Roadside Craftsmen, wrought iron and wood by Roadside Craftsmen."

Avon Coppersmith's advertisements were more likely to describe the materials used to create the product than the product itself. What the ads did not stress—indeed, barely mention—was the handcrafted, handmade virtues of the products. Instead, what the products were *associated* with (celebrations, achievements) and what they were *made* of (copper, brass), the ad copy implies, was more significant than how the skilled individual made the objects. Perhaps a bit too modestly, personality and process were sublimated in favor of the occasion, the giver, and the recipient's anticipated joy, honor, and appreciation upon receipt. This all stands in striking contrast to the earliest, earnest news stories about Coppersmith and touting Wemett's and Cole's personal attributes and skills, though perhaps by the 1950s few remembered or cared about those stories. By midcentury, perhaps handiwork was a quaintly dated sentiment—one better remembered than revisited—and less resonant than, for instance, owning streamline-designed refrigerators to preserve food or fast cars to improve travel efficiency.[13] The copy of these ads lacks language with emotional punch; there were no promises of future satisfaction nor compliments directed at the customer's good taste. When present, Coppersmith's persuasive intent had a singular, soft appeal: we are the place where discerning givers acquire special gifts to be given to significant people for memorable occasions. There was none of the puffery, wry (or even self-deprecating) humor, cloying wordplay, or punning so evident in Hubbard's advertisements for Roycroft products. By contemporary standards, the Avon Coppersmith ads are somewhat lifeless; their "call to action" was a passive invitation to visit and inspect.[14] Avon Coppersmith's display ads inconsistently present the shop's specific street address, business hours, and the firm's circular logo, although sometimes they personalize the enterprise by identifying the Coppersmith's proprietor, Arthur H. Cole, by name. Likewise, the ad copy inconsistently offers the shop's telephone number—perhaps intention-ally, but very subtly, reinforcing the "drop-by and see-it-made" invitation informing both Wemett enterprises.

When visual elements are included in Coppersmith advertisements, photographs of Coppersmith products were not used. Instead, the illus-trated ads feature drawings, representational but not actual illustrations of the products customers could purchase at the Coppersmith. A simple, 1940 vertical Christmas display ad in the *Avon Herald News* presents a line drawing of a candlestick, the Coppersmith's name, and highway loca-tion. Illustrated Avon Coppersmith advertisements used clip art: generic, seasonally or occasion-appropriate visual elements (a lighthouse for New Year's, ribbons and holly leaves or tree ornaments for Christmas, a stork for new babies) occasionally "decorate" the ads, relieving their "textiness" but without advancing their persuasiveness. Most often, though, the only graphic element in the Coppersmith's advertisements was the shop logo, not its inventory.

Most Avon Coppersmith advertisements are informative announce-ments more than they are persuasive overtures. They were virtually interchangeable with many other retail stores. Surprisingly, one genuinely unique Avon Coppersmith solicitation is conspicuous by its omission; an appeal for what Avon craftsmen were perfectly capable of produc-ing and what enhances discrimination between the Coppersmith and department stores. There is no mention of customized commemorative or "presentation"-style products that might be created or commissioned. The seemingly significant (and obvious) gift service had no presence in the Coppersmith's advertising nor in publicity or promotional materials published in local newspapers. Enlisting such an appeal, moreover, would magnify the difference between Coppersmith and mass manufacturers. In fact, Avon Coppersmith offered the service. In nearby Henrietta, just north of Avon, Cole subcontracted with a firm for custom engraving; in Rochester, a Grand Avenue craftsman silver-plated Avon Coppersmith's products at his home.[15] But Avon Coppersmith's advertising made no mention of these personalized, specialized services.

Publicity is a cost-free form of promotion. The trade-off, though, is the publicist's inability to ensure, steer, and control media placements. Publicity for the Avon Coppersmith appeared in local newspapers, usu-ally associated with a variety of community, charitable, and not-for-profit events and causes. Primarily, the publicity was restricted to occasions or events for which the Coppersmith donated (or had sold) an item that functioned as a commemoration or some form of recognition for someone's accomplishment. Publication of such press release–style texts more often than not appeared in the same publications in which the Coppersmith advertised. Message consistency with the paid advertising was achieved for Avon's "public face": The Coppersmith was a local gift store where the gifts to be purchased are created onsite by local craftsmen. The press releases' authors are unknown, but most texts appear to have been prepared by the sponsoring organization, not Avon Coppersmith.

When Avon Coppersmith catered mostly to patrons in their automobiles traveling Route 20 who might stop, browse, and purchase, road signs were the most direct means Coppersmith could use to attract them. Unlike evanescent newspaper ads that travelers were unlikely to encounter, semipermanent signage "met" potential customers at their locations. Large, round, orange-and-black painted metal signs replicating Avon's logo were installed near the Coppersmith's shop. Mounted high atop steel poles, the easily visible signs were placed on Route 20 and the nearby intersecting New York Route 15. They beckoned travelers from all four directions. Almost as well traveled as Route 20, NY-15 runs from Rochester in the north, south to the Pennsylvania border, and beyond. In addition, large, vertically oriented, rectangular hinged metal hanging signs advertising the Coppersmith were placed at roadside in various farmers' fields. Measuring about three by five feet, the signs featured either the Avon logo or the Coppersmith's profile. Since Art Cole personally knew the farmers from whom he rented land for his signs, typically a barter arrangement (farm space for Avon products) in lieu of cash was made.[16] So many signs were present—twenty or twenty-five, son Tom Cole remembers—that collecting the signs to service them (e.g., repainting, ensuring hinges were still functional) was an all-day, 120-mile road trip.[17] On site at the Coppersmith shop, a sign with Art Cole's silhouette personifying the enterprise was present; located first on the front lawn between the shop and highway and with lattice backing, it was later moved atop the building. Similar silhouetted signs identified for customers the entrances to the workshop and the sales room. The painted metal highway signs promoting Coppersmith stand in contrast to the unassuming, matter-of-fact, and graphically dull newspaper advertising.

Advertising for Avon Coppersmith ended as it began. The final ad for the Coppersmith mirrors precisely the location, placement, and form of its first one: at the back of a daily newspaper amid other unillustrated classified ads. This one, though, arranged by a third party, advertised an auction of the Coppersmith's contents. The five-inch, single column advertisement was headlined "Manufacturing and Shop Tool Auction." The ad listed "all tools and equipment at the site of business" including "forms and brass molds," along with "many mallets and hammers" and "several good work benches and cabinets." The ad offered only the slightest hint of Coppersmith's storied past: "All tools [were] used in fine metal work." Maybe more significantly, prospective bidders were advised, "These tools are clean and in good shape."

On Wednesday, January 14, 1970, Tom Coyne Auction Sales of Avon sold nearly forty years of Coppersmith memories beginning at 10:30 a.m. Temperatures for the onsite auction that day were in the teens; twelve inches of snow had fallen the day before. There are no news reports about the auction; we do not know how many attended nor the prices realized. No other advertised local auction competed for bidders' attention that day, though the day before there were auctions for a milking herd in Spencerport and a woodworking machinery auction. One shivering, successful bidder for craftsman Arthur Cole's forms, tools, and related shop materials was Glenn Reece of the Glencroft Coppersmiths in Clarence, New York. Located fifty miles west of Avon, Glencroft was less a competitor for retail customers than a companion enterprise to Avon Coppersmith. Virtually any overlap in copper manufacture was coincidental, and tourists would easily differentiate between the products of each, though direct comparison shopping was unlikely. Each emphasized customer mail-order accessibility and positioned itself as a gift shop, appealing to identical customer motivations, though Glencroft offered a wider range of gift products than Avon.

GLENCROFT COPPERSMITHS

Glenn H. Reece began Glencroft Coppersmiths in 1946 in his South Buffalo basement workshop. Portions of his story mimic those previously told about Roadside Craftsmen, Guy Daugherty, and Homer Bullock. A ten-year fireman with Buffalo's Hook & Ladder 11 and Engine Company 28, Reece purportedly taught himself the craft through trial and error, beginning the enterprise more or less as a hobby. Another report indicates he first started working with metal while a student at Seneca Vocational High School, followed later by evening classes. To supplement his fireman's income, he began selling some of his copper products; his reputation grew, and customers with orders began coming to him for work.[18] Relatively quickly, Reece recognized he was "losing money by continuing his job as a fireman." On August 15, 1953, a few months after Roadside Craftsmen closed its doors, the first Glencroft Coppersmiths shop opened twenty miles northeast of Buffalo at 9385 Main Street (New York Route 5), at the corner at Shisler Road, in Clarence, New York. Operated with his wife, Dorothy Masterson, Reece hired old-time craftsman Fred Niederlander "for shop work." Much like descriptions of Roadside Craftsmen's early years and Avon Coppersmith's original building, "The entire shop, display room and living quarters, to the rear, are a blending of the old and new." Inside, and echoing earlier newspaper reports of Roadside and Coppersmith, journalist Margaret Fess wrote, "The same type of tools used by coppersmiths centuries ago stand next to the most modern in metal working machines." Out in front of the shop, she reported, a hundred-gallon "copper pitcher in the front yard is already a landmark." Unlike work at Roadside or Coppersmith, though, the story did not emphasize handcraftsmanship. Instead, "Unless he is working on a custom order, Reece goes in for mass production. Whether it is candlesticks or trays, he usually makes about 100 at a time."[19]

A 1960 display advertisement in the *Buffalo Courier-Express* Christmas gift guide underplays without disparaging the "mass production" noted in the 1953 report. The ad's text, presumably written or approved by Glencroft, is accompanied by a line drawing of the shop building and more than a half-dozen objects, including a Windsor-style chair, a watering can and tea kettle, and a mailbox and lamp. The copy reads: "An unusual Gift Shop and craft house where each piece shown, whether gift, lamp, or furniture, has been chosen for beauty and good taste in living . . . masterpieces of enduring beauty, worthy of the most beautiful home. Many of our items are wrought in our craft shop adjacent to our Gift Shop, including custom-made items such as fireplace hood and screen combinations and stove hoods of any design to match any décor. Excellent craftsmanship at moderate prices." There is a similarity to some Avon Coppersmith advertisements, and the copy anticipates, especially, the style appearing later during the Parkers' ownership of the Coppersmith.

The early press attention paid to Glencroft was followed by more from others. In 1956 and with a photograph, the *Albany Times-Union* reported Glencroft won a national award for window and interior display from *Gift Art Buyer* magazine.[20] A year later, a *Buffalo Courier-Express* advertising flyer for Loblaws advertised three sizes of Glencroft metal wall plaques with "hand painted fruit pattern on black background,"[21] reminiscent of Kitty Dennison's work for Avon Coppersmith. And Glencroft Coppersmiths made regular appearances in the same newspaper's 1959 "Shop Talk" column "by Marjorie." Advising her readers about where to shop for what, Marjorie presented Glencroft's name and address below such bolded headings as "Good Advice," "Distinctive Pieces," "Charming Pieces," "Home Pieces," "Authentic Pieces," "Home Charm," and "Authentic Early American furniture and other interesting pieces."

On the one hand, business was apparently good and confidence high, as by April 1960 Glencroft was reported as having seven employees who produced "gifts as a manufacturer, wholesaler and retailer." On the other hand, the same article indicated that Glencroft "received conditional approval for" the largest of three small business loans: $35,000 of the $46,000 total loans awarded.[22] Within two years, however, either business or its management soured. The July 11, 1962 *Buffalo Courier-Express* reported Glencroft Coppersmiths had filed for bankruptcy. Debts were listed as totaling $96,845 and assets of $44,026.[23] The *Buffalo Evening News* carried classified ads for Glencroft Coppersmiths' bankruptcy auction in mid-October, 1962; later, in the same newspaper's December 5, 1962 classifieds, "Miscellaneous for Sale" column, a listing offered bankruptcy stock of Glencroft copper gifts. Reece's grandson, William, reports his grandfather had defaulted on the SBA loan.[24]

The next year, though, The Coppersmiths opened at 10210 Main Street in Clarence.[25] Originally built as a church in 1831, the building later became a schoolhouse. In the 1930s, Cape Cod–style architectural features were added to the stone structure and cottages built behind it were rented to passing auto travelers. Glenn Reece's son, Jim (1939–2013), continued the business. Grandson William Reece, and current owner of the now Tonawanda-based copper shop (since 1996), recalls sorting and storing at Glencroft's 10210 Main Street shop all the Avon Coppersmith forms and dies purchased at the 1970 auction. Further, he believed Glencroft had been working with Arthur Cole with the "thought of buying the [Avon] operation and having my father run that shop while my grandfather maintained [the] Clarence" location.[26]

9

Less Copper, More Shoppe

Sometime during the late 1960s, by then legally blind, Arthur Cole acknowledged the end of his professional career. "Forty years," Art said, simultaneously identifying 1970 as both the targeted retirement date and the end of his tenure as the Avon Coppersmith. Neither of his two sons was going to sustain the business; Don shared his father's visual impairment and Tom, recently back from military deployment in Vietnam, was establishing his career as an engineer at Eastman Kodak. Ads placed in local newspapers sought a buyer for one of the village's business icons.[1]

Passing the baton is a sports metaphor used to describe many kinds of change, including when a business transfers ownership. Though well worn, this widely familiar metaphor still resonates. The expression refers to one relay race runner handing off a baton to a second. Conversationally, baton passing suggests a practically effortless, seamless transaction between runners. But in practice, such is rarely the case. Successful, winning baton passes require perfect coordination between the independent, rhythmically synchronous body parts of two in-motion runners. The complexity involved is such that one might reasonably expect more baton "drops" than accomplished passes. Moving the metaphor from a footrace to a business operation does not simplify the process.

Much of the value in Avon Coppersmith's sale was wrapped in the nebulous expression "goodwill." The baton passed to the new owners of the Avon Coppersmith was one weighted with a four-decade, unduplicable, intertwined history of the craft, the craftsman, and the products Art Cole produced, as much as its business name. Skillful and experienced businesspeople though the new owners might have been, the sale of

147

Avon Coppersmith to Don and Joy Parker was as though the relay race runners were on two different tracks: one of packed gravel and the other beach sand. The baton pass occurred in an economic and social climate far different from when Avon Coppersmith debuted.

Spencerport was a small village of about three thousand people in 1970. Located on the Erie Canal, it is some twenty-five miles north and half the population of Avon. The canal, once the singularly powerful transportation engine of New York State commerce, nearly 150 years later had long relinquished its role moving merchandise: first to railroads, later to highways. The Erie Canal had become the backdrop for business of a more sedentary sort: tourism. Immediately adjacent to the canal, the Spencerport "Village Plaza" formed a modest-sized shopping and office complex. Housed there were three Parker family enterprises run by Donald, Erwin, and Clark. Don was born June 30, 1929, about the same time as Clarence Wemett's trip that inspired Roadside Craftsmen and Art Cole's resignation from Roycroft. He worked with his father and brothers at E. J. Parker & Sons, home contractors and builders. Nearby, the Parkers owned Spencerport Lumber and Parker Development Corp., a real estate firm. In 1965 Joy's Lamplight Gift Shoppe, named for Don's wife, Joyce, opened in Village Plaza. Almost immediately successful, Joy's doubled in size two years later. A local newspaper reported it was "one of the most unusual gift shops in the area."[2]

Five years after opening the Spencerport shop, the Parkers purchased the Avon Coppersmith, "relieving the Coles so that they may enjoy their leisure which they so richly deserve."[3] The *Rochester Daily Record* reported on February 9, 1970 that the Coles transferred their interest in the Avon Coppersmith to E. J. Parker & Sons Inc. of Spencerport. The Parker firm, the *Record* indicated, headed by Donald E. Parker, "will lease the premises to Joy's Lamplight Shoppe Inc."[4]

The Parkers' intention was to host a larger, more diverse inventory at Avon Coppersmith than at their Spencerport location, and Coppersmith required remodeling. Completion of the work was anticipated by spring, though the shop did not reopen until summer 1970. Much the way Roadside Craftsmen's repurposed and relocated Baptist church was to feature a display of the latter's history, the new Coppersmith owners connected past to present: a portion of the newly remodeled shop—a glass-enclosed display space to the right of the entrance—offered customers an exhibit of the "material, tools, and finished products that Mr. Cole and his employees worked with over these past years."[5]

But the changes ahead for the Avon Coppersmith were much more than cosmetic. The newspaper report of the Coppersmith's sale advised future visitors they could expect to find "glassware, silver, pewter, brass, copper dinnerware, fine china, California pottery, wrought iron, crystal lamps, Pennsylvania Dutch foods, bridal gifts, invitations, stationery, linen towels, perfume, pictures, and all types of decorative accessories."[6] In other words, customers would see in Avon what they might have already experienced at the Parkers' Spencerport location: ahistorical, manufactured products without a trace of "see-it-made." Perhaps in an attempt to evoke a familiar connection to local customers with long memories, a 1979 supplement to the *Caledonia Advertiser* instructed readers that "particular people" find the "Avon Coppersmith Gift Shoppe [*sic*]" their "complete gift-giving headquarters." Referencing the Coppersmith's past history, the text assured readers that the by then not-so-new management "deals with only established, skilled craftsmen to stock their store with quality, unique merchandise at sensible prices to suit most anyone's budget."[7] In fact, the store was dealing with virtually no craftsmen, and the inventory was composed of almost nothing unique. Instead, the Shoppe stocked goods produced almost exclusively by international factory manufacturers: "Gifts from around the world," as their numerous advertisements exclaimed.

Once the Parkers assumed the Coppersmith's ownership, its advertising took a more aggressive frequency and tone. Ads appear often in community newspapers and shoppers, indicating the store's orientation to the indigenous market. The direction of attention to local customers was sensible, since the transient, peripatetic passersby whose attention Art Cole sought to arrest had long ago abandoned Route 20 for the Thruway. Since there was no longer a coppersmith, and since the shop no longer created anything (aside from the market it sought to build), its display advertising featured lengthy double-column lists and thumbnail photos of brand-name products. Often the merchandise was intentionally created only for the purpose of being collected: "primary," "deliberate," or "born" collectibles, irrespective of any utility.[8] The advertising, in other words, appealed to collectors of products manufactured as collectibles, acclaimed the shop's enormous quantity of inventory as a virtue and frequently offered sales and discount coupons as purchasing incentives for shoppers.

Enhancements to the Avon Coppersmith's inventory were many. The once-singular shop began to resemble a department store: there was the Avon Coppersmith Gift Shoppe, Joy's Lamplight Shoppe, Inc., Joy's Wonderland of Dolls, and the Country Attic Shoppe."[9] For at least a while, floor and shelf display space was rented to independent antiques dealers for their inventory. Populating the store's shelves and display cases were Hummel and Rockwell figurines, Sebastian miniatures, Steiff animals, beer steins, paperweights, and thimbles. A May 1986 advertisement in local papers boasted more than a thousand dolls in stock; within the ad's space, and enclosed inside of a box to separate the feature from the rest of the text, was notice of the Precious Moments "God Bless America" limited edition Uncle Sam figurine.

Instead of the unique, homegrown localism Cole's Coppersmith emphasized, internationalism was the virtue touted by the Parkers' gift shop: "Dolls from around the World" headlined a 1983 advertisement. Inventory quantity and breadth of customer choices were advantages the Parkers' Shoppe offered, instead of the special and fewer hand-worked goods Cole produced. An undated, twofold brochure on green paper breathlessly announced, "NEW Special Blends, Angoras, Mohairs. . . . Hundreds of New Colors!" And a third (1986) advertisement boasted that Avon Coppersmith was "the largest dealer in Collectibles and Limited editions in upstate New York." Coppersmith's sixty-year celebration found Don Parker explaining "the most popular items in their store are lighted houses, miniature designs depicting homes in different seasons and in various architectural styles. They are made of ceramic with electrical illumination."[10] In a perhaps unintentional but nonetheless backhanded comment on Avon Coppersmith's post-Cole operation, Ruth Woodruff, daughter of Clarence Wemett and owner of the "1812 Country Store" in Hemlock, noted, "You don't try and put crystal in a country store." The story's writer did not point out for readers the irony that Woodruff's store (previously Roadside Craftsmen's Forge), like the Parkers', stocked miniatures and dollhouses.[11]

Under the Parkers' ownership, the original Avon Coppersmith logo appears prominently in their advertising. Anniversaries marked in the 1970s and 1980s invariably use the shop logo, sometimes with a photograph of the shop in its earlier days. Advertising copy traced for contemporary readers the modern gift store's history to its 1930s founding, trading on its heritage. Newspaper reporters as much as the advertising refer to the Coppersmith as a "Gift Shop" or "Gift Shoppe"; brides were reminded and invited to register for their wedding gifts. Don Parker continued to claim tourists as among the Coppersmith's biggest clientele, as was true during Art Cole's ownership. The shop's membership in the Finger Lakes [Tourism] Association and its distribution of Coppersmith promotional fliers to nearby merchants sought to stimulate tourist trade. Twenty years after assuming ownership, the Parkers attributed the store's "long success . . . to a good location and the foresight to enter the mail order business."[12] Son Don Parker, Jr. joined the Avon enterprise in 1978 as assistant manager. His "expertise in all phases of mail order has greatly enhanced that aspect of the family business," an anniversary ad for Joy's and the Coppersmith reported. As Cole had accomplished years earlier, the Parker-run Coppersmith "now handles mail orders from all over the United States and Canada."[13] But what the Parkers were mailing differed substantially from what Cole sold: mass manufactured multiples instead of handcrafted originals.

In the mid-1980s, the Parkers' retail empire again expanded, this time much farther south. They opened "Old Town Collectibles" in Kissimmee, Florida, two and a half miles from Walt Disney World. A Spencerport newspaper report of the Florida location indicates it was an imitation of the upstate New York venues. Old Town Collectibles was "located with a group of specialty shops, restaurants and entertainment spots" and its inventory was composed of "limited edition collectibles of every shape, size, subject matter and material," including Hummels, Fenton glass and Precious Moments.[14] As well, advertisements in the *Spencerport Suburban News* from 1988 to 1991 promoted investment properties, including homes, condos, townhouses, and land, in the Disney World-Orlando Florida area, available from real estate agents Don and Joyce Parker of Century 21.

The baton pass to the Parkers in 1970 was economically smooth and mostly seamless, and under their ownership, the Coppersmith shop persisted for nearly three decades until its unfortunate demise. But the "race," the "runners," the "track" on which it was run, and the "spectators" all changed dramatically. Deep social changes, including the subset of consumer retailing, impacted the practice and direction of the Avon Coppersmith's business under the Parkers' ownership. But the most staggering change in the retail landscape was infrastructure: the earlier arrival and broad adoption by drivers of the New York State Thruway. What began as a singularly focused, boutique-sized craft establishment offering itinerant travelers the unique products of Art Cole's talent completely evaporated. Handcraftsmanship was replaced by mass manufacturing and merchandising, the very antithesis to what occurred during the previous four decades. Slight variations in technique, form, and execution are expected and valued in handcrafted objects; the same features are intolerable and viewed as defects in mass-manufactured products.

Avon Coppersmith's claim of exclusivity for its products and evidenced by invitations to "see-it-made" were abandoned in favor of franchised sales pitches for identical products available virtually worldwide. Manufacturers' claims of limited editions, puffery about exclusivity, and the persuasive marketing messages of the merchandise's "collectability" was substituted for the tell-tale, idiosyncratic marks left by the Coppersmith's hammer on metal. Assertions of "collectability" are persuasive claims, not factual ones. And objects marketed as "collectible" are like the old saw about innumerable purported Stradivarius violins: If the label says "Stradivarius," then it isn't.

Gifting as a customer's motivation for purchasing Coppersmith crafts disappeared in favor of inward-directed gratification and acquisition incentives for "building" a collection and accumulating a "complete set" of objects for personal enjoyment and self-reward.[15] Mementos and souvenirs of travelers' trips were no longer apt, since nothing "local" was being produced and the memories being sold were artificial and not unique to the shop. The "limited editions" and any implied scarcity, like the products themselves, was a manufactured one. Collector "clubs" and name brands were the products' marketing features. Illusions of "scarcity" (and correspondingly inflated prices) were unambiguously revealed once eBay arrived in 1995 on the newest superhighway, a few years before the Avon Coppersmith met its demise. The Parkers purchased an inventory, Cole made it; Craft took a backseat to production and the "target" audience moved from the other to oneself.

As with Roadside Craftsmen, the financial underwriter during Avon Coppersmith's formative years is Clarence Wemett, though little of the arrangement with Arthur Cole is known. That Wemett would evolve a second, sympathetic craft operation from his first is sensible, maybe even logical, especially given the shops' geographical proximity—if in fact that is what happened. Granddaughter Laurel Wemett believes Clarence's "plan was to link the handcraft businesses in a cooperative marketing arrangement."[16] But in mid-1933, when Avon Coppersmith launched, it would have been premature for Wemett to judge Roadside's profitability forecast and, still deep in the Depression, the fiscal sensibility for Coppersmith would have been unknown but likely fragile. Further, and chancier still, unlike the multimedia and multiple craftsmen populating Roadside, from its inception the Avon Coppersmith was singular in its product focus and was managed and later owned by a single craftsman trained in a single craft, Arthur Cole.

The current work leaves a number of questions unanswered. When and how did the idea for the copper shop come about and whose was it? To what extent was Avon Coppersmith conceived as a quasi-partnership with or companion craft business to Roadside Craftsmen and what relationships were present and practiced when both establishments were simultaneously in business? What explains the difference in business longevity between Roadside Craftsmen and Avon Coppersmith? Since Wemett already had a metal shop at his Hemlock Forge location, what appealed to him about separately launching the Avon Coppersmith? To what extent was the medium and the product produced at Avon thought to be more accessible, attractive, and with greater purchase appeal to traveling tourists than the iron work? How did the copper products' requirements for manufacturing, retailing, and shipping compare to those for the Hemlock Forge? How much shipping of Avon's products in fact took place and what was the division between retail and wholesale orders at Coppersmith?[17] What or who persuaded Arthur Cole to leave his home of thirty years and move to a place where, as best we can tell, he had no connection? How was Walter Jennings involved in Avon Coppersmith, with whom, and how long did the relationship last? Why does Cole and Jennings's close colleague Karl Kipp appear to play no role in Avon Coppersmith? Were other former Roycrofters recruited to Avon Coppersmith as either craftsmen or consignors? What was Wemett and Cole's relationship during the thirteen years they were partners and how formal was the partnership? How hands-on was Wemett relative to Cole in business decisions for the Avon Coppersmith? Which partner paid how much for what and under whose authority and direction was the Coppersmith operated? It is plausible to believe Wemett was the silent funding partner and Cole, more or less, an employee but one with considerable managerial latitude. Rival scenarios, though, are equally tenable in the absence of evidence. Neither the broader nor the precise arrangement of agreements and obligations, in written form, are currently known.

Arthur Cole's lengthy, solo craft career in metal has few parallels. At Roycroft's copper shop, a rotating staff of metal craftsmen were part of the factory-like enterprise's two decades of glory in a forty-year lifespan. For comparison, nearby, in Syracuse, Gustav Stickley's factory, including its metal shop, failed to reach even half that length; on the other end of the continent, and on a much smaller scale than Stickley's, Dirk van Erp's tenure as a coppersmith was nearly as long as Roycroft's.[18] Avon Coppersmith began to flourish, expanding its physical facility and, presumably, profitability by the end of the 1930s, the same time Roycroft slid toward the drain, finally dissolving into bankruptcy by the end of the decade. The apprenticeship with Kipp and Jennings, and especially the creative work innovated and produced by them, informed Cole's aesthetic sensibilities and perfected his craft skills. But Arts and Crafts artistic inspiration yielded to the vicissitudes of commercial pressures—fashion, style, taste, and transient consumers' interests—presenting themselves during the much lengthier post–Arts and Crafts period. Cole's adaptable, accurate understanding of his customer base produced nearly forty successful business years. Working within the Arts and Crafts aesthetic, the Avon Coppersmith exploited and expanded it, better serving and fitting contemporary customers' gifting motivations for purchasing the objects. With Clarence Wemett far in the background, Art Cole led a largely one-man operation that stayed in business longer than virtually any Arts and Crafts peer.

The fire inside Art Cole that began in his teens was his passion for the craft, fueling and powering his artistic expression. The passion was fanned and endorsed by strangers driving by who stopped at his Coppersmith shop in Avon. There, he built and sustained a singularly focused craft enterprise enabling a lifelong professional career as a commercial enterprise where the "report card" for Craft as much as craftsman was delivered daily at the shop's cash register. Perhaps it was a fire born of frustration that ended the Avon Coppersmith shop's life—and its owner's—twenty-eight years after Cole's retirement. When Art Cole sold the Avon Coppersmith in 1970, the New York State Thruway was mature and heavily traveled. East-west traffic on Route 20 had long before tapered off and drivers favored the alternative's speedy efficiency. In the early 1970s, under the Parkers' ownership, Interstate 390 was completed, connecting Rochester to Corning and the state's Southern Tier. A north-south alternative to New York Route 15, the interstate was just a few miles east of the Avon Coppersmith, entirely bypassing the village. Though less commercial than Routes 5 and 20, traffic on Route 15 was usurped by the nearly parallel I-390, and the commerce bordering state highway suffered the same fate as those had on Route 20 earlier. Regional locals, travelers with unhurried leisure, and drivers with the patience to bear with a slow-moving, traffic light-dotted, two-lane highway aside, there were few reasons to stop at, never mind pass (near) by, Avon, New York.

At the same time Arthur Cole retired from the Avon Coppersmith, a young assistant professor at Princeton University was planning the first United States exhibition of American Arts and Crafts. Cole was unlikely to have known of Robert Judson Clark's celebration of the movement of which Cole was so much a part. And when the exhibit opened in 1972, no one predicted the Princeton exhibit, as it became known, would inspire a stream of scholarship on Arts and Crafts subjects.[19] The revival of interest in the movement grew steadily and strongly beginning in the '70s, and its persistence has now outlasted the duration of the movement's original popularity. After Princeton, other Arts and Crafts exhibitions launched at venues across the nation and internationally and have been presented continuously for four decades. About as long as the Avon Coppersmith was under Cole's stewardship.

10

No Shortcuts

Half a century before Clarence Wemett came up with his idea for roadside commerce, Fred Harvey invented it. In the third quarter of the nineteenth century, two thousand miles southwest of Avon and Bloomfield, Harvey observed growing numbers of post–Civil War passengers headed west on railroads. At the time, few passenger trains had dining cars. His empire of restaurants, eventually numbering eighty-four, began in Topeka, Kansas, in 1876 with one alongside the Atchison, Topeka, and Santa Fe Railway. Soon, he became the pioneer of roadside commerce. "Harvey House" trackside restaurants were a monopoly, and hungry passengers had no alternative. "The Civilizer of the West," as Harvey was known, should also be credited as creator of the literal tourist trap.[1] Digging deeper into his captive railroad customers' pockets, Harvey created attractions to accompany the restaurants: theme parks "of sublime natural wonders, prehistoric and colonial historic significance, and colorful, tamed, native peoples,"[2] as inventive as Disney would be later. As the new century began, a little more than twenty-five years after establishing the first Harvey House, the personal freedom of automobiling down open public highways liberated rail tourists from the confines imposed by privately owned tracks—and Harvey. But by then, Fred Harvey (who died in 1901) and his achievements in hospitality and tourism were fading memories. Clarence Wemett's two craft shops were modern adaptations of Harvey's business instinct for freewheeling travelers, regardless of the purpose or destination of their journeys.

Wemett did not seek to create a "tourist trap," if only because replicating the monopoly Harvey held trackside was impossible on a public

157

highway. As well, Wemett likely recognized the circularity of the tourist trap: Purely invented places—theme parks, including Fred Harvey's, and so-called fossil and shell museums, for instance—they would not otherwise exist and serve no function other than to attract tourists. Roadside Craftsmen and Avon Coppersmith's reason for being was manufacturing and their location was thought to be commercially advantageous. They were business ventures established to perform the work to produce a product. By locating them on Route 20, the work product might attract the interest of retail passersby, including tourists tooling along the horizontal spine stretched across the top of New York State. Roadside and Coppersmith's modest, quietly dignified physical appearance was without the garish ostentation so often associated then and today with roadside "attractions." Softly, each beckoned visitors to stop, browse, and "see-it-made," without demanding purchasing, though that clearly was the intention.

Entrepreneurship in curbside commerce and monetizing crafts were not twentieth-century novelties. Whether surplus crop or a chair in disrepair, the yard sale existed long before it was so named. The twentieth-century difference was twofold: the customer base expanded beyond that of immediate neighbors, family, and friends, and the inventory morphed from "previously enjoyed" personal possessions to goods created specifically for sale and intended for profit. Wemett's innovation was favorably marshaling these factors for newly mobilized citizens driving their personal transportation. Nor was longevity for craft-based gift shops begun at Roadside Craftsmen or Avon Coppersmith something new. On the opposite side of the continent, at a place every bit as remote as Upstate New York, coppersmith Albert Berry's Arts and Crafts Shop opened in Juneau, Alaska, in 1913. A student of Theodore Hanford Pond's (who we meet later in the chapter), Berry moved his shop to Seattle, Washington in 1918. Two of Berry's product labels plainly state, "Gifts of Character," an expression Art Cole would have appreciated. Berrys' Craft Shop (their maker's mark) persisted until his death in 1949. Edwina, his wife, assumed control and, following her death in 1957, the shop was run by the Berrys' bookkeeper, Hilda Bale, until 1971 or 1972.[3] Portable, handmade objects, suitable for souvenirs or mementos, were also earlier produced for the tourist trade by contemporaneous ceramists, including George Ohr (Biloxi, Mississippi) and Cornwall and Wallace Kirkpatrick (Anna Pottery, Anna, Illinois). They were unapologetically marketed as novelties and whimsies.

Coincidentally and, as it turned out, ominously prophetically, the very first strip of the New York State Thruway open to traffic was the short, four-mile leg between Canandaigua and Victor. Within ten miles of East Bloomfield, it opened toll free in 1948.[4] Following a pattern begun in the nineteenth century, older man-made transportation routes' response to emerging ones was to sequentially exhibit complacency, then competitiveness, and, last, cooperation.[5] Shortly after midcentury, one New York State route dominated. The Thruway was "a billion-dollar triumph of engineering" that "ranks with the old Erie Canal" *National Geographic*'s reporter Matt McDade breathlessly wrote. So speedy, traveling its entirety "was four hours better than . . . on the old cross-State roads."[6] McDade's lengthy, color-photo-filled essay made scant mention of the displacements necessary for the Thruway's construction.[7] Perhaps the article's 1956 publication meant discussion of the new roadway's rippling, broader consequences was premature. But one thing was clear: Route 20, once one of the state's most significant transportation arteries, was soon relegated to merely one of its many capillaries. It survived the Erie Canal and the railroads, but Route 20 could not defeat the Thruway.

It was an ironic twist. Federal highway support for Route 20 benefitted the launch and sustained the maturity of Roadside Craftsmen and Avon Coppersmith. In the 1930s and 1940s, Route 20 was New York's "superhighway." A quarter century later, as part of an ambitious federal Interstate highway program, the introduction of the Thruway spelled one craft shop's demise and modified the business practice of the other. The Thruway infringed on the most significant element in Wemett's business model: its customer base. It diverted overwhelmingly substantial numbers of drivers from passing by to bypassing Roadside Craftsmen and Avon Coppersmith. Unaware of either shop, Thruway drivers could never be persuaded and never had the opportunity to "see-it-made." Or buy it. Roadside Craftsmen was shuttered just before the Thruway's wider, official opening; its passing was hastened by two factors: artificiality and nature. The completion of the Thruway (the former) most assuredly accelerated it, but the process was sealed by the latter: the aging of the initiative's underwriter, Wemett, and its chief craftsman, Daugherty. Wemett turned to nurturing new interests; some, such as his Egypt Valley camp, loosely aligned with his earlier craft operations. Daugherty returned south to ply his craft for a few years until his death in 1958. The Avon location persisted under the guidance of the shop's original craftsman until 1970. Clarence Wemett's relationship to Guy Daugherty differed from that with Arthur Cole. Both Daugherty and Cole were experienced, skilled craftsmen; neither required tutoring.

The shops' names suggested different orientations, between the singular and the plural: Coppersmith versus Craftsmen. The Avon operation was personalized as much by the business name and the craftsman who personified it. Roadside Craftsmen suggested multiple talents and, as one early report expressed it, a "cooperative" style that arranged craftsmen harmoniously working in different media under a single roof with a shared mission. Operationally, as well, the two craft shops differed. At Roadside, the shop was managed by Norris, Wemett's oldest son. Cole managed the Coppersmith shop's business, especially after 1947 when he acquired sole proprietorship, and it became a one-man, family-run operation. Avon Coppersmith enjoyed lower overhead costs by employing relatively few, most part-time. The Coppersmith's post-1950 advertising presence in local publications signaled a change in sales emphasis: from peripatetic automobiling tourists to the geographically proximate customer base. As railroads had done to canals, and highways to railroads, advances in transportation systems made older ones less vital and the new system "shaped the economic and social landscape."[8] Interest in crafts did not diminish with the arrival of the Thruway, even though public access to the products produced at Roadside and Coppersmith lessened. Just the opposite, in fact. But well before the Thruway's arrival, Wemett's enterprises curiously overlooked an opportunity in their own backyard that might have firmed their foundations.

Rochester's Arts and Crafts Tradition

The Arts and Crafts movement was the aesthetic touchstone for Roadside Craftsmen and the Avon Coppersmith. The shops' craftsmen both created the goods and performed the work required to produce them. From a Texas potter to an East Aurora metalsmith and a handful of Alfred University student ceramists, except for the woodworker virtually all the principal craft creators at Roadside and Coppersmith were "imported." Yet little more than two dozen miles away was a substantial cohort of equally skilled, experienced craftspeople—and many more apprentices "in-training." Despite the proximity, the neighbor nearby went curiously untapped by Wemett's enterprises. Because by conviction, coincidence, or convenience, Rochester and the Mechanics Institute (MI) were among the earliest adopters, most visible proponents, and keenest practitioners of the Arts and Crafts movement's philosophy and, especially, its material output. Just before the turn of the twentieth century, an Arts and Crafts society was formed in Rochester, the first in the nation. Shortly thereafter, a craft curriculum was initiated at Mechanics Institute and, almost immediately following, a significant Arts and Crafts exhibition installed. Later, at exactly midcentury, Rochester became a leader in Craft education and craft retailing when the School for American Craftsmen (SAC) moved to Rochester Institute of Technology (RIT), and shortly thereafter, a center-city Rochester retail craft shop named Shop One opened.

Theodore Hanford Pond initiated the Department of Applied and Fine Arts at Rochester's Mechanics Institute beginning in 1902. Instruction and training in crafts became an intimate part of MI's largely vocational training curriculum. The department's very name, much as the movement's, interlaced the expressive "purity" of art with the pragmatic functionality of Craft. The "and" linking the two suggests equality as much as it expresses a tension: the personally expressive self-indulgence of fine arts and the market-driven practicality of applied arts. At Mechanics Institute, utility is positioned before expression, just the reverse of the movement's arrangement.[9] Likewise, Roadside Craftsmen's and Avon Coppersmith's intentions prioritized commercial ones, even as they blended in art; and unlike some Arts and Crafts movement manufacturers, the two businesses exclusively practiced handcraftsmanship for their products. Mechanics Institute joined a number of other schools across the nation offering training in traditional crafts to citizens.[10] Pond, educated at Pratt Institute in Brooklyn, taught design, wood carving, and metalwork modeling at Rhode Island School of Design beginning in 1896. During his last two years at RISD, 1900–1902, he was director of its Department of Design and Applied Art.[11] Arriving in Rochester, he literally put his stamp on Mechanics Institute almost at once; Pond designed the graphic treatment for the diplomas issued to MI graduates.

The Rochester Arts and Crafts Society began in 1897, the same year the first Arts and Crafts exhibition took place in Boston.[12] Rochester's Society was the earliest of such groups populating cities across the nation, including Boston, Chicago, and Minneapolis. Tightly knit, the Rochester group's members intersected in social and professional circles. The society's president, Harvey Ellis, was a draftsman, architect, and faculty member at Mechanics Institute.[13] Claude Bragdon, the group's treasurer, also taught at MI and was a well-established Rochester architect; later, he designed the Bevier Memorial Building—housing art galleries, studios, and class-rooms—for Mechanics Institute.[14] Its secretary, M. Louise Stowell, was also on the MI faculty and, following Ellis's death in 1904, represented his art at her gallery.

Nearly coinciding with the founding of the Applied and Fine Arts Department, the Rochester Arts and Crafts Society collaborated with Mechanics Institute and brought Gustav Stickley's United Crafts exhibition from Syracuse to Rochester, April 15–25, 1903. Sponsored by Stickley and Pond, the exhibition was organized by Irene Sargent, editor of Stickley's still relatively new monthly magazine, *The Craftsman*.[15] Ellis designed the exhibit's poster and supervised the exhibit's installation. Hosted at the Mechanics Institute's recently built Eastman Building, more than a thousand examples by 150 craftsmen were on view. To encourage wide attendance, admission was ten cents, compared to twenty-five cents for the exhibit's earlier (March) Syracuse edition at the Stickley firm's commercial showroom.[16]

A tremendous success, the exhibit's halo effect provided hard-to-dispute legitimation as much for the Arts and Crafts movement and the Rochester Society as for the Mechanics Institute and Pond's recently formed academic department. "An unexpected interest has been taken in the exhibition," reported Rochester's *Democrat and Chronicle*. "Throughout the ten days there has been large attendance." The boosterish article also noted that "the creditable showing made by Rochester craftsmen" included furniture assembled at the Mechanics Institute and a stained-glass and ironwork fire screen designed and executed by Pond's decorative art class.[17]

Pond left Rochester in 1908 to head the department of design at the Maryland Institute for the Promotion of the Mechanic Arts in Baltimore (today Maryland Institute College of Art). At virtually the same time Pond was leaving, thirty-seven-year-old ceramist Frederick E. Walrath arrived. An 1897 graduate of the Geneseo Normal School (today SUNY at Geneseo), Walrath trained under Charles Fergus Binns at Alfred University from 1900 to 1904. Walrath taught summer ceramics classes at Chautauqua Institution while an Alfred student and was awarded a bronze medal at the 1904 Louisiana Purchase Exposition. He was ceramics instructor at the University of Chicago, 1904 to 1906, and a member of numerous professional artistic organizations and craft guilds.

During 1907, Walrath was a ceramic chemist at Grueby Faience, thanks to Binns's recommendation to the Boston firm's owner, William Grueby. But, within a year, personal and professional disagreements with the company's namesake prompted Walrath's departure. Thanks again to his mentor's recommendation, this time to MI's Pond, Walrath joined the

Mechanics Institute faculty and worked there for a decade, until 1918. Walrath's MI work was recognized widely, and he was featured in several local newspaper stories.[18] He left Mechanics Institute for Newcomb College in New Orleans where he replaced Paul Cox, another Alfred-Binns graduate, as ceramic chemist. Walrath died during a trip home to Jasper, New York, in 1921.[19]

Almost immediately stepping in to keep the kick wheel spinning at Mechanics Institute following Walrath's departure, and for the next thirty-four years, was Lulu Scott Backus. Throughout all of Roadside Craftsmen's years of operation, Backus was a prominent faculty member at Mechanics Institute until her retirement in 1952. By that time MI's name had changed, in 1944, to Rochester Institute of Technology. Backus first appears in the 1919 Rochester Athenaeum and Mechanics Institute yearbook, where she is listed as an instructor of metal work, jewelry, and pottery.

Lulu Scott Backus and the Mechanics Institute

Few Mechanics Institute faculty are more frequently and prominently featured in Rochester's daily newspapers than Lulu Scott Backus. In large part, this was thanks to a column, variously entitled "Artists and Craftsmen" and "Concerning Interests of Artists and Craftsmen." There, Backus's recognition, professional achievements, and exhibitions for her work, and that of her students and adult learners, received regular play.

Born in the hamlet of Town Pump, in the town of Ogden, New York, Backus graduated (1895) from Brockport State Normal School (today SUNY, the College at Brockport), taught drawing and music, and became a Brockport grade school principal. She enrolled in the Rochester Athenaeum and Mechanics Institute (1902–1905 and 1907–1910), completing the art and craft teaching training curriculum. Her postgraduate work in metalry and jewelry was with Pond and, at Alfred, she trained in ceramics under Binns. Shortly after accepting the Mechanics Institute faculty position, she enrolled in the Alfred ceramics summer session as part of her continuing education.[20]

Recognition for Backus's ceramic work was rapid. In 1927, nine years after joining the MI faculty, she was awarded the fourth Lillian Fairchild Award from the University of Rochester. The annual award recognized "the finest contribution to art and literature by a citizen of the Rochester area."[21] With Backus, for the first time the Fairchild was awarded to a ceramist. Award notes indicate it was "for pottery and new ceramic glazes, shown at [the University of Rochester's] Memorial Art Gallery." A newspaper story was more expansive: "For contributions to the art of ceramics through the origination of new glazes for pottery, made possible by her own experimentation in the field."[22] Subsequent Fairchild Awards recognized accomplishments in music, sculpture, architecture, textile design, painting, literature, printmaking, and drama. But not until 1953 was another given for ceramics; and then, the Fairchild Award to Frans Wildenhain was bestowed for mixed media in ceramics, painting, and sculpture. He joined Rochester Institute of Technology's faculty with the arrival of the School for American Craftsmen faculty in 1950.[23]

Amy H. Croughton, initially a movie critic and later a cultural critic, was the "Artists and Craftsmen" columnist for the *Times-Union*, Rochester's afternoon daily newspaper. She reported on Rochester's art scene, including Wemett's Roadside Craftsmen enterprise. Readers could almost count on regular appearances by Backus in Croughton's column beginning in the early 1930s and nearly until the columnist's death in 1951, shortly before Backus's retirement. As well, Backus and her ceramic work were extensively covered by such regional New York newspapers as the *Livonia Gazette*, *Clinton Courier*, *Geneva Daily Times*, and the *Elmira Star Gazette*. Nationally, she was profiled in a four-page May 1942 story published in the *Bulletin of the American Ceramic Society*.[24] Backus's pottery was exhibited in the company of such other well-known ceramists as Arthur E. Baggs (Marblehead Pottery), Binns, Mary Chase Stratton (Pewabic Pottery), and Waylande Gregory.[25] One thumbnail sketch of Backus's career notes her work had been "shown in exhibitions of the American Ceramic Society, the New York Society, the Federation of Arts, the Art Alliance of Philadelphia, and at the Art Museum at Syracuse in its annual National Ceramic Exhibition. Examples of her work are in American galleries and several pieces are on exhibition in Europe."[26]

Lulu Scott Backus's lengthy career at Rochester Institute of Technology concluded in 1952 with a faculty-staff dinner at the Powers Hotel honoring her and six others.[27] Three years later, at eighty-two, she died on August 27, 1955, and was buried in Lakeview Cemetery, Brockport. The *Rochester Democrat and Chronicle* obituary, drawing on Croughton's previous reporting, credits Backus with establishing the Industrial Ceramics Group, notes her substantial exhibition record, and explains that she "conducted extensive experiments in new techniques of glazing and coloring pottery."[28]

Beginning at the turn of the twentieth century, Rochester and the Mechanics Institute were populated with professional craftsmen and bursting with students gaining instruction in and pursuing a variety of crafts: ceramics, metalworking, furniture building, textiles (embroidery), stained glass, and book design. Yet none of this talent found its way to or was tapped by Roadside Craftsmen or Avon Coppersmith.

The Alfred Connection

The absence of any connection between Roadside Craftsmen and Avon Coppersmith with Rochester and the Mechanics Institute is puzzling, especially in contrast to Roadside's connection to Alfred University, situated nearly three times the distance from Bloomfield than Rochester. Today, a trip from the Bloomfield location to Alfred is a ninety-minute scenic drive; in 1930 it would have been a lengthier, albeit no less scenic one. The presence of Alfred University's School of Ceramics and, later, Glidden Pottery, a commercial manufacturer, suggests a reason for the connection between Roadside Craftsmen and Alfred. As with the Mechanics Institute, neither the ceramics school nor the pottery were secrets; the press covered each extensively and favorably.

Alfred University's School of Clay Working and Ceramics is the nation's oldest college ceramics program. Englishman Charles Fergus Binns, today regarded as the "father of American studio ceramics," founded the school in 1900. Author of *The Story of the Potter* (1898), he later contributed regularly to Syracuse ceramist Adelaide Robineau's *Keramic Studio* and Stickley's *Craftsman* magazines. Highly regarded and with widely dispersed professional connections, he helped place Alfred ceramics alumni at commercial manufacturers and educational institutions across the United States. Among them were Arthur Baggs (Marblehead Pottery, Ohio State University), Guy Cowan (Cowan Pottery), Elizabeth Overbeck (Overbeck Pottery) and, as noted above, Paul Cox, Frederick Walrath, and Lulu Scott Backus.[29]

One Alfred ceramics graduate student (1937 to 1939), Glidden Parker, was especially entrepreneurial. From 1940 to 1957, his Glidden Pottery became nationally known and its products widely adopted. Parker intended Gliddenware as much for the dinner table as for the gift shop. The former made production demands and the latter artistic ones. Almost immediately, though the pottery then had a staff of only one or two, he acquired a New York City sales representative to market the wares and showed Glidden Pottery samples at the annual New York Gift Show.[30] A local newspaper's misleading 1941 front-page headline about the firm, ALFRED HAS A CERAMIC INDUSTRY UNKNOWN TO MANY, detailed Glidden's rapid success after only a year.

With Manhattan marketing representation, national advertising exposure, and an affordable price point, Glidden Pottery's popularity grew remarkably quickly. After two years, production had doubled,[31] and four years after opening, the production facility's size substantially increased with a new building. Moreover, the local newspaper reported that "the clay, which previously came by the ton in sacks, will now be purchased in carload lots."[32] In 1944, 50,000 Glidden Pottery pieces were sold and another 100,000 awaited shipping.[33] Midway through the firm's tenure, as many as fifty-five people were employed at Glidden. Department stores stocked Glidden, and Lucille Ball (who grew up an hour west in Jamestown) and Desi Arnaz owned Glidden dinnerware; it was a set piece on their *I Love Lucy* CBS television program. At least one postcard depicting the interior of the Avon Coppersmith shows Glidden pottery on the shelves.[34]

Alfred's single-craft focus was a fertile training ground for ceramists. The university's faculty were arguably better known than those in Rochester. Certainly, Binns was, not in the least due to his extensive publications. Glidden Pottery modeled commercial ceramic manufacture and its marketing and retailing in ways the university could not promise its students. Roadside Craftsmen's personnel included nearly a half-dozen recent Alfred University ceramics graduates. Most were hired during Roadside's earliest years and before Glidden Pottery began: Doris Marley (graduated 1933 and later Norris Wemett's wife), Elizabeth L. Rogers (1932), Richard Thomas (1939), Emil "Chick" Zschniegner (1931), and Heinz George Rodies (1943). University records indicate Rogers had a relatively long tenure at Roadside: six months in 1932 and 1933, seven in the two following years, and five months in 1936. Ceramics professor Marion Fosdick, who spent more than three decades at Alfred, beginning in 1915, may have played some role in helping young graduates find work at Roadside Craftsmen; it was she who suggested that Rogers, for one, work there, and Clarence Wemett reportedly visited Alfred to recruit ceramists.[35] Once initiated, nearby Glidden Pottery may have attracted Alfred students who otherwise would have sought employment at the more distant Roadside Craftsmen (see figure 10.1).

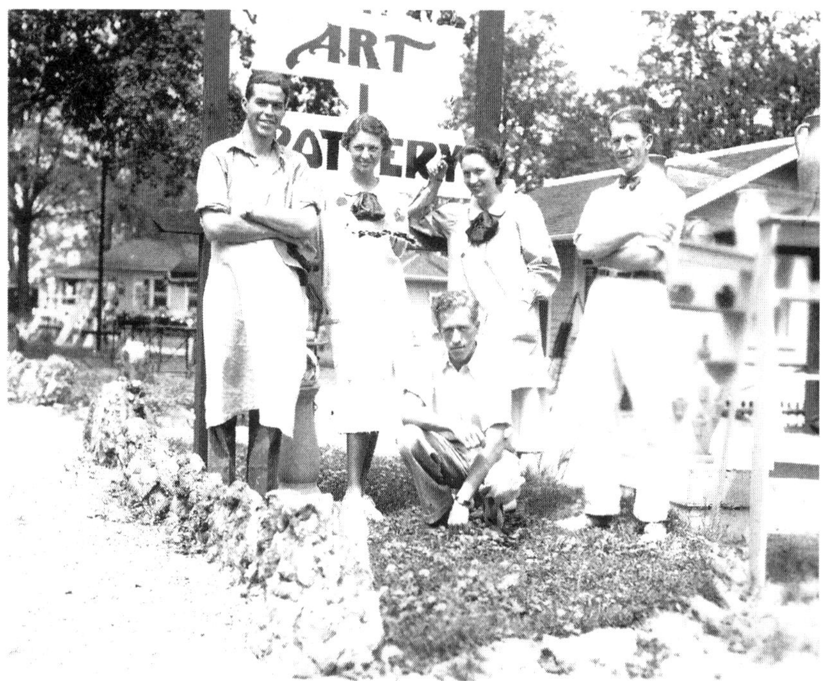

Figure 10.1. Workers circa 1934 at the Bloomfield Art Pottery, later renamed Roadside Craftsmen. From left: Norris G. Wemett, Clarence Wemett's son and manager; Alfred ceramics alumni Elizabeth (Betty) Rogers Sarver, Doris Marley Wemett, and Emil ("Chick") Zschiegner; kneeling is Guy Merlin Drumm who pursued wholesale business. Photograph from the Norris G. Wemett collection, courtesy of Laurel C. Wemett.

Midcentury Rochester Developments

Shortly before Roadside Craftsmen phased out of business, and not long after Avon Coppersmith came under the sole ownership of its principal craftsman, two early 1950s developments occurred in nearby Rochester: the introduction of a crafts school and the initiation of a retail store exclusively focused on Craft. Each enterprise dovetailed with interests Wemett expressed two decades earlier. In 1950, the School for American Craftsmen arrived at Rochester Institute of Technology, ironically from its previous home at Alfred University; and in 1953, four SAC faculty members opened Shop One.

SAC was founded by Aileen Osborn Webb, a wealthy New York philanthropist deeply devoted to Craft and its artists. Her lifelong accomplishments on behalf of Craft include initiating a school[36] that would both train artists in their craft *and* provide them with the tools to earn a living by working at their craft, precisely what Glidden Parker had accomplished.[37] First begun at Dartmouth College in 1944, SAC moved to Alfred in 1946. Internal friction at Alfred, though, precluded SAC's continuance there. The 1950 move to Rochester Institute of Technology was thanks to active recruitment by RIT's president, Mark Ellingson, and facilitated by Osborn Webb. SAC's curriculum mirrored the media plied by Roadside: metal, wood, clay, fiber.

Begun by four SAC faculty—a ceramist, a woodworker, and two metalsmiths—Shop One distinguished itself from other retail stores that sold decorative art or gifts by offering customers only work produced by the shop's principals. Roadside's inventory matched nearly exactly that of Shop One's. But Shop One's guiding philosophy could not have been more different than Roadside's and Coppersmith's. Shop One sought (perhaps "demanded") artistic legitimation for Craft that the more "folksy," everyday Wemett enterprises either ignored or eschewed. Shop One also avoided being lumped into the category of a rural "roadside" merchant; its model was Webb's urban craft store, America House.[38] But Roadside and Coppersmith had already done for Craft in the country what Shop One and America House now did for Craft in the city: elevate its status.

That Avon Coppersmith and Roadside Craftsmen's interests never meshed with talent at Mechanics Institute and, for that matter, Rochester's wider cultural art and craft leaders, institutions, and artists, is a curiosity without satisfactory explanation. Together, all shared matching craft product interests and were geographically close. The prominent, consistent media presence of Lulu Scott Backus in the Rochester press beginning in the early 1930s suggests broad public awareness of Backus herself, her academic department, and the many students enrolled in ceramics courses. Moreover, Roadside's pottery and Backus's work would have been aesthetically compatible, albeit with discernible differences. But the historical record offers no mention of any relationship. Instead, farther away in Alfred, a connection was formed, albeit briefly, between Roadside Craftsmen and the ceramics school, and up to a half dozen of their alumni were employed there.

Perhaps conversations took place and either never reached the point of formalization or were not publicly acknowledged. Perhaps those working at Mechanics Institute were so fully engaged they did not seek out additional work or were not approached about doing so. On the other hand, perhaps Wemett's two enterprises *did* reach out to Mechanics Institute, and for equally mysterious, unreported reasons, the entrée was rejected. Maybe Mechanics Institute was perceived as little more than a trade school serving such local and unrelated industries as Eastman Kodak or Bausch + Lomb. Or maybe MI's academic bona fides seemed slight compared to those of Alfred's. Nonetheless, mutually beneficial opportunities were missed. Either one of Wemett's commercial businesses would have gained by the geographic convenience of collaborating with the Rochester craftsmen. If nothing else, Mechanics Institute students—as much as those at Alfred—would have been a reliable pool from which to select apprentices. And Roadside and Coppersmith's commercial interests were aligned with Mechanics Institute's;[39] after 1950, when SAC moved to RIT, the alignment of interests was further strengthened. Timing is everything, the cliché asserts, but it certainly was not a propitious one at midcentury. Roadside Craftsmen's waning days began just as the School for American Craftsmen moved to RIT. In the end, all failed to take advantage of potentially valuable alliances.

Conclusion

Heading north from Hemlock toward the Route 20 intersection in Lima, a mid-nineteenth-century forester's horses would have strained to pull loads up the hill on the modern, rough-sawn wooden pavement. Just beyond the crest, Clarence Wemett later located his iron forge. But, except for where glaciers carved a deep cut, producing the hill leaving the village, the ten-mile stretch of Plank Road to Lima is mostly flat and as straight as it is lonely. Farmers' fields on either side are interrupted only sporadically by structures and the small Baptist cemetery that opened at the beginning of the nineteenth century on the east, closed shortly after the new one began. Lush and green in the spring, the snow fences built there are impotent barriers to the fierce wind that whips snow across Plank Road in winter. By the time he was ready to open his craft shops, Wemett enjoyed modern advantages of automobility on better paved roads.

Despite the Great Depression's fraught social and economic climate, Wemett's counterintuitive craft enterprises had long lives. Modern transportation systems and publishing liberated businesses from the restrictive confines of localism. Railroads facilitated mail-order catalogue shopping with an efficient means for shipping products to customers. Catalogues, gatekeepers for product distribution, revolutionized the retail industry, redirecting sales from brick-and-mortar stores. In cooperation with the emergence of personal leisure, the introduction of automobiles and the expansion of surfaced highways formed a commercial circulatory system prompting opportunities for Craft (singular or plural, upper- or lower-case): nudging it forward, helping it evolve up a hierarchical ladder from necessity in service to human convenience to social utility for rehabilitative therapy and, beginning in the twentieth-century, decorative art if not an art form. Highways *delivered* customers to manufacturers and retailers, including Wemett's. With strategic business planning and tactical execution and, doubtless, a dose of serendipity, Clarence Wemett's two examples of entrepreneurial capitalism persisted despite factors otherwise militating against them. Roadside Craftsmen was in business from 1929 until 1953 and letterhead bearing its Hemlock iron forge's name is extant as late as 1962. Avon Coppersmith, initiated in 1933, remained under the principal's management until his retirement in 1970 and in name until 1998. Their stories expand and enhance commercial Craft history, case studies of Craft emerging during the years between the two world wars, an era that, as Kardon notes, has "been undervalued, even neglected."[1]

Called a "craft revival," most authors locate the onset of the movement elevating Craft and their makers' status to the second half of the twentieth century, placing it during the 1960s.[2] An alternate reading of Craft's ascent suggests its genesis with two not-for-profit developments in the Depression: the introduction of Craft in college-level curricula (e.g., Penland [1923], Cranbrook [1928], and Black Mountain College [1933]) and government initiatives growing out of the Depression and associated with the New Deal. Both noncommercial developments coincide with Wemett's commercial craft shops' opening, marking a greater prominence for Craft and the profession. Also, characterizing New York State as a "center" or "hotbed" for crafts is not entirely hyperbolic given such earlier turn-of-the-century examples as Elverhoj (Milton-on-Hudson), Briarcliffe (Ossining), and Byrdcliffe (Woodstock).[3] Measuring the status of Craft and craftsman is inexact, and their proxies are imperfect. Arguably, the clearest, widest form of support came from such programs as the Works Progress Administration, Federal Art Project, Public Works of Art Project, and even the Civilian Conservation Corps. These empirical actions kickstarted a Craft movement under the guise of government-sponsored economic relief. Localized actions mixed art with craft. At least 3,000 WPA craft projects provided "income, self-help and rehabilitation for the unemployed."[4] The initiatives were double-edged: they unambiguously offered relief during desperate economic times although were sometimes accompanied by the pejorative of pity or derision.

The professionalization of Craft is documented by Aerni.[5] She summarized research on Craft as performed by governmental, philanthropic, and not-for-profit agencies and for-profit organizations in the United States.[6] Aerni reports "impressive" and "significant growth," beginning in the mid-1960s,[7] in the number of retail craft firms and galleries, fairs and shows, college curricula, and professional organizations—all markers of an elevated status for Crafts and their makers. Although the Southern

Highland Handicraft Guild began in 1929, by 1978, only 30 percent of all craft organizations had been initiated prior to 1958. In 1980 there were 1,000 to 1,250 professional craft organizations. While colleges offering Crafts curricula began in the 1920s, there were only 19 such programs by 1962; the number jumps to 750 in 1973. Craft fairs can be traced to as early as 1942 (Highland), but did not reach 10 annually until 1970. Between 1966, when the American Craft Enterprises held its first craft show, and 1985, the number of commercial exhibitors grew from 60 to 626 and gross sales expanded from $18,000 to $5.4 million. Until 1960, the number of American craft shops and galleries remained in single digits, rising to 100 that year; by 1975 there were 950. In the mid-1980s, there were 12,000 to 15,000 self-reported full-time craftspeople and 51,000 to 61,000 part-timers. Less easily enumerated are the number of not-for-profits supporting Crafts in one fashion or another and the number and frequency of museum exhibitions featuring (exclusively or not) crafts and their makers. Aerni's summary of past research conservatively demonstrates the growth of the Craft marketplace only after the mid-twentieth century.

The movement professionalizing the craftsmen and heightening the profile for Craft is personified and largely driven by Aileen Osborn Webb. Her life's work, she wrote in her unpublished memoir, was "helping to develop the status of craft in the United States."[8] She shared with Wemett's enterprises "an appreciation of beauty that was inspired by the Arts and Crafts Movement."[9] With counterintuitive timing, beginning during World War II and through the Cold War, her support for crafts and their makers was indefatigable and generous. A 1953 exhibition survey of American crafts, "Designer Craftsmen U.S.A.," organized by Webb's American Craftsmen's Educational Council and the Brooklyn Museum, traveled to more than eleven museums.[10] The 1956 opening of her Museum of Contemporary Crafts in a renovated New York City Victorian brownstone, next door to the Museum of Modern Art, placed Craft "symbolically on par with that prestigious art institution."[11] Thanks, especially, to Webb's numerous, visible initiatives, Craft moved into an increasingly prominent position.

Legs and Legacy

Whether cognizant of the fact or not, Aileen Webb's America House and the SAC craftsmen's Shop One inherited a legacy created well before either was actualized. Roadside Craftsmen's demise in the early 1950s is coincidental with the School for American Craftsmen's move to Rochester Institute of Technology. As tempting as it seems to draw a genealogical line from the older to the newer enterprise, no evidence supports this. Instead, another Rochester organization is closest to inheriting Roadside Craftsmen's legs: the Rochester Folk Art Guild (1957 to present). Its story in many ways mirrors scripts already written for and enacted by Roadside Craftsmen. Ever present in the newer narrative are nostalgic elements of the past: for the honest and primitive, and for the virtues of handcraftsmanship.

Louise March (1900–1987) was the Rochester Folk Art Guild's "founder and guiding spirit."[12] Begun in Rochester in 1957, a decade later the group's half dozen members moved fifty miles south to an 1850 farmhouse in Middlesex, New York, a structure nearly as old as the Branchport church Wemett moved to Bloomfield to house Roadside Craftsmen. There, on the three-hundred-acre East Hill Farm, Guild members worked the land by hand along with clay, wood, and fiber crafts. It was, as a Woodstock-era photographic feature in the Sunday magazine for Rochester's daily newspaper expressed it, a "Return to Simple Life."[13] "We weren't expert craftsmen when we started," said one member, "but some are now."[14] Newspaper reports about March and the Guild mimic without mentioning dramatic tropes journalists previously applied to the Roadside Craftsmen enterprise.[15] The Guild was personified by March, and her exotic biography. Swiss-born, she managed the Opportunity Art Gallery in Manhattan in the late 1920s for famed photographer Alfred Stieglitz. As significant to the colorful narrative, she was a student and translator of Armenian mystic-philosopher, George Ivanovich Gurdjieff (1866–1949). An article about the Guild described Gurdjieff's beliefs: "Modern men and women are enslaved by old attitudes and outside influences—such as the weather and criticism—which prevent them from controlling their lives."[16] In some ways, Louise March's and the Guild's stories fit the contemporary throwback memory of the late 1960s, as well as the present story's narrative of Wemett's enterprises.

While old attitudes held by modern people were to be purged, reporters' descriptions of the Rochester Folk Art Guild liberally, literally, and positively referenced medieval guilds, where "an individual was an instrument of the whole."[17] The Guild's persona also bears passing familiarity to those expressed earlier by late nineteenth- and early twentieth-century New York utopian craft communities seeking to connect head, heart, and hand: "The folk art guild is a place where the craft work and activities of daily living are outer expressions of inner work."[18] In a 1981 article, March said: "Man himself is a vessel."[19] At least one earlier report sought to dispel the Guild's "spiritual mumbo-jumbo and commercialism" and draw attention to the quality and beauty of its products.[20] Writing in the *Auburn Citizen Advertiser*, and using language mirroring in sentiment that of 1930s Roadside Craftsmen newspaper descriptions, Ruth Ann Appelhof affirmed the Guild creates for those "disillusioned with the wasteland of manufactured products stamped out in wood-grained plastic or peeling chrome."[21] Most articles, including one from 1969, note that Guild membership led to personal transformation. Before becoming Guild members, "Their so-called education was lopsided and their knowledge too specialized. They came to understand that they were not to embark on manual work for name or fame, but to discover their own nature."[22] Fifteen years later, a Guild spokesman explained to a reporter: "We are a community of craftsmen who use crafts as a means to explore ourselves."[23] Self-discipline and self-discovery were virtues shared and benefits earned by Guild members.[24] And it is there that Wemett's enterprises and the Rochester Folk Art Guild diverge: personal enlightenment, transformation, or redemption held no part of any promise extended to those who worked at or purchased from Roadside Craftsmen and Avon Coppersmith.

Instead of internal growth, Craft and craftsmen at Wemett's shops became part of a wider, external "movement." Unlike other organized, early twentieth-century social movements, this one was leaderless, without a manifesto, and geographically dispersed. It was, nonetheless, a movement that shook up business practices and realigned artistic aspirations and consumer expectations. The movement, including Roadside Craftsmen and Avon Coppersmith, traveled a convoluted route leading to Craft's maturation: from necessity to luxury, passing by such disparate outposts as industrial product and rehabilitative therapy, tchotchke and souvenir, garage hobby and juvenile camp activity. The movement's speed was imperceptibly slow, its destination unmapped, and signage was indistinct or ambiguous when present at all. Its travelers were as unaware of their status as they were their journey. In that way, they were much like subjects in "just-noticeable difference" experiments unable to discriminate among small changes. Wrapped inside, Craft's evolution was a bundle of paradoxes. Jane Kessler identified some of the late 1920s tensions: "Crafts were hybrids of both past and future, often embodying conflicting attributes. They were authentic as well as affected. They were conceived within a barter system and matured within a market system. They were silent in terms of authorship, yet uniquely individual."[25] Clarence Wemett, Roadside Craftsmen, and Avon Coppersmith's accomplishment was far more than a business innovation. As movement members they facilitated the evolution of Craft from lower- to uppercase and the professionalization of those who worked the materials to create the goods, advancing the status for each. The outcomes were neither intended nor anticipated when Wemett launched the enterprises.

Preindustrial Craft's pragmatism was self-legitimizing. No one wondered, "What is it good for?" or "What do I do with it?" Likewise, solitary craftsmen did not justify or explain themselves. Practiced in the home, Craft required no philanthropy or underwriting. Craft was something made by someone, often for the same one. When Wemett's enterprises began, standardization, uniformity, and mass production in service to efficiency and product volume were well established and viewed as virtuous modern achievements. Wemett's enterprises moved Craft's noncommercial, personal, and utilitarian roots from the singular to the many and from self- to other-directed by tying the Craft attributes to the increased numbers of paved highways and broad public adoption of automobiles. The shops exploited newfound personal mobility and bound traditional methods of decorative expression to modern industrial practices, only on a smaller scale. A quieter form of industrialism. Trade-offs between efficiency and quantity on the one hand were offset by personal skill and product quality on the other. Wemett may have recognized that without the pretensions of art, Craft avoided art's accompanying burdens: for credibility, endorsement, and reputation. And public subsidy. As commercialized in East Bloomfield and Avon, Craft's unapologetic, transferable utility was made affordably available to many.

Avon Coppersmith and Roadside Craftsmen mostly welcomed and exploited the modern age. Unlike when the Arts and Crafts movement emerged, neither Wemett craft shop protested a gloomy future. Although there was good reason to expect grim times, since their opening coincided with the onset of the Great Depression. Instead, the shops' "protest" was businesslike product differentiation married to pride of workmanship. As if to say: "Our handmade alternatives to mass production set them apart from the rest." Incongruously, the otherwise humble Coppersmith and Roadside simultaneously assumed a superior, elitist position but one without any twinge of martyrdom that begs for sympathy as incentive for purchase. Rather, as undifferentiated mass production dominated many industries, Roadside's and Coppersmith's craft work asserted and evidenced individuality, personal competence, and artistry.

This transitional phase of the movement located craftsmen in a murky double-bind between "professional" and "amateur," as Kessler suggests. When compensation and profit for the latter begins, then amateurs are accused of "selling out" to commercialization. Or, as Bourdieu wrote, a form of "reversed economics," that takes "failure as a sign of election and success as sign of compromise."[26] As craftsmen professionalized, any association with weekend hobbyists faded. Home crafts created by DIY amateurs had had their moment in the spotlight. Apotheosized by such narrowly focused publications as Gustav Stickley's *The Craftsman*, the amateurs were tutored by ones with broader editorial scope and wider dissemination such as *Popular Mechanics*. Wemett's shops evolved "do-it-yourself" to "see-it-for-yourself" and manufactured products with benefits shared by craftsman, customer, and owner. But above all else, among the craftsmen at Roadside and Coppersmith, the work was the way they made their living.

Wisely, Clarence Wemett's craft enterprises rejected or ignored the platitudes of the earlier design movement, Arts and Crafts, thereby avoiding wrestling with its contradictions and conceits. Roycroft, where Art Cole worked, was among the most successful early twentieth-century Arts and Crafts operations. But Roycroft quickly transformed to factory-scale production set inside a large physical plant. The Roycroft campus was complete with an inn for lodging, buildings for manufacturing, and even one for generating its own power. Media, including serial publications and product catalogues, promoted the enterprise. Wemett mimicked almost none of Roycroft's accoutrements for his craft enterprises. Neither Roadside nor Coppersmith leveraged the persuasive advantages of modern printed media and their professional practitioners to promote and market their products. Their efforts to widen public awareness of their operations beyond point of creation and purchase were mostly nineteenth-century ones. Coppersmith's understated ads in local newspapers and its network of roadway signs served geographically narrow retail interests and serendipitous discovery by highway motorists. It is unlikely either shop meaningfully engaged sales representatives to place their products in distant retail craft and gift shops. Neither shop offered especially robust product catalogues, and the received history reveals no information about catalogue dissemination, never mind the publications' success at stimulating business. Unlike earlier Arts and Crafts proponents, including those in upstate New York, Avon Coppersmith and Roadside Craftsmen were undistracted and unburdened by responsibilities to publications for polishing reputations or preaching philosophy. Without the diversions of proselytizing or didacticism, the two shops' focus was singular: build their businesses by creating work passing travelers would purchase.

What are we to make of what the Avon Coppersmith wrought from his metal and the Bloomfield Potter formed from his clay? Although aesthetics are the quality collectors most value and the criterion by which they judge all other products in the class, Roadside's and Coppersmith's artistic contributions are their least significant. Few objects created at either shop rise to anyone's estimation of fine art. While the quality of their work was uniformly high, the aesthetic treatment was uneven. Technically proficient, and in some cases exemplars for that attribute, much of the two firms' output is unremarkable. Not "bad" or "off-putting." But rarely magnetic or evocative.

The passion exemplified by Arts and Crafts was not present, as though the Roadside and Coppersmith objects sought to remain impersonal, anonymous, without self-disclosure or transparency. Well-made, perfectly functional, and quite suitable for gifting or commemorating occasions, they possess little of the design or aesthetic pizzazz of either Arts and Crafts or midcentury modern style. Among Coppersmith's output, there is none of the geometric elegance demonstrated by Roycroft's Secessionist-style work; Roadside Craftsmen's monochromatic ceramics lack the painterly qualities of Rookwood's art pottery, Grueby's sculpted plant motifs, or Teco's architectonic references. The shops' products also almost defiantly swim against the currency of precisionism, streamlining, and the other aesthetic impulses that gripped the modern worlds of art and design when the two shops began business. Coppersmith's and Roadside's aesthetic was an affirmation of Craft and its traditions. One likely to be embraced by travelers and tourists whose interests would find the work comfortably familiar. The shops' aesthetic aspiration was to meet the mainstream, maybe a common denominator, that gift recipients would appreciate and that would find favor as decoration enlivening domestic spaces. Their work better represents modern business methods than modern aesthetics. Coppersmith and Roadside's sophistication is found in the enterprise more than in the objects. The business enterprise and the people involved in perpetuating these businesses form the story.

Technically, there is little to fault about the products produced at either shop. The pots thrown in Bloomfield exhibit the same balance in weight and execution as better-known, earlier art potteries. But it is difficult to describe Roadside's work as "refined." Its pottery is composed of mostly conventional forms distinguished by the narrow albeit attractive range of monochromatic colors. Everyday wares—jugs, vases, bowls—they occasionally feature such decorative flourishes as mustache-shaped or rat-tail handles. When the glazes offer a bit more chewing gum for the eye, it is as much due to their difference from those most customarily encountered for the Pottery's output as to any unique properties. Among the more interesting Bloomfield glazes, polychrome examples seem almost end-of-day style creations, less a function of intention than happenstance. Daugherty's work at Roadside Craftsmen fits neatly beneath a broadly sheltering, but stereotypically confining, umbrella of "Southern Pottery" or "Southern Folk Art." The labels discriminate between utilitarian and artistic wares, exemplifying a similar tension as between "craft" and "art": art potteries created work on a canvas of clay, the rest formed mud for utility. Attractively arranged on today's shelf, table or mantel, Roadside Craftsmen's pottery looks nice and is quite capable of performing their function.

The best metal created at Avon Coppersmith is every bit as good as that produced by Roycroft. But Roycroft produced consistently high-quality work across a much broader product line than Coppersmith, which perhaps bowed to perceived whims and fancies of the tourist trade. Like its neighbor fifteen miles down the highway, Avon Coppersmith made unsurprising, conventional forms. As with the pottery, most Coppersmith products were utilitarian or decorative. The hammered copper vases would hold water and flowers, even for customers unlikely to ever use them for that purpose. Trays had the strength to transport and serve food or drink, even if more often than not they found a place only in the plate-rail of a sideboard or the grooved shelf inside of a china cabinet. The Coppersmith's forms lack the design heterogeneity and ambition of those Roycroft produced. Most Avon vases are clunkier, their proportions less refined than Roycroft's. Art Cole's Coppersmith objects did not exhibit the whittled-down decorative restraint exemplified in the best work produced by his mentors, Karl Kipp and Walter Jennings. Significantly, all three experienced commercial craft production uniformity in a near-assembly-line context. Examples produced by Cole and Jennings outside of Roycroft and the Coppersmith are typically more aesthetically refined than work done at either shop. Avon Coppersmith's output was more homogenous and its execution more conservative than at many other Arts and Crafts period metal shops.

BOOKENDS

An object's aesthetic appeal is typically the first magnet pulling collectors' interest. A three-part, nearly simultaneous visceral reaction occurs: the eye's attention is drawn, the mind's processing system is engaged, and the heart is stimulated. Curiosity might be piqued following initial attraction, perhaps prompting the collector's closer inspection or deeper investigation of the object. When aesthetics is coupled with (perceived) rarity, desirability increases and prices escalate.

Among collectors of Arts and Crafts hammered copper products, bookends' rank on the list of objects coveted and in the hierarchy of significance is, in most cases, low or last. Commonly found and usually inexpensive, ownership can telegraph status as a beginning collector. Virtually any reference to them is prefaced apologetically (i.e., "they're *just* bookends"). No matter the bookends' salability to, say, (rare) book collectors or even their function among writers desperate for a metaphor. Bookends are an example writers trot out for either the addiction or illness metaphor used in genesis stories about collecting. New metal collectors are said to pass through a "bookend stage" before sophistication and maturity set in. Bookends are the initial "taste," sample, or point of contagion that got the otherwise unsuspecting, un-addicted and perfectly healthy started down a meandering, not-so-miserable lifelong road of being "hooked on" or "infected by" the collecting "habit" or "ailment" from which, happily, few recover. Bookends are a measure of snootiness among a self-identified elite and the yardstick by which growth and connoisseurship is measured: while I began *there*, now I am *here*. Humble at best, ridiculed at worst, bookends are only memorable (if at all) if they serve a role for their primitive primacy, often destined only as a double entendre in autobiographical articles about collecting (e.g., "My First Piece").

Roycroft, where Arthur Cole worked, began as a publishing enterprise. Their deluxe edition books with tooled leather covers were retail priced up to $250. An outgrowth of the book cover work, Roycroft produced other leather goods: table mats for vases, lamps, and bowls, one catalogue advised, as well as picture frames, purses, and clutches; there was even a tooled leather cover enclosing an inexpensive desk clock. Only later, as the Roycroft commercial enterprise expanded, were objects of copper and furniture of oak or mahogany manufactured. Drawing on Roycroft's bookish beginnings, manufacturing bookends was a sensible, organic extension of an already established product line. A few bookends were of (weighted) wood and a couple with tooled leather inserts. Roycroft's copper shop obligingly created more than two dozen design variations on the form. Indeed, of all the Arts and Crafts–era metal shops, Roycroft's production of bookends had no rival; it was the most prolific and varied. A few were plain and simple, differentiated only by shape and size. Many were decorated in one fashion or another: geometric designs evoking a European Secessionist-style, animal (peacocks, an owl's head) or floral motifs (trillium, poppy), and structural bookends with riveted straps for support as though buttresses on a building. Even among the scant dozen or so special finish Roycroft copper pieces, named Italian Polychrome, were three models of bookends.

Unsurprisingly, Avon Coppersmith made several models of copper bookends. The best set is the simplest. Just over four inches tall and three inches wide, their slightly curved bend near the base suggests a spring-loaded tension powerfully capable of snugly containing the books in between. The undulating top of the bookend flares out slightly. Picking them up, their weight unambiguously telegraphs the medium's thick gauge without need for any other form of measurement. They have the heft and substance of structure well beyond that which seems required, almost no matter the size and number of the shelf's volumes. Otherwise unadorned, the Coppersmith's hammer marks are broad for visual discrimination but tightly spaced without seeming mechanical or crowded; just enough idiosyncrasy in the planishing to clearly demonstrate the craftsman's presence. A mellow brown patina covers the copper with lighter highlights, allowing light to play off the form and engage the eye. While overall, the design of Avon Coppersmith's products is uneven, when its product was good, it was *really* good (see figure C.1).

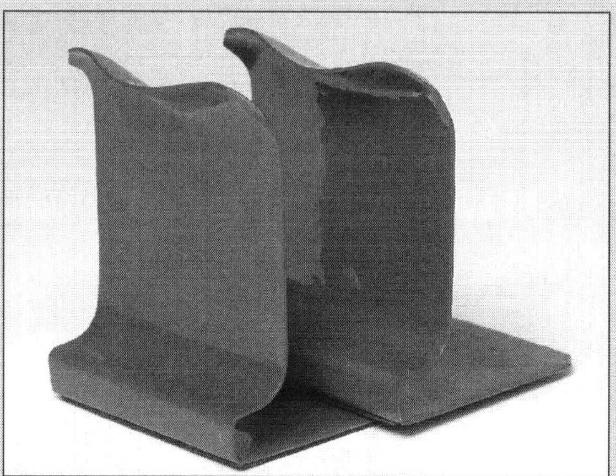

Figure C.1. Bookends by the Avon Coppersmith, 4.25 inches tall, 3.33 inches wide, 3.25 inches deep. Joseph A. DiTucci collection. Photograph by A. Sue Weisler.

Despite aesthetic shortcomings, the businesses' longevity *suggests* their economic viability. Short-term success might be due to novelty; longer-term endurance is more difficult to explain, though persistence is no assurance of profitability. Industrialization resulted in cheaper, more efficient ways to manufacture and distribute product; it did not guarantee cash at the retail register. An old chestnut about a related trade, the antiques business, is that buying is easy, selling is hard. Accumulating an inventory, in other words, requires only money; selling the inventory at a profit is the measure of business success. Product adoption is the criterion that measures economic approval. Creating something few want produces only a large inventory occupying long shelves. To what extent was Clarence Wemett's investment in the two craft operations financially successful? We do not know. If his business records are extant, they were not located for the present study. Nonetheless, it is hard to imagine a businessman such as Wemett would continue to pour resources into an enterprise not worth his while.

Good luck and timing are sometimes invoked as explanations for an innovation's success. In Clarence Wemett's roadside crafts case, timing played no role since no one would characterize an economic depression as good. "Luck's" explanatory power is amorphous, beyond anyone's control, and trivializes Wemett's work. And his work was not the craft, it was the idea, the vision, the investment and, not at all least, the long-term underwriting of craft and craftsmen. Clarence Wemett's two enterprises coincidentally aligned with an expanding highway system, increasing numbers of automobile drivers, and the growth of leisure travel. He could not have forecast the infrastructure and social changes nourishing his two enterprises, any more than he could have predicted the length of the Depression's endurance or that, harmoniously paralleling his initiatives, Craft would transition toward a form of art and its producers would achieve professional status. If luck was part of the "mix," its significance was minor. Instead, the development and history of Roadside Craftsmen and Avon Coppersmith suggests personal qualities of visioning, careful initial strategizing, and a long-term profit horizon as more credible evidence explaining longevity than ethereal ones. Wemett's confident, active role in initiating and supporting the two craft shops was the essential ingredient.

The Roadside Craftsmen and Avon Coppersmith narrative resets the maturation date for the professionalization of Crafts to the early 1930s, at least a decade before most other reports.[27] Much of the credit for the modern, twentieth-century Crafts movement is justifiably due to philanthropist Aileen Webb. Her carefully drawn, multiprong, and symbiotic strategy advanced the status of Craft and craftsmen. Wemett's approach differs from Webb's in scope, ambition, and timing: hers was a broad, carefully mapped plan, while his was a more narrowly focused, intuitive idea; his happened before hers. Unbeknown to Wemett, Craft began taking on a larger role because his shops leveraged wider societal advances in federalized, paved highways and public adoption of automobiles to grow his enterprises' businesses. Wemett's shops exploited the highway and all those it brought. Theirs was a business literally driven by tourism with the unintended consequence of transforming Craft from isolated, individualized enterprises serving localized needs for utilitarian objects yielding personal income to enterprises where one could earn a living solely by making artistic objects for itinerant customers. Each shop is an exemplar of early twentieth-century entrepreneurship for which Craft was the vehicle.

Avon Coppersmith and Roadside Craftsmen's story is a localized one of two shops in close proximity under a single owner. Case studies, including this one, produce a lot about a little.[28] We do not know much about where else Wemett's experience was duplicated. Scientists call this external or population validity and ask: to what extent is the Coppersmith-Roadside story generalizable? Their stories may be like those of dozens, perhaps hundreds, of others that to date have not achieved the visibility and prominence—relatively speaking—of Roadside Craftsmen or Avon Coppersmith.[29] Unrecorded, undocumented, and by now lost from the memory of all but a few, they cannot be dismissed as simple hobbyists. The Roadside Craftsmen-Coppersmith story is one patch to be stitched into a broader Craft quilt that will together cover the Depression to mid-century historical bed.

Fred Harvey introduced modern roadside commerce to the hospitality industry. Clarence Wemett's highway entrepreneurship built a retail environment for twentieth-century Craft by exploiting modern roadways, personal transportation vehicles, and passengers. He saw opportunity and took action. Wemett's venture into modern handcrafts was no revolution to change the world; it was a means to become a seamless part of an emerging and evolving one. A modern model for commerce was firmly in place at the beginning of the twentieth century, and Wemett gained instruction and drew inspiration as much from Sears and Larkin as he did Stickley and Hubbard.

What is the two craft enterprises' legacy? While referencing the past, both lived very much in the present. The shops were genuinely old fashioned, both by their standards and today's. Neither, for instance, sought to meaningfully expand its footprint beyond a single physical location. But each exploited infrastructure innovations and contemporary social behaviors for operational (and, presumably, personal) profit. Both offered customers quality merchandise. Roadside Craftsmen and Avon Coppersmith produced products people found worthy of purchasing, providing pleasure and an aesthetic reward, and the work found its way well beyond local living rooms. Cleverly, the shops' objects were marketed to satisfy a dual function: they were for gifting or as a souvenir memorializing a customer's trip. In each case, owners gained a form of decorative art enlivening their domestic space. Gift-given objects were proxies for the purchaser's esteem, respect, and affection for the recipient. The objects did not make their owners aesthetes; they made them happy.

The East Bloomfield and Avon, New York curbside businesses were the antithesis of the ostentatious flamboyance and garish excess of the now-iconic roadside structures later featured in slick, coffee table-style books. Unpretentious, they were in a dignified way more monochromatic than rainbow. Roadside Craftsmen and Avon Coppersmith seduced passing tourists with their invitation to observe firsthand the creation of handicrafts: see-it-made. Behind both enterprises was the ambitious, entrepreneurial businessman whose "reading" of social, transportation, and consumer behaviors optimized an opportunity for commercial success. The "fit" between a sales initiative to transcend localism and exploit the recreational travel market, and Craft and its professionalization, makes Roadside Craftsmen and the Avon Coppersmith's story consequential.

Today, "craft," "craftsmanship," and "artisan" are as indiscriminately applied to cupcakes as they are to beer. "Curating" once meant the scholarly process art museums followed to assemble a cohesive exhibition; the same vocabulary on social media pages today describes snapshot assemblages of puppies or yesterday's lunch. Wemett's prescience in touting "see-it-made" for his highway shops seems even more forward thinking today than it did in 1930 when authentic vestiges of craftsmanship were more readily located. Writing on the cusp of the digital age, Flink summarized the dramatic significance of the automobile and roadways: "During the 1920s automobility became the backbone of the new consumer-goods-oriented society and economy."[30] The commercial venue for twenty-first century Craft, unsurprisingly, is the internet. The digital superhighway's lanes and shoulders are longer, broader, and better interconnected than any imaginable at Wemett's time. Beginning with eBay, followed in short order by Etsy, Instagram, Pinterest, and others, the creators, their products, and buyers' migration to digital highways parallels what happened decades ago when paved roads and automobiles were introduced. A nonphysical environment this time, the internet's ever-replenishing stream of potential customers affords opportunities as much for part-time hobbyists as the professional craftsperson. Though much has changed in the years since Wemett grew his roadside businesses, in at least some ways, little has.

Notes

Introduction

1. An example, one neither glossy nor colorful, is Liebs, *Main Street to Miracle Mile*. The black-and-white photos in the large-format book have the grittiness of a documentary film, rather than sensational or voyeuristic qualities. At the time of its publication, reproducing color photography was expensive.

2. Sontag, "Notes on 'Camp.'"

3. See Bergman, *We're in the Money* and Schatz, *Hollywood Genres*.

4. The Depression-era decorative arts tension was akin to though qualitatively different from the one experienced by Arts and Crafts. The unresolved difference was in location: a tension between and one within. Colonial Revival's timeless, traditional past ran headlong into the hyper-timely, very much in-flux present of Modernism. Now and then simultaneously juxtaposing an antiseptic, streamlined environment with a soft focus but literal and familiar life.

5. Before giving it a name or placing a label on it, often in uppercase so as to signify the properness of the noun, Craft was the stuff that was made in order to live and make living easier. Once monetized, then Craft allowed one to "make" a living. Though one means of status-raising is an object's monetization, that can be a double-edged sword. Commercialization is sometimes construed as evidence of the art or artist's corruption. As though authenticity is to be equated only with poverty and the misery derived from and caused by it.

6. Kardon, "Within Our Shores," 23.

7. Craft, with or without an uppercase "c," as a noun and as a verb, has been defined as often as it has been debated. One such discussion is offered by Kardon ("Within Our Shores," 23–24) who also discriminates between craft and folk art. See also Denker, "Aileen Osborn Webb."

8. Kurp, "Road to History"; Porter, "Route 20 Ribbon of Memories"; Jaramillo, "Roadside Attractions."

9. Howland, "Route 20 is for Travelers Who Want to 'Stop and Smell the Roses.'"

10. Hedglon, "The Road Less Traveled"; see also Cantor, *Where the Old Roads Go*, 235.

11. Kates, "Preserving a Trip Across N.Y."

12. Hedglon, "Area Shop Keepers Try to Thrive in Shadow Cast by Retail Giants"; Hedglon, "Along the Way."

13. Nelson, *Twenty West*, 32–68.

14. Weisberg, *Talking to the Dead*.

15. Rae, *The Road and the Car in American Life*, 34, 17.

16. Lewis, *Divided Highways*, 10.

17. Liebs, *Main Street to Miracle Mile*, 170.

18. Gimigliano, "Experiences Along the Cherry Valley Turnpike," 197.

19. See Gimigliano, "Experiences Along the Cherry Valley Turnpike," 1–80; Werbizky, "Accommodating the Traveler," 64–133.

20. Lewis, *Divided Highways*, 20.

21. Machmer and Machmer, *Just for Nice*.

22. Ludwig, *The Arts & Crafts Movement in New York State*, 24–25.

23. Educational institutions closest to Roadside Craftsmen and Avon Coppersmith were Alfred University and Mechanics Institute. Others include Cranbrook Academy, Black Mountain College, Carnegie Institute of Technology, Chicago School of Design, Cleveland School of Art, and the WPA's Design Laboratory. See Manhart, "Charting a New Educational Vision" and Grieve, *The Federal Art Project*. Perkins, "Education in Ceramic Art in the United States," offers a focused history of ceramics education through the mid-twentieth century.

24. America House opened in October 1940. Webb's work on behalf of Craft is the most successful and best known, including her downstate Putnam County Products. Other examples, predating Webb's initiatives, are the Southern Mountain (later "Highland") Handicraft Guild and Berea Student Craft Industries.

25. Perkins, "Education in Ceramic Art," 29.

26. Prip's snarky comment pertained to the midcentury novelty and success of the craftsmen-initiated and operated retail craft store, Shop One (Austin, "Selling Crafts at Mid-Century"): "Every time there was a craft venture, you'd scratch beneath the surface and find some wealthy person supporting it" (quoted in Brown, "Shop One," 22). Prip's comment is ironic insofar as one such "wealthy person" was Mrs. Webb, one of Prip's own patrons through his faculty position at School for American Craftsmen, which Webb founded and funded. Arguably, Clarence Wemett might be considered Roadside Craftsmen's and Avon Coppersmith's patron. But his business approach to business, compared to Webb's philanthropic impulse, suggests otherwise.

27. Cole, personal interview with Bruce A. Austin.

28. For instance: Why did Arthur Cole leave East Aurora, the place where he established himself as a professional at Roycroft, and move fifty miles east

to Avon to establish his business? Another: Because no business records were located, any assumption of the two enterprises' profitability is no more than that.

29. Clark and Thomas-Clark, "Arthur H. Cole and the Avon Coppersmith."

30. Cathers, "Pioneers."

31. *Style 1900* was first named *Arts & Crafts Quarterly*. The publication began as an inexpensively reproduced and stapled newsletter initiated in 1986 by antiques dealer David Rago. Evolving to a slick, glossy magazine format, it sought to tap into revived interest in Arts and Crafts, fueled a half century after the Movement's demise by the 1972 "Princeton exhibit" (Clark, *The Arts and Crafts Movement in America*). Likely, the subjects of the Clarks' columns improved the status of collections (and collectors) that may not otherwise have met the exacting standards of connoisseurship set by others.

32. Austin, *The American Arts & Crafts Movement*.

33. Austin, "Widescreen."

34. Simonet, "Industry," 72. Simonet wrote about empirical research on the audiences for theatrical motion pictures.

35. As a simple, anecdotal example, exploration of the disconnect between the movement's philosophy and practice is rarely discussed. Years before contemplating the present project, a conversation with a woman then in her nineties illustrates the point. She had worked in the Roycroft book bindery where her blinding, painstaking job was to apply gold leaf to the page edges of deluxe edition Roycroft books using an incredibly fine brush. Mr. Hubbard, she reported, encouraged the improvement and education of "his" workers. When a famous person came to campus to lecture, all the Roycroft workers were assembled to listen. "Of course," she said, "if the talk lasted 45 minutes, we had to work 45 minutes longer that day." There were things, she implied, to be professed and those to be done; accomplishing the first would not excuse neglecting the latter.

36. Austin, *The American Arts & Crafts Movement*; Austin, "Selling Crafts at Mid-Century."

Chapter 1

1. "High School Note."

2. One pronunciation of "Wemett" follows that of its original French spelling: "Ouimet" (oui-met). Most commonly, I hear it pronounced "Wem-ett."

3. L. Wemett, email to Bruce A. Austin, 2020.

4. "Old Halfway House."

5. L. Wemett, email to Bruce A. Austin, 2020; quoted in Alvord, "Peeping Into the Local Past."

6. L. Wemett, email to Bruce A. Austin, 2020.

7. Boorstin, *The Image*, 57.

8. January 9, 1914.

9. *Livonia Gazette*, November 25, 1921.

10. "Shell Service Station to Mark."

11. "Wemett Leases."

12. "Wemett & Co."

13. August 3, 1922; "Neighborhood News," 1924.

14. "Wemett Leases."

15. "More About." See also "Should be in the Museum."

16. "Appreciation Dinner." A business card in the collection of the East Bloomfield Historical Society indicates Jean L. WeMett (*sic*) operated a "DeLuxe" tourist cabin court in Lima, located next door to her Gulf gas station on Routes 5 and 20.

17. *Livonia Gazette*, June 3, 1932.

18. Connor, "Tales of the Past"; "First Toll His Last."

19. Arthur Cole considered the cobblestone house as a venue for his Avon Coppersmith (T. Cole, personal interview).

20. Except for a short, four-mile stretch between Farnham and Silver Creek, New York to the west.

21. See Werbizky, "Accommodating the Traveler," 72–76; and Gimigliano, "Experiences Along the Cherry Valley Turnpike."

22. Mac Nelson (*Twenty West*) points out famous places, famous residents, and famous occurrences along Route 20. Often the road serves as his foil for sometimes touristy and other times promotional profiles. The once-tiny hamlets bordering Route 20 became pressure valves relieving over-inflated metropolises of the strain produced by population growth and density during the second half of the twentieth century.

23. Schlenker, *Elton Park and the Monument of East Bloomfield*; Schroeder and Herr-Gesell, *Memories and Traditions of Bloomfield*.

24. Shelgren et al., *Cobblestone Landmarks*, 15; Freeman and Freeman, *Cobblestone Quest*, 7; Peterich, "Cobblestone Architecture," 18.

25. Shelgren et al., *Cobblestone Landmarks*, 5; Cobblestone Museum, "Frequently Asked Questions."

26. Lewis, *Divided Highways*, 314.

27. Werbizky, "Accommodating the Traveler," 87.

28. Surdam, *Century of the Leisured Masses*, 61.

29. See Fuller, "Good Roads and Rural Free Delivery of Mail" and Wells, *Car Culture*, 12.

30. See Quinan, *Frank Lloyd Wright's Larkin Building*; Quinan, "Elbert Hubbard's Roycroft"; and Stanger, "The Larkin Club of Ten."

31. See Stanger, "From Factory to Family."

32. See Moody, "Sears, Roebuck & Co." Ironically, 130 years later, in 2018, Sears filed for bankruptcy, the victim of a still-newer transportation route: the World Wide Web.

33. Rae, *The Road and the Car in American Life*, 166.

34. Surdam, *Century of the Leisured Masses*, 203.

35. Hart, *The Story of American Roads*, 173, 171; see also Gimigliano, "Experiences Along the Cherry Valley Turnpike."

36. See Rae, *The Road and the Car*, 27–33; Mason, *The League of American Wheelmen*.

37. Hart, *The Story of American Roads*, 194.

38. See Kay, *Asphalt Nation*, 150–51.

39. Quinn, "The League of American Wheelmen," 40. The League of American Wheelmen (LAW) believed good roads would enable farmers to haul their produce to rail lines "at minimal cost and effort" and sought to produce better transportation facilities for railroads and "meeting the needs of the automobile age." Quinn, "The League of American Wheelmen," 8 and preface. Herbert Hoover, then US food administrator, believed "that half the country's farm produce did not make it to market before it spoiled because of woefully inadequate transportation." Gutfreund, *20th-Century Sprawl*, 22. The league's publications included *The Wheelman* (1883–1884), founded by Pope, and *Good Roads* (1885–1902) magazines; twenty-thousand copies were sold of *The Gospel of Good Roads*, an 1891 LAW publication by Isaac Potter, later editor for *Good Roads*. In 1892, LAW sponsored the National League for Good Roads Convention in Washington, DC. Quinn, "The League of American Wheelmen," 3, 6, 27.

40. Lewis, *Divided Highways*, 31.

41. Lewis, *Divided Highways*, 10.

42. Gutfreund, *20th-Century Sprawl*.

43. Lewis, *Divided Highways*, 11.

44. Fuller, "Good Roads and Rural Free Delivery," 67.

45. Gutfreund, *20th-Century Sprawl*, 237.

46. Wells, *Car Culture*, 129.

47. Green, "Culture and Crisis," 37.

48. Willey and Rice, "The Agencies of Communication," 175.

49. Patton, *Open Road*, 13.

50. Readers of Rochester, New York daily journalism know the lengths to which seemingly every story reported is somehow connected to the city, no matter how remote or tenuous. Herewith the obligatory Rochester automobile connection: George Selden, a Rochester patent attorney whose clients included Eastman Kodak founder George Eastman, claimed to be inventor of the gas-powered automobile, filing more than five hundred auto-related patent applications. Seiler, *Republic of Drivers*, 2. Based on an 1895 patent, Selden filed suit for infringement against the

Ford Motor Company in 1903, shortly after the motor company was founded. In 1911, the court decided in Ford's favor. Selden became a folk hero to some and a patent troll to others. See Snow, "The Father of All Patent Trolls."

51. Scott and Kelly, *Route 66*, 3.

52. Seiler, *Republic of Drivers*, 46.

53. The parallel between the highway and the automobile on the one hand and mass media on the other is not entirely whimsical. Toll roads were mirrored by early attempts at forming broadcast radio networks; at the end of 1924, AT&T connected twenty-six radio stations over its long lines by toll for a coast-to-coast broadcast. Broadcasting, like highways, facilitated consumerism by adopting advertising as means for financial support. Roads connected farmers to rail heads in the same way radio would connect advertisers to customers and citizens to government; commerce was a common cause. Goods to multiple rail heads would ensure fair, competitive pricing; broadcasting would ensure a national (or, at least a regional) conversation in an open marketplace of ideas leading to better policymaking and governance. The socially cohesive consequences of automobility on the road were paralleled at home with the family bonding afforded by the new medium of radio. Belasco, in his study of Americans on the road in the first half of the twentieth century, noted: "Like another recent innovation, the motion picture, the automobile offered unprecedented experiences of time, space, and movement" (*Americans on the Road*, 17). Movies, even more so than cars and highways, were democratic. They were inexpensive, did not require literacy, were widely available within a narrow geographic context, and offered rapid turnover of subjects and stories. At least during their formative first quarter century, movies were a neighborhood-based urban experience served by mass transit. And, at least initially, movies were not present in the countryside. The famous *Variety* headline, STICKS NIX HICK PIX, was not published until 1935 (McCall, "Sticks Nix Hick Pix"). The entertainment trade paper's story was about rural audiences' negative reaction to movie depictions of rural life. Their diffusion there occurred later, thanks to roadways that accommodated the delivery trucks carting reels of film.

54. Gutfreund, *20th-Century Sprawl*, 21.

55. For instance, music recording and reproduction replicated the sound of live musical performances, but records and phonographs were an on-demand medium. They changed our understanding of music as performance, as an art form—it was no longer a unique, here (hear) and now expression—and how we experienced it: from one as presented at some place and in the company of others to at-home and private. Likewise, commercial network radio drove an at-home leisure industry. And, with the arrival of the internet, there was no more waiting for the newspaper to arrive at the doorstep or, for that matter, any notion of a journalist's deadline or a "final" edition. The edition was never final, and deadlines occurred on a rolling basis instead of a fixed one. With digital media, movies or TV shows begin when you want—not when Warner Bros., NBC or the Rialto wants—and on a screen of your choice, no matter how tiny.

Chapter 2

1. Nelson, *Twenty West*.

2. See Green, *Byrdcliffe*. Byrdcliffe is conceptually related to the Rochester Folk Art Guild, the group inheriting Roadside's legacy and discussed in the conclusion.

3. Family lore reports C.E.'s fascination with ironwork, enjoyment of woodworking, and, later in life, painting (L. Wemett, email to Bruce A. Austin, 2020).

4. See Revels, *Sunshine Paradise*.

5. "Roadside Handcraft Shop."

6. "Rotarians Hear."

7. Initially, pottery was also purchased from Bybee Cornelison Pottery (Bybee, Kentucky) and sold at Bloomfield Pottery. Wemett's hardware partner, Hugh Drain, made several trips south in order to stock Bloomfield's shelves until sufficient locally made inventory was built (L. Wemett, email to Bruce A. Austin, 2020).

8. The Route 20 establishments were not alone in the practice. Ronan ("Painting Print," 46) describes an earlier example at illustrator Howard Pyle's Wilmington, Delaware School of Art.

9. Croughton, "Concerning Interests of Artists and Craftsmen," July 30.

10. Chester, "Turning Back History."

11. Bullock, "Things I Think I Remember."

12. Bullock, "Things I Think I Remember."

13. Seiler (*Republic of Drivers*, p. 4) defines automobility as "The act of driving and all of those components that make driving possible, practical, empowering, fun, salutary, and imperative." He traces the term's etymology to 1903, after which it quickly dropped from common usage. See, too, Flink ("The Three Stages," 473) who notes: "Automobility has had more important consequences for 20th century American man than even Frederick Jackson Turner's frontier had for our 19th century forebears." Arts and Crafts manufacturer Gustav Stickley initially responded negatively toward automobiling: "You can hardly cross the highway on a Saturday or Sunday afternoon for dodging the procession of flying motor cars" ("Als ik Kan: Life on the Automobile," 711). Six months later he reversed himself, acknowledging the benefits of the "motor-car," especially for farmers ("Als ik Kan: The Motor-Car"), and later for families and those wishing to escape the city ("Als ik Kan: The Motor Car and the City Man"), for vacations ("Als ik Kan: A Vacation") and for hygiene ("Als ik Kan: The Motor Car for Hygiene").

14. Steiner, "Recreation and Leisure Time Activities," 921–22.

15. The Commission on Recent Social Trends documented patterns and changes in seemingly everything about the United States during the first three decades of the twentieth century with social scientific authority. Its summary volume, published in 1933, was the product of more than three dozen researchers' efforts and reported results in twenty-nine chapters composed of just under sixteen

hundred pages of text. Among the findings was the population shift from rural to urban centers and coining the expression "metropolitanism." But even as people moved toward more condensed spaces, highway development and construction occurred principally outside the urban areas. This, of course, benefitted Wemett first for his oil and, later, his craft enterprises.

16. Halbert, "Oil Jobbers Provide Tourist Camp."

17. "Oil Company Tourist Camp."

18. Brimmer, *Autocamping* and *Motor Campcraft*; Long and Long, *Motor Camping*.

19. Gladding, *Across the Continent* and Massey, *It Might Have Been Worse*.

20. "You Sing America."

21. See Till, *Along New York's Route 20*, 90–91; Werbizky, "Accommodating the Traveler," 151, 193; Schmit, "Overnight Rest-Cabins Spreading"; and "Vagabonds."

22. Belasco, *Americans on the Road*, 129; McCarthy and Littell, "Three Hundred Thousand Shacks."

23. Willey and Rice, "The Agencies of Communication," 172.

24. Belasco, *Americans on the Road*, 121–22; Gudis, *Buyways*, 44, 47.

25. Hoover, "Camps of Crime"; see also "Couples Trade"; "Good and Bad"; and Henry, "Camps of Crime."

26. We witness this today when reporters add "gate" as a suffix to nouns referencing a (frequently political) scandal or a similarly unsavory event, often involving a cover-up. The trope invokes an early 1970s presidential misdeed that few may remember well and most understand perfectly by reputation.

27. Belasco, *Americans on the Road*, 3, 7.

28. Miller's song sentimentalized the carefree life ("I don't pay no union dues") of the hobo aboard a freight car (an "eight by twelve, four-bit room") free of the torturous restrictions of modern civilization ("no phone, no pool, no pets") bound for Bangor, Maine. The song's destitute and homeless protagonist, wears "old worn out clothes and shoes," smokes "old stogies I have found, short but not too big around" and still proclaims himself to be "a man of means by no means, king of the road."

29. "Unable to Use."

30. See, for example, McGovern, *Sold American* and Cohen, *A Consumers' Republic*.

31. See Belk, "Possessions and the Extended Self"; Horowitz, *The Morality of Spending*; Lears, "From Salvation to Self-Realization."

32. Steiner, "Recreation and Leisure Time Activities."

33. Thompson and Whelpton, "The Population of the Nation"; McKenzie, "The Rise of Metropolitan Communities."

34. Willey and Rice, "The Agencies of Communication," 186–87.

35. Lynd, "The People as Consumers," 860, 862, 864; see also Olney, *Buy Now, Pay Later*.

36. Weinberger, "Economic Aspects of Recreation," 448.

37. Kolb and Brunner, "Rural Life," 523.

38. Witzel, *Route 66 Remembered*, 65; see too Belasco, "Commercialized Nostalgia."

39. Bluestone, "Roadside Blight."

40. Hart, *The Story of American Roads*, 63.

41. Scott and Kelly, *Route 66*, 37.

42. Belasco, *Americans on the Road*, 140; see also Wik, "The Early Automobile."

43. Belasco, *Americans on the Road*, 90; Wells, *Car Culture*, 169.

44. Gudis, *Buyways*, 40.

45. Scott and Kelly, *Route 66*, 45.

46. Belasco, *Americans on the Road*, viii.

47. "Road trip" movies are almost as numerous as books. Perhaps most famously, the dustbowl desperation depicted in *The Grapes of Wrath* (1939) was the Depression's emblematic road trip; late-'60s counterculture was typified by the doomed optimism of *Easy Rider*'s (1969) freewheeling, drug-dealing motorcyclists. A handsome guy on the back of an outrageously chopped motorcycle (Peter Fonda) and, thirty years earlier, his equally handsome father (Henry Fonda), a paroled murderer struggling in a dilapidated, overburdened jalopy. The Fondas traveled in opposite directions on Route 66.

48. MacCannell, *The Tourist*, 6, 8. MacCannell's work, originally published in 1976, draws theoretically more than thematically on, especially, Goffman (*The Presentation of Self in Everyday Life*) and Boorstin (*The Image*). MacCannell's interpretative, critical analysis of the cultural experience of tourism follows Goffman's dramatic framework. He characterizes tourism in developing regions as "the social production of highly fictionalized versions of everyday life of traditional peoples, a museumization of their quaintness" (178). Skvirsky (*The Process Genre*, 67–70) traces the practice of human showcases in themed historical exhibitions for public viewing to the 1859 Jardin d'Acclimation, Paris. MacCannell uses the trope of "museum" in a way that suggests fictionalization and romanticizing the actual for purposes of capitalizing on tourism. But he also acknowledges the museum institution's own fictional genesis: something invented, not organic, for purposes of consecration of "*social, historical, cultural,* and *natural* objects" (78, emphasis in original), a fiction of fiction, in other words—an inauthentic representation of the authentic. For a critique of MacCannell see Schudson ("Review Essay"); Kammen (*In the Fast Lane*, 139–42) discusses exploiting people (e.g., Wallace Nutting) and places (e.g., Colonial Williamsburg) of America.

49. Surdam, *Century of the Leisured Masses*, 155–56.

50. Ramsaye, *A Million and One Nights*. On film regulation see, for example, Jowett, *Film*; Randall, *Censorship of the Movies*; Sklar, *Movie-Made America*.

51. Belasco, *Americans on the Road*, 150–51.

Chapter 3

1. "Hemlock Man Establishes," 1.

2. Croughton, "Concerning Interests of Artists and Craftsmen," *Rochester Times-Union*, July 30.

3. Willms, "A Practical Spirituality," 63; see, too, Fariello, "Arts and Crafts in Appalachia."

4. Quoted in Edwards, "Historic Champion of the Craft Movement."

5. Braznell, "The Early Career of Ronald Hayes Pearson," 212.

6. Denker, "Aileen Osborn Webb," 14, 18–19.

7. Quoted in Denker, "Aileen Osborn Webb," 19.

8. Quoted in Edwards, "Historic Champion."

9. Reynolds, "Wayland Resident Keeps."

10. "All Around the Towns."

11. "Thoughts by a Country Woman"; "Wayland Ready."

12. "Thoughts by a Country Woman."

13. Mukerji, *Chinese Sewing Baskets*, 87.

14. Mukerji, *Chinese*, 87; Reynolds, "Wayland."

15. Mukerji, *Chinese*, 88.

16. See Woloson, *Crap*, 205–7.

17. Merrill, "Wayland"; Merrill, "A Visit with Sally Patchin."

18. "Plail Family Legacy."

19. "Sally Patchin Funeral"; see, too, "All Around the Towns" and "Mrs. Patchin Dies."

20. Clarence Wemett's obituary indicates he had purchased the building in 1933 one year before the razing. "Obituary: Clarence E. Wemett."

21. " 'Roadside Craftsmen' at East Bloomfield." Wemett's remarks are quoted in an article reporting on the building's lease to Woodcroftery Shops following the dissolution of Roadside Craftsmen. The story nonspecifically references the *Livonia Gazette*'s files from 1934, where Wemett's either well-rehearsed or well-edited remarks were first published.

22. "History of the Branchport Baptist Church"; "Old Branchport Church is Razed on 100th Birthday."

23. "Happening around Penn Yan."

24. "Baptist Church Torn Down"; "Old Branchport Baptist Church is Razed"; "Old Branchport Church is Razed."

25. "Old Branchport Baptist Church is Razed."

26. " 'Roadside Craftsmen' at East Bloomfield."

27. "Century-Old Records"; "Former Church Fire."

28. " 'Roadside Craftsmen' at East Bloomfield."

29. Bullock, "Things I Think I Remember."

30. Bullock, "Things I Think I Remember."

31. L. Wemett, "The Roadside Craftsmen," typescript included in New Hope Fellowship, historical documents, vertical file folder, reviewed November 28, 2018.

32. The Arts and Crafts movement can also be understood as one stop in the longer evolution of Craft history where Craft moved from that which was needed to objects that were appreciated and desired as much for their own sake as for their artistry and functionality. Originally, handcraft was the human response to necessity and desire. Thanks to ingenuity and creativity, handcraft was transformed during the Industrial Revolution by mechanized advances coupled with economic incentives. At the beginning of the twentieth century, Craft existed in a mixed world of skillful necessity and as a therapeutic, rehabilitative remedy for various afflictions. By midcentury, perhaps most thought Craft(s) a harmless weekend avocation performed in suburban garages and basements. The commercialization of Craft occurred in tandem with enhanced public mobility beginning during the first quarter of the twentieth century as travel became a form of leisure rather than strictly a necessity.

33. How the name "mission" came to be applied to American Arts and Crafts period objects, especially furniture, prompts different replies. One references Louis Sullivan's dictum that form follows function; for example, a chair's function, or "mission," is seating, and its form should accommodate that. Another, somewhat more romantic explanation, suggests a relationship to the furnishings populating old California Spanish missions. Perhaps, too, the term "mission" was used as an assertion discriminating the American expression for a style first introduced elsewhere. The mid-nineteenth century crafts movement began in England, drifted to Europe as Art Nouveau in Belgium and France, and Secessionism in Austria (see Livingstone and Parry, *International Arts and Crafts*). In America, the aesthetic saw distinctive interpretations on the East Coast, Midwest, and West Coast; each, though, retained fidelity to basic if not entirely consonant principles. Gustav Stickley ("How 'Mission' Furniture was Named") was dismissive of the term and the second explanation as sentimental, commercial puffery, while taking thinly veiled swipes at his competitors, Joseph McHugh and George Clingman (Tobey Furniture). Stickley used "Craftsman" to describe the style of furniture he made. Elbert Hubbard discriminated between "mission" style furniture and his Roycroft products. New York City furniture maker Joseph McHugh was "the self-proclaimed originator of 'Mission' style furniture in America" (D'Ambrosio, *The Distinction of Being Different*, 11). As late as 1915, and just before declaring bankruptcy, display ads for Stickley asserted: "We are not 'the originators of mission furniture.' We are the originators of Craftsman Furniture, from which mission furniture is copied" ("Craftsman Building"). A second ad, "Praise from Our Competitors," read: "All the Stickley family are famous as makers of good furniture, and particularly of mission furniture. I am the eldest of the five Stickley brothers and have no desire to quarrel with the above statement, except that I

cannot be included as a maker of 'mission furniture.' Mission furniture is slavishly copied from my Craftsman patterns."

34. David Cathers (*These Humbler Metals*, 11) summarized the Arts and Crafts aesthetic and method of metalwork: "It was antithetical in almost every way to the metalwork of the preceding decades. It repudiated the expensive, highly elaborated (though expertly handcrafted) domestic objects made of precious metals that had been prevalent during the latter part of the nineteenth century."

35. See Green, "The Promise and Peril of High Technology."

36. Rhoads, "Colonial Revival in American Craft," 49.

37. Electra Havemeyer Webb was sister-in-law to Aileen Osborn Webb. Each came from wealthy Hudson Valley families and both married into the Vanderbilt railroading family. Closer to East Bloomfield and fewer than ten miles from Avon, but arriving much later than the three historic villages noted, is another: the Genesee Country Village and Museum (Mumford, New York), founded by collector (and then-president of Rochester's Genesee Brewing Company) John (Jack) L. Wehle in 1966. For more about Colonial Revivalism and American nationalism, especially architecture, see Rhoads, "The Colonial Revival and American Nationalism."

38. Greenfield, *Out of the Attic*, 4; see also Stillinger, *The Antiquers*, and Wilson et al., *Re-creating the American Past*.

39. See Schinto, "Good Fellows."

40. Ludwig, *The Arts & Crafts Movement*, 9.

41. Much of the readily accessible, published research is found in exhibition catalogues. Revived attention to the American Arts and Crafts movement is typically traced to Robert Judson Clark's 1972 exhibition at Princeton University. Unsurprisingly, the evolutionary path taken by Arts and Crafts exhibits (and scholarship) followed a deductive trajectory with earlier exhibitions presenting a broad, "waterfront" approach to the Movement (e.g., Clark, *The Arts and Crafts Movement*; Kaplan, *"The Art That is Life"*; Bowman, *American Arts & Crafts*) and later ones focusing on more specific and particular aspects such as geography (Ludwig, *The Arts & Crafts Movement*; Trapp, *The Arts and Crafts Movement in California*; Barons and Nelson, *Severity and Simplicity*), manufacturer (Lamoureux, *The Arts & Crafts Studio of Dirk Van Erp*; Bartinique, *Gustav Stickley: His Craft*; D'Ambrosio, *The Distinction of Being Different*) or medium (Darling, *Teco*; Marek, *Grand Rapids Art Metalwork*; Parry, *Textiles of the Arts and Crafts Movement*).

42. Likewise, each was devotional: Shakers to a deity, Arts and Crafts to a (fuzzy) philosophy. Reflecting on the Arts and Crafts Movement in 1914, Gustav Stickley remarked that he did not realize the significance of his "strong, simple furniture" at first. But, he said, "Others saw it and prophesized a far-reaching development. To me it was only furniture; to them it was religion. And eventually it became religion to me as well" ("Founder Tells Growth"). Gustav Stickley gives a nod to the Shakers, their influence on his pre–Arts and Crafts furniture, and

contrasts their style to the "cheap ornamentation" of late 1800s furniture. Stickley wrote: "The only decoration that seems in keeping with simple structural forms lies in the emphasizing of certain features of the construction, such as the mortise, tenon, key and dovetail. If these are added purely for the sake of decoration, they are as out of place as any other applied ornament; but where they really do the work for which they exist they are legitimately ornamental and add much to the strength of the piece as well as to its interest and beauty." See also Smith (*Gustav Stickley: The Craftsman*, 3) and Archer ("Lessons from Utopia").

43. Very briefly, and with little apparent success, Roycroft dabbled in pottery, Roadside Craftsmen's original craft and mainstay (see Via, "The Roycroft Pottery"). There is no record of Roycroft ever being involved with textiles. As with the Roadside Craftsmen and the Avon Coppersmith, metalsmithing and woodworking flourished as craft trades, helping support the Roycroft enterprise, along with the book arts of printing, binding, and publishing. Painting and sculpture had a place at Roycroft, though to a much lesser extent than the crafts, but not at either Roadside or Coppersmith.

44. See Manchee, *Sutures and Spirits*. There were no nationally distributed daily newspapers at the time; they were a medium bounded by geography and thus tapped only local markets. Radio was a nascent medium still developing its national (network) reach and commercial legs; nationwide network commercial radio coverage emerged about 1925. Advertising on theatrical motion picture screens had only modest penetration in the United States, though it was far more common in Europe (see Johnson, "Cinema Advertising"; Austin, "Cinema Screen Advertising"; Rotzoll, "The Captive Audience"). Billboards and posters, like newspapers, were trade stimulators for local interests and served the functional purpose of directing or alerting tourists to unfamiliar locations and businesses.

45. Ward, "Crafty Ads," 2,15–16.

46. Runyan, "A Content Analysis of Advertisements."

47. See Stickley "The Use and Abuse of Machinery." That much of what was produced during the Arts and Crafts period was financially out of reach for most and an indulgence for the few is discussed in Austin's ("Product Price Structure") case study of Roycroft; see, too, Bowman ("Industry and Ideals," 28) and Wilson ("Introduction," 19–20). Ostensibly democratic, the movement rarely achieved the aspiration commercially. For instance, the principal means for disseminating the Arts and Crafts "philosophy" was print. And the admission ticket for that medium is literacy and financial ability. High-minded ideals espoused by elite writers in various publications may have made for good, inspirational reading, but only among a narrow audience. Then, as now, reading, like writing, occurred among equally elite circles by those with an abundance of time and funding to do so. Among those working to produce Arts and Crafts products, the Movement was much more about earning a living and, most immediately, putting bread on their

tables (Austin, *The American Arts & Crafts Movement*). The same might be said of today's collectors of the period's work: Resources uncommitted and free from any obligations drive and make possible the collector and collection.

48. Edwards, "The Art of Work," 230–31.

49. Stickley, "The Use and Abuse of Machinery," 204.

50. Dormer, "Craft and the Turing Test for Practical Thinking," 143; see also Pye, *The Nature and Art of Workmanship* and Osborne, "The Aesthetic Concept of Craftsmanship," for further refinements on craftsmanship relative to work, labor, and the machine.

51. See Via, "The Roycroft Pottery."

Chapter 4

1. Porter, "Avon Landmark Consumed."

2. Porter, "Avon Landmark Consumed."

3. Appell, ". . . Fire at Avon Coppersmith"; "Livonia Man"; Livadas, "Gift Shop Owner Mourned."

4. "Livingston County Sheriff's Report"; Hand, "Avon Fire is Determined."

5. Parker, *Rochester Democrat and Chronicle*, March 24, 1998; Parker, *Mendon-Honeoye Falls-Lima Sentinel*, April 2, 1998.

6. Porter, "Avon Landmark Consumed"; see too Livadas, "Gift Shop Owner Mourned" and Mayron, "Firefighters Find Body."

7. "Owner of Avon Copper Shop Dies."

8. January 18, 1973.

9. The *Rochester Democrat and Chronicle* (January 16, 1973) obituary noted, "Mr. Cole is a former Roycroft Coppersmith and also a former owner of the Avon Coppersmith which he operated for 40 years." Cole's obituary in the *Avon Herald News* included an unfortunate typo, "Coppersmith Learned Trade at Roycrafters [*sic*]"; the *Tonawanda News* (January 15, 1973) headlined its obituary "Owner of Avon Copper Shop Dies" but located the shop in East Aurora instead of Avon. The *East Aurora Advertiser*'s obituary (January 18, 1973) for Cole reports his forty-year ownership of Avon Coppersmith and his status as a former Roycroft coppersmith. It also notes that he was a fifty-year Mason and a member of the American Legion and the First Baptist Church of East Aurora. The other details presented inadvertently suggest equal weight to his craft work. For instance, Cole was elected a member of the American Legion's executive committee early in 1928 and later the same year vice commander ("Legion Meeting," 1928; "American Legion Elects New Officers," 1928). Married three times, Cole was predeceased by Alice Mae Olds (1888–1932) and Mildred Esther Corby (1904–1957); Harriet Haskell Newell survived him (Goller, email correspondence, 2020).

10. "Avon Coppersmith Makes Bow."

11. "Clarence Wemett of Hemlock Presents 'The Avon Coppersmith' to the Public."

12. East Aurora is, in fact, west of Aurora, New York. East Aurora was located on Route 20 until the highway's renumbering in the mid-'30s to today's Route 20A; see Till, *Along New York's Route 20*.

13. For a discussion of Roycroft's pricing relative to the potential customer base for its products see Austin, "Product Price Structure."

14. Hubbard and his work at Larkin and Roycroft are detailed by Quinan, *Frank Lloyd Wright's*; Quinan, "Elbert Hubbard's Roycroft"; Stanger, "From Factory to Family"; and Stanger, "The Larkin Club of Ten." Woloson (*Crap*, 130–135) discusses consumer premiums.

15. Elbert Hubbard's death aboard the torpedoed *Lusitania* in 1915 was at the height of Roycroft's prosperity and popularity. Despite the sizeable estate Hubbard bequeathed to his son and successor, "Bert" (Elbert II), hard times at Roycroft followed. Bert inherited about $210,000 ($5,243,000 in 2018 dollars) and was awarded subsequent arbitral judgment for lost business training ($25,000 plus 5 percent interest annually from 1915) and as executor for Elbert and his wife's estates ($1,000 each plus interest) (Reports of International Arbitral Awards). The luxury liner's final voyage and passengers final moments are vividly reported by Larson, *Dead Wake*.

16. See Kornacki, "The Secret Life of Karl Kipp" for further discussion of Kipp's colorful biography. Newspapers reported on Kipp's embezzlement and life on the lam. For example: "Karl Kipp an Embezzler to the Extent of $6,428," *Daily Saratogian*, April 18, 1904; "Bank Clerk Had New Scheme," *Glens Falls Morning Star*, April 20, 1904; "Officers Leave St. Paul Tonight with Karl Kipp," *Daily Saratogian*, October 31, 1904; "Karl Kipp A Bookkeeper in Dannemora Prison," *Daily Saratogian*, December 22, 1904; "Embezzler Will Plead Guilty," *Troy Times*, December 6, 1904; "[Unreadble] Ask Clemency for Kipp," *Troy Times*, December 7, 1904; and "On Way to Federal Prison," 1906.

17. Roycroft Campus Corporation.

18. Rust, Turgeon-Rust, Via and Searl, "Alchemy in East Aurora," 82.

19. "East Aurora, N.Y."

20. "The American Santa Claus."

21. Advertising copy in a 1929 *Saratogian* for a Saratoga Springs, New York shop, Robson & Adee, promoted Kipp's work. Kipp "now heads his own organization" the advertisement reports, and the craftsman's "standard is: Not how many things I can make, but how fine I can make a few." A profile of Kipp in a hometown newspaper column lists him under "Class Artists" describing him as "the real McCoy when it came to the artistic. In case you don't know it, he designed the lamps and much of the interior decorations of the famous Roycrofters Inn at East Aurora. . . . The last I heard from him he was designing artistic pewter ware of his own" ("35 Years Out of School").

22. Cole, personal interview.

23. "Clarence Wemett of Hemlock," 1.

24. Clark and Thomas-Clark, "Arthur H. Cole"; Cole, "The Avon Coppersmith"; Swanton, "Arthur H. Cole."

25. "The Old Guard to Return."

26. "Former Saratogian Succeeds."

27. "More Men Leave"; Cole, personal interview.

28. "Company O."

29. Cole, personal interview.

30. Cole, personal interview; Rust et al., "Alchemy in East Aurora," 96.

31. Clark and Thomas-Clark, "Arthur H. Cole," 22.

32. Cathers, *These Humbler Metals*, 134.

33. Goller, email to Bruce A. Austin, 2019.

34. February 7, 1928, 30.

35. Rust et al., "Alchemy in East Aurora," 90; Clark and Thomas-Clark, "Arthur H. Cole," 22.

36. Cole, "The Avon Coppersmith."

37. Cathers, *These Humbler Metals*, 135; Goller, email to Bruce A. Austin, 2019.

38. Cole, personal interview.

39. Wemett is described as a "silent partner" by Clark and Thomas-Clark, "Arthur H. Cole," 23.

40. Cole, "The Avon Coppersmith."

41. Clark and Thomas-Clark, "Arthur H. Cole," 23.

42. Very likely, the Jennings' visited Chester W. Crumrine, developer of "the first commercially successful electric typewriter." Crumrine held more than seventy-five patents, including one for a camera designed with Walter Dorwin Teague for Kodak (see "Family Planning" and "14 Inventors"). Reports such as this were regularly published in community papers. Typically cryptic, often no more than a sentence, they served to alert readers to such happenings as their neighbors' guests, travels, and even their medical procedures. By today's standards simultaneously quaint and an invasion of privacy, community papers served as the fence over which social news was shared.

43. L. Wemett, email to Bruce A. Austin, 2020.

44. "Clarence Wemett of Hemlock," 1, 9.

45. L. Wemett, email to Bruce A. Austin, 2020.

Chapter 5

1. Green, "Culture and Crisis," 32.

2. MacCannell, *The Tourist*, 8, 6, 178.

3. MacCannell, *The Tourist*, 54, 83.

4. Belasco, *Americans on the Road*.

5. See Ward, "The Automobile in the Suburbs."

6. Bassett, email to Bruce A. Austin.

7. Werbizky, "Accommodating the Traveler."

8. Stanger, "From Factory to Family."

9. Sennett, *The Craftsman*, 8.

10. Sennett, *The Craftsman*, 20.

11. Flink, "The Three Stages of American Automobile Consciousness," 458–59.

12. Shell, *Cheap*, 141.

13. Lazarsfeld et al., *The People's Choice*; Katz and Lazarsfeld, *Personal Influence*. Early in the twentieth century, conventional wisdom held that media messages produced strong, nearly immediate, and uniform effects on recipients. This powerful—often called "hypodermic needle"—media effects model was supported by anecdote and casual observation of the impact of World War I propaganda. In the wake of increasingly sophisticated and empirical social science research—exemplified, especially, by the president's Social Trends studies and the Payne Fund studies on motion pictures, both initiated in 1929—a more subtle, nuanced model emerged. By the late 1930s and early 1940s, a "limited effects" model conservatively predicted some media messages' effect on some people, under some conditions, some of the time—intervening factors moderating the power of media. (For a summary of this history, see DeFleur and Ball-Rokeach, *Theories of Mass Communication*.) Personal influence through "opinion leaders" and the power of word of mouth were seen as mediating agents for the effects of mass communications messages on the public. Early work in rural sociology (Ryan and Gross, "The Diffusion of Hybrid Corn Seed") grew to include broader research on the diffusion of innovations (Rogers, *Diffusion of Innovations*) leading, more recently, to Gladwell ("The Science of the Sleeper" and *The Tipping Point*) who refers to the interpersonally driven diffusion process as one working through "Mavens" and "Connectors," instead of the 1940s term, "opinion leaders." Wemett would likely have been as unaware of these scientific studies and theories as he was of the craft movement.

14. See Lazarsfeld et al., *The People's Choice*; Katz and Lazarsfeld, *Personal Influence*.

15. Belasco, *Americans on the Road*, 37.

16. See Woloson, *Crap*, 169–96.

17. Pooler, *Why We Shop*, 76.

18. See Schwartz ("The Social Psychology of the Gift") for an alternate view. Rather than philanthropy or altruism, he argues that gift-giving is a means for developing and maintaining the giver's identity and as a way of exerting control and subordination.

19. "East Aurora, N.Y."; "The American Santa Claus."

20. Patton, *Open Road*, 17.

21. Denenberg, *Wallace Nutting*, 141; Rhoads, "Colonial Revival in American Craft," 42.

22. See Cathers, *Gustav Stickley*; Tucker, *Gustav Stickley*.

23. Ashby, *With Amusement for All*, 107.

24. Shell, *Cheap*, 18.

Chapter 6

1. Frelinghusen et al., *American Art Pottery*, 27, 138.

2. "Hemlock Man Establishes." Pottery making in Bloomfield was not a twentieth-century novelty. Charles Kimball established a pottery in West Bloomfield about 1811; his brother, Herber, was a red earthenware potter from 1822 to 1832; and Alvin Wilcox operated a West Bloomfield pottery, 1800–1862 (see Thomas, "Herber C. Kimball").

3. "Hemlock Man Establishes."

4. Frelinghusen et al., 233.

5. Riddle, email to Bruce A. Austin.

6. "Hemlock Man Establishes."

7. Croughton, "Concerning Interests of Artists and Craftsmen," July 2 and July 30, 1932.

8. Denton County History.

9. Croughton, "Concerning Interests of Artists and Craftsmen," July 2, 1932.

10. Riddle, email to Brue A. Austin.

11. For example, Bullock, "Things I Think I Remember."

12. Croughton, "Concerning Interests of Artists and Craftsmen," July 30, 1932.

13. See "Visit Shop"; "Kick-Wheel Potter."

14. Bullock, "Things I Think I Remember."

15. Elliott, "Voice from the Gallery."

16. "Rotarians Hear."

17. L. Wemett, email to Bruce A. Austin, 2018.

18. Daugherty's loss doubtless resonated for Clarence Wemett, who, we expect, was empathetic. Coincidentally, Ada Jennings Wemett, Clarence's first wife, died of pneumonia on December 16, 1934, at age forty-seven. Like Daugherty, the Wemetts had five children: Ruth, Mary, Norris, Bruce, and Mark. Clarence later married Ada's sister, Anna Jennings. How much of the year Daugherty spent in East Bloomfield and how often that occurred is not entirely clear. The Roadside woodworker's son, Paul Bullock, claims Daugherty "was never there during the winter" and that the Texan potter "had jobs in other parts of the country including the Carolinas and Texas" (see Bullock, "Things I Think I Remember," 2007). Hamell's ("Earthenwares and Salt-Glazed," 11–12) essay on Rochester-Genesee

Valley stoneware labeled Daugherty's work "folk pottery" and him "the last traditional potter to work in this region."

19. O'Connor, "Tompkins County" and O'Connor, "State Fair."

20. O'Connor, "Tompkins County" and O'Connor, "State Fair."

21. "Hemlock Ye Observer."

22. "Had Two Cousins."

23. Hollingshead patented the clamshell-shaped landscape design for the rows of ramps that pointed cars at the large outdoor movie screens. On drive-ins, see Austin, "The Development and Decline" and Fox and Black, "The Rise and Decline"; the drive-in theater as an element in roadside commerce is discussed by Liebs, *Main Street to Miracle Mile* (152–67) and experiential consumption by Holbrook and Hirschman, "The Experiential Aspects."

24. See Cole, personal interview, 2019 and Cole, "The Avon Coppersmith," 1984.

25. Cole, personal interview, 2019.

26. Clark and Thomas-Clark, "Arthur H. Cole," 1998, 23; Cole, personal interview, 2019.

27. November 23, 1950, 52.

28. Cole, personal interview.

29. Cole, "The Avon Coppersmith."

30. Cole, "The Avon Coppersmith"; Cole, personal interview; Clark and Thomas-Clark, "Arthur H. Cole."

31. Cole, personal interview.

32. "New Building is Being Erected."

33. Cole, personal interview.

34. "New Vacation Center"; "Egypt Valley Opens."

35. Costa and Tranquille, "Rte. 20 Revisited."

36. "Thruway and Freeway," *Albany Knickerbocker News*, September 9, 1955; "Out of Step."

37. "Luring the Tourist."

38. "Thruway and Freeway," *Rochester Democrat and Chronicle*, September 6, 22, 1955.

39. "Rt. 20 Association."

40. "Freeway Ass'n to Issue Brochure"; "Rt. 20 Association."

41. Gallinger, "Route 20 Assn."

42. "Freeway Group Adopts"; "Thruway and Freeway," 1955b; "State Group to Plug."

43. "Rt. 20 Association"; "Route 20 Businessmen."

44. "Freeway Group Adopts"; "Freeway Ass'n Names Directors"; "Rt. 20 Freeway Assn."; "Rt. 20 Freeway Group"; "Routes 5 & 20"; "Freeway Association Will Incorporate"; "Rt. 20 Freeway Assn."

45. Cole, personal interview.

46. Cole, personal interview.

47. Loeper Gaylord, 1977; Edna Roberts, 1965.

48. Braznell, "The Early Career," 187.

Chapter 7

1. "Novelty Factory Located Here."

2. Bullock, "Things I Think I Remember."

3. *Rushville Chronicle and Gorham New Age*, January 10, 1919.

4. Chester, "Turning Back History."

5. Bullock, "Things I Think I Remember."

6. "Penn Yan Corporations."

7. Bullock's son, Paul, remarked in his memoir that on Homer's death in 1957, "He still had a supply of exotic wood from the Isle in storage" and equipment from the failed Woodcraft enterprise (Bullock, "Things I Think I Remember"). Older brother Phil, Paul recalled, took a large lathe and some of the Isle wood and tried to turn a bowl: "But dry rot had made it impossible to work the wood. My guess is that the wood died with Homer" (Bullock, "Woodcraft Products Corporation"). Paul Bullock acknowledges the frailty of memory, confessing, "I couldn't always distinguish between my own recollection and my recollection of someone else's recollection" (Bullock, "Things I Think I Remember"). Bullock's "Woodcraft" is not to be confused with John P. Coley's "Woodcroftery."

8. "A New Factory."

9. "Prizes Awarded Winners at Fair."

10. *Penn Yan Democrat*, February 4, 1927, 4.

11. "Sheriff's Sale"; "Woodcraft Firm Dissolves."

12. Bullock, "Things I Think I Remember."

13. Bullock, "Things I Think I Remember."

14. Bullock, "Things I Think I Remember."

15. Steele, "East Bloomfield Craftsman."

16. Quoted in Wade, *The War Years*.

17. Bullock, "Things I Think I Remember"; L. Wemett, email to Bruce A. Austin, 2020.

18. While artist signatures for fine art (e.g., paintings and sculptures) is commonplace and expected, the same tradition does not hold true for crafts. There, the history is a bit uneven. Among Arts and Crafts–era art pottery manufacturers, for instance, some include artist signatures while others did not. At Grueby and Rookwood, it was not unusual to see an artist's or decorator's cipher. Pottery produced at Newcomb College routinely includes the mark of the one who threw the pot as well as its decorator. At Teco, the designer's name is noted only in the printed catalogue descriptions.

19. "New Building is Being Erected."

20. Wemett, "A Group of Spirited Workers."

21. "Roadside Handcraft Shop."

22. Croughton, "Concerning Interests of Artists and Craftsmen," July 2, 1932; L. Wemett, email to Bruce A. Austin, 2020.

23. L. Wemett, email to Bruce A. Austin, 2020.

24. Elliott, "Voice from the Gallery."

25. "Roadside Handcraft Shop."

26. "Neighborhood News," 1937. Manchester's obituary reported he was a silversmith at Wemett's "art shop, 'The Smiths.'" See "Silversmith at Hemlock Dies."

27. "A Bit of Yesteryear."

28. L. Wemett, email to Bruce A. Austin, 2020.

29. "Hemlock Forge."

30. See Wemett.net.

31. "Wemett & Co. Host to Shell Station."

32. "Wemett Pottery."

33. "Local Brevities," 1941; "Roadside Handcraft Shop."

34. "Pottery Making to be Demonstrated."

35. *Otsego Farmer*, 4.

36. "Local Brevities," 1943.

37. *Penn Yan Chronicle Express*, February 3, 1944, 7.

38. "New Building."

39. King, "Through the Skioscope."

40. *Livonia Gazette*, May 26, 1949.

41. "New Vacation Center"; "Grand Opening"; "Egypt Valley Camp."

42. "Egypt Valley Opens."

43. "Wemetts Sell Camp."

44. "Keuka College."

45. "Pottery Making Is Fun."

46. "White Horse Inn."

47. "Wemett Corp. Buys."

48. "Out of the Past."

49. "Restored White Horse Tavern."

50. "White Horse Tavern"; "White Horse Inn."

51. "White Horse Inn."

52. "First Unit in White Horse Shopping Plaza"; "Market Building Starts at E. Avon"; "Nunda Men Open Avon Supermarket."

53. "'Roadside Craftsmen' at East Bloomfield."

54. Avon Preservation & Historical Society, "White Horse Tavern."

55. "'Roadside Craftsmen' at East Bloomfield."

56. A profile is offered in "Our Industries."

57. See "Obituary: Mrs. Honni [*sic*] Coley"; Thwing, "What's Business Reverse?"

58. *Bath Farmers Advocate*, July 17, 1907; *Steuben Courier*, July 26, 1907.

59. See Clark and Thomas-Clark, "The Majestic Furniture Company."

60. See Clark and Thomas-Clark, "The Plail Brothers."

61. "The Woodcroftery Now Located in Batavia."

62. "Wayland Industry Moves."

63. "Resort Near Bushville." The campground was opened in May 1923 by Charles F. Miller who sold the Inn to William A. Jermyn of Rochester in 1925 ("Jermyn-Miller Case"). Woodcroftery's history and origins are discussed in "Woodcroftery Shop."

64. "Roadside Business Expanded."

65. "The Woodcroftery Now Located in Batavia."

66. "Woodcroftery in Wayland Plant."

67. "Woodcroftery in Wayland Plant."

68. Trietley, "Artistry is Interesting Work."

69. New Hope Fellowship.

70. "In Area Churches"; "Obituary: Mark Wemett."

71. Parshall, email to Bruce A. Austin.

72. "Ann Mattison Assisting."

73. L. Wemett, email to Bruce A. Austin, 2018.

Chapter 8

1. See http//www.wemett.net/roadside_craftsmen/roadside_craftsmen_photo_index.html.

2. "Clarence Wemett of Hemlock," 1.

3. "Woman Painter."

4. T. Cole, personal interview, 2019.

5. Cole, "The Avon Coppersmith," 1984.

6. Clark and Thomas-Clark, "Arthur H. Cole."

7. T. Cole, personal interview, 2019.

8. Cole, "The Avon Coppersmith," 1984.

9. Clark and Thomas-Clark, "Arthur H. Cole," 22; Swanton, "Arthur H. Cole."

10. "East Aurora, N.Y."

11. "East Aurora's Shop of Beautiful Gifts."

12. The contrast is to practices followed at Roycroft. In East Aurora, the locals could come by the inn or the Copper Shop and make purchases at their convenience. Out-of-town travelers staying at the Roycroft Inn had nearly inexhaustible opportunities and perhaps good reasons to make purchases: items for their use (a vase to hold flowers), for its beauty (the same vase, displayed on a mantel), and as a gift (the identical vase, wrapped in tissue and placed in a Roycroft gift box). More significant—in number and volume—were out-of-town

Roycroft customers who "arrived" by mail. Readers of Roycroft periodicals and recipients of Roycroft's product catalogues were scattered across the nation. Thanks to rural free delivery and parcel post, most anything could be shipped just about anywhere in the United States. Roycroft's "Goodie Box" was intended for shipment and both the tabletop and floor models of the Roycroft "Little Journeys" book stand would disassemble for flat, easy packing and shipment. Copper products were easily boxed and shipped.

13. That the speed of the automobiles might also mean we missed seeing and appreciating the countryside we were racing past may have been much lower on the list of important virtues than quickly getting from A to B.

14. Using contemporary standards to judge past actions is, of course, exactly the wrong criterion to apply for almost anything. Invariably the present appears superior to the past.

15. T. Cole, personal interview, 2019.

16. T. Cole, personal interview.

17. T. Cole, personal interview.

18. Fess, "Coppersmith Hobby"; Hunt, "Let's Go Behind."

19. Fess, "Coppersmith Hobby."

20. *Albany Times-Union*, October 14.

21. *Buffalo Courier-Express*, April 14, 1957.

22. "Three Firms OKd."

23. "Coppersmith Firm." Two days later, July 13, the *Rochester Daily Record* indicated the bankruptcy petition was dated June 27, 1962, and, perhaps a typo, liabilities were $94,845.

24. Reece, email to Bruce A. Austin.

25. "Glencroft Coppersmiths."

26. Reece, email to Bruce A. Austin.

Chapter 9

1. T. Cole, personal interview, 2019.
2. "Avon Coppersmith: Widely Known Firm Changes Hands."
3. "Avon Coppersmith: Widely Known Firm."
4. "Business Briefs."
5. "Avon Coppersmith: Widely Known Firm." Later, one panel (of six) of a promotional brochure reported the Shop's history, noting that "Joyce and Don Parker have set aside a portion of Avon Coppersmith's building to display Mr. Cole's thirty-seven years of operation."
6. "Avon Coppersmith: Widely Known Firm."
7. "Do You Know Your Business Community?"
8. See Gelber, *Hobbies*, 63; Woloson, *Crap*, 221–48.

9. "Avon Coppersmith Celebrates 60th Year." The Parkers claimed to have expanded Coppersmith's operation "to accommodate four stores under the same roof."

10. "Avon Coppersmith Celebrates 60th Year."

11. "A Bit of Yesteryear Changes Hands."

12. "Avon Coppersmith Celebrates 60th Year."

13. "25th Anniversary Sale."

14. "Former Local Couple's Shop."

15. See Wolfe, "The 'Me' Decade" and Lasch, *The Culture of Narcissism*.

16. L. Wemett, email to Bruce A. Austin, 2020.

17. At Glencroft Coppersmiths in Clarence, New York, a complementary operation to Avon, a considerable portion of its business was wholesale to other gift shops. Reece (email correspondence) reports, following Glencroft Coppersmiths' 1962 bankruptcy filing, work there may have been somewhat spotty and Glenn's son, Jim, took "a factory job until 1976 when they [Glencroft] got a large mug contract with Things Remembered and sold 50,000 copper mugs a year to them." Begun in 1967, Things Remembered was a retailer specializing in personalized gifts.

18. Likewise, two other Syracuse Arts and Crafts metal shops, Benedict Studios and Onondaga Metal Shop, were short-lived. For information on Dirk van Erp, see Lamoureux, *The Arts & Crafts Studio*.

19. Alan Crawford ("Review: Inspiring Reform," 28) wrote that the Princeton exhibit "established the subject, gave it some visual coherence, and opened out prospects for future research and collecting." The consumer market for Arts and Crafts developed and grew in the first quarter of the twentieth century and did so again (this time among collectors) in the fourth quarter. In no small part, the drivers for each were exhibitions: Stickley's 1903 Syracuse-Rochester and Clark's Princeton exhibits. Journalism flourished in the wake of the first wave, scholarship in the second.

Chapter 10

1. Among the best sources on Fred Harvey is Fried, *Appetite for America*; see also Poling-Kempes, *The Harvey Girls* and Howard and Pardue, *Inventing the Southwest*. The 1946 *Harvey Girls* MGM musical starred Judy Garland and was based on Samuel Hopkins's 1942 novel.

2. Weigle, "From Desert to Disney World," 115.

3. See Farmarco, "Berry Picking"; Fish, "Two Smiths of the West"; Hill, "Albert Berry."

4. *Thruway Chronology*, n.d.

5. Murray ("Complacency, Competition and Cooperation") earlier used the alliteration to discuss the interaction between an established media form (motion pictures) and a new one (television).

6. McDade, "New York State's New Main Street," 567, 591, 618.

7. But see McDade, "New York State's New Main Street," 594.

8. Patton, *Open Road*, 13.

9. Craft is emblematic of *function*: purpose, utility, reason. And the object *functions* as much for the creator as the customer. The craft object's logic is, typically, self-evident, with little mystery or need for an intermediary to explain or enhance the holder's understanding. Also craft is often made in multiples, in contrast to unique art objects. In at least some instances, crafted objects are the beginning point for industrial ones. Preindustrial crafts are the template, test lab, and useability experience for mass-manufactured duplicates; the craftsman's one-off prototype for the factory-made product. A good idea's design problem is how to re-create it on a large scale for customer adoption and make it available for affordable purchase anywhere. Perhaps a subset of craft is the folk or naïve art made "just for nice." Unaware of their status as "artists," untutored artisans created (what was later appreciated as art) objects that, as the Pennsylvania-Germans said, were "just for nice" (Machmer and Machmer, *Just for Nice*). The objects were created and existed not for any utilitarian purpose but simply for one's pleasure. The art-craft divide was one subtext in a 1968 public controversy about a San Francisco public sculpture (see Isenberg, "Culture-a-Go-Go"). Laura Morelli discusses the distinction in a Khan Academy talk ("Is There a Difference between Art and Craft?"). "Fine arts" seems for some as much a justification as an assertion, while "decorative arts" suggests an apologetic minimizing of aspiration. If so, then "Craft," is a distant third-tier with some unsure whether crafts can be squeezed into the same category as "art." The distinction between art and craft (applied art) has been traced as far back as the fifteenth century, widely discussed and parsed along philosophical, rhetorical, aesthetic, technical, and semantic lines. A brief, accessible overview is presented in Lauria and Fenton (*Craft in America*); see also Auther, *String, Felt, Thread*, Lugowska, "The Art and Craft Divide," Markowitz, "The Distinction Between Art and Craft," and Risatti, "Metaphysical Implications").

10. Manual training in educational settings predates the Arts and Crafts period. Some authors trace it back to the seventeenth century. For discussion of manual training within the context of the Arts and Crafts movement, see, for example, Clark and Thomas-Clark, "Manual and Industrial Training," 1997, and Floyd, "The Skillful Hand," 2001.

11. Brown, "Theodore Hanford Pond."

12. See "On Japanese Art" and "Society of Arts and Crafts."

13. One month after the Rochester exhibit of Arts and Crafts concluded, Ellis went to work for Gustav Stickley's Craftsman Workshops in Syracuse (Ludwig,

The Arts and Crafts Movement, 1983). His tenure there was brief, as he died in 1904.

14. See Massey, *Crystal and Arabesque*; Ellis and Reithmayr, *Claude Bragdon*.

15. Hewitt, *Gustav Stickley's Craftsman Farms*, 42. The exhibition is more fully discussed by Austin, *A Symbiotic Partnership*.

16. "A Fine Display of Handiwork."

17. "Large Crowd on Closing Night."

18. Today, Walrath's pots are often compared in form and decoration to those produced at Marblehead Pottery, though Walrath's decoration tends to be more subtle than Marblehead's. Arthur Baggs, another one of Binns's students, headed up Marblehead.

19. Austin, "Rediscovering Frederick E. Walrath" and Austin, "Fred Walrath, Part Two."

20. "Alfred's Summer Session."

21. Collins, "The Lillian Fairchild Award."

22. "Fairchild Award for Fine Arts."

23. Austin, *Frans Wildenhain*.

24. "Lulu Scott Backus"; Croughton, "Artists and Craftsmen."

25. Croughton, "Interests of Artists and Craftsmen."

26. Croughton, "Artists and Craftsmen."

27. "RIT Honors 7."

28. "Mrs. Lulu Scott Backus Dies." Later, a classified ad in the same paper (November 2, 1955, 34) advertised a sale from her estate of household goods, "including books, pottery, and antiques," and held at her South Goodman Street home.

29. The most extensive treatment of Binns is by Carney (*Charles Fergus Binns*). One of Binns's students and the second graduate of the Ceramics School, Paul E. Cox, memorialized his professor at the 1935 dedication of Binns Hall: "Instruction by him consisted of beautifully worded lectures, kindly criticism of laboratory work, encouragement in the type of things that most present day engineering schools catalog as 'special problems,' and gentle but firm insistence that quality rather than [quantity] be the goal" ("Dedicate Binns Hall").

30. Carney, *Glidden Pottery*, 16–17.

31. "Glidden Pottery Plant Has Doubled Production."

32. "Glidden Pottery Plant Being Extensively Enlarged."

33. Carney, *Glidden Pottery*, 1.

34. For a collector's perspective on Glidden, see Kransler, *Glidden Pottery*.

35. Kowalczyk, email correspondence, 2018; McFadden, email correspondence, 2018.

36. See Braznell, "The Early Career of Ronald Hayes Pearson," 1999, 189. Mrs. Webb's prodigious successful efforts on behalf of craft and craftsmen is documented by Braznell ("The Early Career"), Denker ("Aileen Osborn Webb"),

Hintze ("Cultivating the Crafts"), Lovelace ("Who Was Aileen Osborn Webb?"), and Zaiden ("An Unyielding Commitment").

37. For a brief history of SAC at RIT, see Simmons, "Craft Education." In 1951, *Popular Mechanics* wrote that SAC was a "down-to-earth school" providing training in pricing and marketing trends for students who study craft "as a paying career" (Eris, "They Learn Crafts," 143).

38. The gift dimension of Coppersmith might have accommodated some work retailed at Shop One. However, Shop One's scope was far broader than Avon's; exhibiting metalsmiths and sculptors in metal, such as Ruth Asawa and later, Albert Paley, were more abstract, less functional, and more adventuresome than anything ever produced at Avon. From the start, Shop One was a full-time operation run by the four partners. Trying to squeeze creative work out of their own studios and into a schedule already crowded with classroom teaching and student studio time at RIT would have been challenging. Promoting and publicizing Shop One ate up time, as did private commissions. And the financial returns were slender; partner Frans Wildenhain reported $706 in Shop One income, including sales of his own ceramics and any profit generated by the store, on his 1971 federal tax return (Austin, "Selling Crafts at Mid-Century," 212). Adding on additional responsibilities elsewhere and for someone else would have required a twenty-five-hour day and was unthinkable.

39. As far back as Frederick Walrath's tenure at Mechanics Institute, he exhibited, advertised, and sold his wares, as did his employer before MI (Grueby Pottery) and after (Newcomb College).

Conclusion

1. Kardon, "Within Our Shores," 23.

2. For example: Aerni, "The Economics of the Craft Industry"; Lugowska, "The Art and Craft Divide"; Markowitz, "The Distinction Between Art and Craft."

3. See Ludwig, *The Arts and Crafts Movement*; Eisenstadt, *The Encyclopedia of New York State*.

4. York, "New Deal Craft Programs," 60–61.

5. Aerni, "The Economics of the Craft Industry."

6. The timeline for the professionalization of Canadian crafts and their makers parallels that of the United States, and Aileen Webb also plays a role north of the US border (Alfoldy, *Crafting Identity*, 4, 52). Professionalization for craft makers parallels initiatives for such diverse occupations as journalism and public relations, teaching and design and, more recently, international intelligence, as well as a host of others; see for instance Wilensky ("The Professionalization of Everyone?") and Beegan and Atkinson ("Professionalism, Amateurism").

7. Aerni, "The Economics of the Craft Industry," 18, 121.

8. Quoted in Hintze, "Cultivating the Crafts," 4.

9. Hintze, "Cultivating the Crafts," 2.

10. Hintze, "Cultivating the Crafts," 34.

11. Zaiden, "An Unyielding Commitment to Craft," 13.

12. "Area Folk Art."

13. Bergmanis, "Return to Simple Life in Upstate."

14. "Folk Art Guild Sale."

15. "Area Folk Art"; "Folk Art Guild Slates."

16. Edmonds, "Work Ethic Isn't Their Only Bond."

17. "Area Folk Art."

18. Edmonds, "Work Ethic Isn't Their Only Bond."

19. "Folk Art Guild Slates."

20. Lippincott, "Arts in My View."

21. Appelhof, "A New World."

22. "Area Folk Art."

23. "Exhibition Features."

24. Another craft school briefly operated later, not far from the Rochester Folk Art Guild's Middlesex location. On the other side of Canandaigua Lake in Naples, New York, the Naples Mill School of Arts and Crafts (January 1971–August 1979) offered classes in ceramics, glass-blowing, fiber, blacksmithing, photography, drawing and painting, according to its founder, R. Bruce Lindsay's 2018 LinkedIn profile. Some of the school's instructors, including Wendell Castle and Frans Wildenhain, were also on the faculty of RIT's School for American Craftsmen. The twelve-acre campus included an 1880s grain mill, warehouse, and train depot with more than forty-thousand square feet of studio space.

25. Kessler, "From Mission to Market," 129.

26. Bourdieu, "The Field of Cultural Production," 40.

27. For example, Braznell, "The Early Career of Ronald Hayes Pearson," 187.

28. For one response to the limitations, including those of idiosyncrasy and empiricism, of case studies see Flyvbjerg, "Five Misunderstandings About."

29. As one example, little is known about Richcraft Pottery in Cohocton, New York, though what is known is intriguing. Owned and operated by Richard Thomas and Charles Dispenza in the years following World War II, their advertising was connected to the Richcraft appliance store, and the pottery was a free premium "with all purchases in our electrical shop" ("Says Richcraft"). One of the appliance store's ads states: "Your gift problem for Christmas is SOLVED at NO additional cost." Thomas, a ceramics graduate of Alfred University and member of their Ceramic Guild, and Dispenza both served in the armed forces. Their pottery shop opened January 23, 1946 ("Alfred Man") and by 1949 Dispenza was identified as proprietor of the Richcraft Inn. Thomas exhibited his ceramics "hobby" in Geneva, New York ("Spare Time Profits") and a Richard Thomas judged ceramics at an Erie, Pennsylvania Art Club show and was identified as a

faculty member at Cranbrook Academy of Fine Arts ("Erie Art Club"). But the only "Richard Thomas" listed by Cranbrook as a faculty member was the head of the metalsmithing department, 1948–1984.

30. Flink, *The Car Culture*, 140, emphasis added. See, too, Rae, *The Road and the Car* and Flink, *The Automobile Age*.

References

"A Bit of Yesteryear Changes Hands." *Livonia Gazette*, January 10, 1985.

"A Fine Display of Handiwork." *Rochester Democrat and Chronicle*, April 8, 1903.

"A New Factory." *Penn Yan Democrat*, March 20, 1925.

Aerni, April Laskey. "The Economics of the Craft Industry." PhD diss., University of Cincinnati, 1987.

Alfoldy, Sandra. *Crafting Identity: The Development of Professional Fine Craft in Canada*. Montreal: McGill-Queen's University Press, 2005.

"Alfred Has a Ceramic Industry Unknown to Many." *Alfred Sun*, July 10, 1941.

"Alfred Man Located at Cohocton." *Alfred Sun*, July 31, 1947.

"Alfred's Summer Session." *Alfred Sun*, July 9, 1919.

"All Around the Towns." *Rochester Democrat and Chronicle*, November 22, 1956.

Alvord, Florence A. "Peeping Into the Local Past, April 14, 1933," *Livonia Gazette*, April 15, 1943.

"American Legion Elects New Officers." *East Aurora Advertiser*, September 20, 1928.

"The American Santa Claus and His Gifts." *The Craftsman*, December 1914, 338–43.

"Ann Mattison Assisting." *Dansville Genesee Country Express and Advertiser*, July 20, 1933.

Appelhof, Ruth Ann. "A New World." *Auburn Citizen Advertiser*, 1975.

Appell, Howard W. "Fire at Avon Coppersmith." *Geneseo Lake & Valley Clarion*, n.d. Clipping in the Avon Preservation & Historical Society, Avon, NY.

"Appreciation Dinner Held by Wemett Co." *Livonia Gazette*, January 19, 1950.

Archer, Sarah. "Lessons from Utopia." *American Craft*, October/November 2020, 70–77.

"Area Folk Art Guild to Exhibit at D.C." *Penn Yan Chronicle Express*, October 2, 1969.

Ashby, LeRoy. *With Amusement for All: A History of American Popular Culture*. Lexington: University of Kentucky Press, 2006.

Austin, Bruce A. "The Development and Decline of the Drive-In Movie Theater." In *Current Research in Film: Audiences, Economics, and Law*, edited by Bruce A. Austin, 59–91. Vol. 1. Norwood, NJ: Ablex, 1985.

Austin, Bruce A. "Cinema Screen Advertising: An Old Technology with New Promise for Consumer Marketing." *Journal of Consumer Marketing* 3, no. 1 (Winter 1986): 45–56.

Austin, Bruce A. *The American Arts & Crafts Movement in Western New York, 1900–1920*. Rochester: Rochester Institute of Technology, 1992.

Austin, Bruce. "Rediscovering Frederick E. Walrath," *Arts & Crafts Quarterly*, August 1993, 20–23.

Austin, Bruce. "Fred Walrath, Part Two, How Walrath Marked His Work: Signature as Evidence." *Arts & Crafts Quarterly*, November 1993, 22–24.

Austin, Bruce A. "Product Price Structure at the Roycroft and the Creation of Consumer Culture." In *Head, Heart and Hand: Elbert Hubbard and the Roycrofters*, edited by Marie Via and Marjorie B. Searl, 149–55. Rochester: University of Rochester Press, 1994.

Austin, Bruce A. *Frans Wildenhain, 1950–75: Creative and Commercial American Ceramics at Mid-Century*. Rochester: Printing Applications Laboratory, 2012.

Austin, Bruce A. "Selling Crafts at Mid-Century: Moving the Merch at Shop One." In *Frans Wildenhain 1950-75: Creative and Commercial American Ceramics at Mid-Century*, Bruce A. Austin, 161–221. Rochester: Printing Applications Laboratory, 2012.

Austin, Bruce A. "Widescreen: Expanding the Research Agenda for Arts & Crafts." Paper presented at "Frank Lloyd Wright and the Buffalo School of Arts and Crafts: An International Conference." University at Buffalo, Buffalo, New York, October 2017.

Austin, Bruce A. *A Symbiotic Partnership: Marrying Commerce to Education at Gustav Stickley's 1903 Arts & Crafts Exhibitions*. Rochester: RIT Press, 2022.

Auther, Elissa. *String, Felt, Thread: Art and Craft in American Art*. Minneapolis: University of Minnesota Press, 2010.

"Avon Coppersmith Celebrates 60th Year." *Avon Herald News*. 1992.

"Avon Coppersmith Makes Bow to the Public." *Mount Morris Enterprise*, June 21, 1933; also *Nunda News*, June 30, 1933.

"Avon Coppersmith: Widely Known Firm Changes Hands." *Geneseo Livingston County Leader*, January 21, 1970; also *Mount Morris Enterprise*, January 31, 1970.

Avon Preservation & Historical Society. "White Horse Tavern," three-ring binder, reviewed July 21, 2019, Avon, New York.

"Baptist Church Torn Down; Branchport Loses Old Landmark." *Penn Yan Democrat*, September 28, 1934.

Barons, Richard, and Lucie Nelson. *Severity and Simplicity: The American Arts and Crafts Aesthetic in the Northeast*. Binghamton: University Art Museum, 1997.

Bartinique, A. Patricia. *Gustav Stickley: His Craft*. Parsippany, NJ: Craftsman Farms Foundation, 1992.

Bassett, Mark. Email to Bruce A. Austin, February 4, 2021.

Beegan, Gerry, and Paul Atkinson. "Professionalism, Amateurism and the Boundaries of Design." *Journal of Design History* 21, no. 4 (Winter 2008): 305–13.

Belasco, Warren James. *Americans on the Road: From Autocamping to Motel, 1910–1945*. Cambridge: MIT Press, 1979.

Belasco, Warren. "Commercialized Nostalgia: The Origins of the Roadside Strip." In *The Automobile and American Culture*, edited by David L. Lewis and Laurence Goldstein, 105–22. Ann Arbor: University of Michigan Press, 1983.

Belk, Russell W. "Possessions and the Extended Self." *Journal of Consumer Research* 15 (September 1983): 139–68.

Bergman, Andrew. *We're in the Money: Depression America and Its Films*. New York: Harper Colophon, 1971.

Bergmanis, Talis. "Return to Simple Life in Upstate." *Rochester Democrat and Chronicle, Upstate* magazine section, January 5, 1969.

Bluestone, Daniel. "Roadside Blight and the Reform of Commercial Architecture." In *Roadside America: The Automobile in Design and Culture*, edited by Jan Jennings, 170–84. Ames: University of Iowa Press, 1990.

Boorstin, Daniel J. *The Image: A Guide to Pseudo-Events in America*. New York: Harper Colophon, 1961.

Bourdieu, Pierre. "The Field of Cultural Production, or: The Economic World Reversed." In *The Field of Cultural Production*, 29–73. Translated by Richard Nice. New York: Columbia University Press, 1983.

Bowman, Leslie Greene. *American Arts & Crafts: Virtue in Design*. Boston: Bulfinch Press/Little, Brown. 1990.

Bowman, Leslie Greene. "Industry and Ideals: McHugh, Stickley, and the American Arts and Crafts Movement." In *The Distinction of Being Different: Joseph P. McHugh and the American Arts and Crafts Movement*, Anna Tobin D'Ambrosio, 27–30. Utica: Munson-Williams-Proctor Institute, 1993.

Braznell, W. Scott. "The Early Career of Ronald Hayes Pearson and the Post-World War II Revival of American Silversmithing and Jewelrymaking." *Winterthur Portfolio* 34, no. 4 (Winter 1999): 185–213.

Brimmer, F. E. *Autocamping*. Cincinnati: Stewart Kidd, 1923.

Brimmer, F. E. *Motor Campcraft*. New York: Macmillan, 1923.

Brown, Conrad. "Shop One: Here is a Model for Craftsmen Who Dream of Opening a Retail Outlet." *Craft Horizons*, March/April 1956, 18–23.

Brown, Wilmer. "Theodore Hanford Pond, Craftsman." *International Studio* 47 (1912): xliii–xlv.

Bullock, Paul D. "Things I Think I Remember: Part I (1929–1947)," October 2007. http://bullock1.com/PDBAutoPartIEdited.pdf. Accessed November 13, 2018.

Bullock, Paul D. "Woodcraft Products Corporation," August 2012. http://bullock1.com/HomerWoodcraftProductslorez.pdf. Accessed November 13, 2018.

"Business Briefs." (Rochester) *The Daily Record*, February 9, 1970.

Cantor, George. *Where the Old Roads Go: Driving the First Federal Highways of the Northeast*. New York: Harper and Row, 1990.

Carney, Margaret. *Charles Fergus Binns: The Father of American Studio Ceramics*. New York: Hudson Hills Press, 1998.

Carney, Margaret. *Glidden Pottery*. Alfred: Schein-Joseph International Museum of Ceramic Art, 2001.

Cathers, David. *Gustav Stickley*. New York: Phaidon Press, 2003.

Cathers, David. "Pioneers." *American Bungalow*, no. 58 (Summer 2008).

Cathers, David M. *"These Humbler Metals": American Arts & Crafts Metalwork from the Two Red Roses Foundation*. Palm Harbor, FL: Two Red Roses Foundation, 2014.

"Century-Old Records Endangered as Fire Damages Former Church." *Rochester Democrat and Chronicle*, October 21, 1940.

Chester, Eleanor. "Turning Back History to the Day When Horsepower Was Just That." *Rochester Democrat and Chronicle*, August 4, 1935.

"Clarence Wemett of Hemlock Presents 'The Avon Coppersmith' to the Public." *Lima Recorder*, June 16, 1933.

Clark, Michael, and Jill Thomas-Clark. "The Plail Brothers Chair Company: Design and Gender." *Style 1900* (Spring 1996): 35–39.

Clark, Michael, and Jill Thomas-Clark. "Manual and Industrial Training at the Oswego School: Heart, Hand, and Head." *Style 1900* (Spring/Summer 1997): 20–23.

Clark, Michael, and Jill Thomas-Clark. "Arthur H. Cole and the Avon Coppersmith." *Style 1900* (Spring/Summer 1998): 22–25.

Clark, Michael, and Jill Thomas-Clark. "The Majestic Furniture Company: Gus Meets Frank Lloyd Wright." *Style 1900* (Spring/Summer 1999): 21–25.

Clark, Robert Judson, ed. *The Arts and Crafts Movement in America, 1876–1916*. Princeton, NJ: Princeton University Press, 1972.

Cobblestone Museum. "Frequently Asked Questions." http://www.cobblestonemuseum.org/cobblestone-masonry/. Accessed May 9. 2019.

Cohen, Lizabeth. *A Consumers' Republic*. New York: Knopf, 2003.

Cole, Jennifer. "The Avon Coppersmith: Arthur H. Cole." Term paper (1984) in the collection of the Avon Preservation & Historical Society, Avon, New York.

Cole, Thomas. Personal interview with Bruce A. Austin, September 5 and 19, 2019.

Collins, Rowland L. "The Lillian Fairchild Award, 1924–74." *University of Rochester Library Bulletin* 29, no. 1 (Autumn 1975): 1–12.

"Company O Looses [sic] Half Its Men." *East Aurora Advertiser*, November 27, 1919.

Connor, Frank. "Tales of the Past." *Livonia Gazette*, January 16, 1931.

"Coppersmith Firm Files for Bankruptcy." *Buffalo Courier-Express*, July 11, 1962.

"Coppersmith Learned Trade at Roycrafters [sic]." *Avon Herald News*, January 24, 1973.

Costa, Richard H., and Dante Tranquille. "Rte. 20 Revisited: 'Save Toll, See State' Drive Begins to Click." *Utica Observer Dispatch*, August 13, 1954.

"'Couples Trade' in the Tourist Camp." *New Republic*, July 29, 1936, 10.

"Craftsman Building" (advertisement). *New York Sun*, January 14, 1915.

Crawford, Alan. "Review: Inspiring Reform." *Archives of American Art Journal* 37, no. 3/4, (1997): 28–31.

Croughton, Amy H. "Artists and Craftsmen." *Rochester Times-Union*, June 19, 1942.

Croughton, Amy H. "Concerning Interests of Artists and Craftsmen." *Rochester Times-Union*, July 2, 1932.

Croughton, Amy H. "Concerning Interests of Artists and Craftsmen." *Rochester Times-Union*, July 30, 1932.

Croughton, Amy H. "Interests of Artists and Craftsmen." *Rochester Times-Union*, September 21, 1934.

D'Ambrosio, Anna T. *The Distinction of Being Different: Joseph P. McHugh and the American Arts and Crafts Movement*. Utica, NY: Munson-Williams-Proctor Institute, 1994.

Darling, Sharon S. *Teco: Art Pottery of the Prairie School*. Erie: Erie Art Museum, 1989.

"Dedicate Binns Hall." *Alfred Sun*, June 13, 1935.

DeFleur, Melvin L. and Sandra J. Ball-Rokeach. *Theories of Mass Communication*, 5th ed. New York: Longman, 1989.

Denenberg, Thomas Andrew. *Wallace Nutting and the Invention of Old America*. New Haven, CT: Yale University Press, 2003.

Denker, Ellen Paul. "Aileen Osborn Webb and the Origins of Craft's Infrastructure." *Journal of Modern Craft* 6, no. 1 (March 2013): 11–34.

Denton County History. "Native American Heritage Month: Denton County's Original Settlers." Blog posted November 10, 2017. https://dentoncounty-historyandculture.wordpress.com/page/6/.

"Do You Know Your Business Community?" *Caledonia Advertiser*, October 4, 1979.

Dormer, Peter. "Craft and the Turing Test for Practical Thinking." In *The Culture of Craft*, edited by Peter Dormer, 137–157. Manchester: Manchester University Press. 1997.

"East Aurora, N.Y., Resplendent in Homelikeness and Artistry." *Christian Science Monitor*, June 9, 1913.

"'East Aurora's Shop of Beautiful Gifts'" (advertisement). *Christian Science Monitor*, January 17, 1917.

Edmonds, Elizabeth. "Work Ethic Isn't Their Only Bond." *Finger Lakes Times*, June 8, 1985.

Edwards, Julie Eldridge. "Historic Champion of the Craft Movement." Shelburne Farms, Blog posted March 21, 2019. https://shelburnefarms.org/blog/historic-champion-of-the-craft-movement. Accessed 22 June 2020.

Edwards, Robert. "The Art of Work." In *"The Art That is Life": The Arts & Crafts Movement in America, 1875–1920*, edited by Wendy Kaplan, 223–236. Boston: Little, Brown, 1987.

"Egypt Valley Camp Proves Very Popular." *Lima Recorder*, July 23, 1953.

"Egypt Valley Opens in Bristol Hills." *Bath Steuben Advocate*, June 24, 1949.

Eisenstadt, Peter B. *The Encyclopedia of New York State*. Syracuse: Syracuse University Press, 2005.

Elliott, E. Peabody. "Voice from the Gallery." *Livonia Gazette*, July 17, 1941.

Ellis, Eugenia Victoria and Andrea G. Reithmayr, eds. *Claude Bragdon and the Beautiful Necessity*. Rochester: RIT Press, 2010.

"Erie Art Club to Open Annual Show on May 1." *Jamestown Post-Journal*, April 11, 1953.

Eris, Alfred. "They Learn Crafts for Careers." *Popular Mechanics*, May 1951, 143–45.

"Exhibition Features Picnic." *North Tonawanda News*, July 21, 1984.

"Fairchild Award for Fine Arts Work Goes to Mechanics Institute Teacher." *Rochester Democrat and Chronicle*, November 11, 1927.

"Family Planning Private Rite for C.W. Crumrine." *Rochester Democrat and Chronicle*, February 8, 1962.

Fariello, Anna. "Arts and Crafts in Appalachia: The Third Wave." *Style 1900* (Winter/Spring 2003): 70–75.

Farmarco, Joe. "Berry Picking: A Personal Portrait of the Craft of Albert & Edwina Berry." *Style 1900* (Spring/Summer 1998): 64–70.

Fess, Margaret. "Coppersmith Hobby Now Is Full Business." *Buffalo Courier-Express*, October 11, 1953.

"First Unit in White Horse Shopping Plaza." *Lima Recorder*, May 17, 1956.

"First Toll His Last." *Rochester Democrat and Chronicle*, June 20, 1954.

Fish, Marilyn. "Two Smiths of the West: Albert Berry and Dirk Van Erp." *Style 1900* (Summer/Fall 2006): 60–67.

Flink, James J. "The Three Stages of American Automobile Consciousness." *American Quarterly* 24, no. 4 (October 1972): 451–73.

Flink, James J. *The Car Culture*. Cambridge, MA: MIT Press, 1975.

Flink, James J. *The Automobile Age*. Cambridge, MA: MIT Press, 1988.

Floyd, Barbara. "The Skillful Hand, the Cultured Mind." *Style 1900* (Fall/Winter 2001): 46–53.

Flyvberg, Bent. "Five Misunderstandings About Case-Study Research." *Qualitative Inquiry* 12, no. 2 (April 2006): 219–45.

"Folk Art Guild Sale Today – Direct from D.C.!" *Rochester Democrat and Chronicle*, November 20, 1969.

"Folk Art Guild Slates Holiday Exhibition, Sale." *Geneva Chronicle Express*, November 12, 1981.

"Former Church Fire Loss $500." *Canandaigua Daily Messenger*, October 21, 1940.

"Former Local Couple's Shop is 'Rare Find.'" *Spencerport Suburban News*, March 17, 1987.

"Former Saratogian Succeeds." *The Saratogian*, August 6, 1917.

"Founder Tells Growth of the Craftsman Idea." *New York Press*, April 12, 1914.

"14 Inventors Get Patents." *Rochester Democrat and Chronicle*, June 19, 1936.

Fox, Mark, and Grant C. Black. "The Rise and Decline of Drive-in Cinemas in the United States." In *Handbook on the Economics of Leisure*, edited by Samuel Cameron, 271–98. Northampton, MA: Edward Elgar, 2011.

Freeman, Rich, and Sue Freeman. *Cobblestone Quest: Road Tours of New York's Historical Buildings*. Englewood, FL: Footprint Press, 2005.

"Freeway Ass'n Names Directors." *Seneca County News*, August 23, 1956.

"Freeway Ass'n to Issue Brochure." *Nunda News*, March 15, 1956.

"Freeway Association Will Incorporate." *Geneva Times*, October 6, 1955.

"Freeway Group Adopts Slogan." *Geneva Times*, March 6, 1956.

Frelinghusen, Alice Cooney, Martin Eidelberg, and Adrienne Spinozzi. *American Art Pottery: The Robert A. Ellison Jr. Collection*. New York: Metropolitan Museum of Art, 2018.

Fried, Stephen. *Appetite for America: Fred Harvey and the Business of Civilizing the Wild West -One Meal at a Time*. New York: Bantam, 2010.

Fuller, Wayne E. "Good Roads and Rural Free Delivery of Mail." *Mississippi Valley Historical Review* 42, no. 1 (June 1955): 67–83.

Gallinger, Roy. "Route 20 Assn. to Ask Road Name by Changed to State Freeway." *Oneida Daily Dispatch*, November 6, 1955.

Gaylord, Ivy Loeper. Obituary. *Auburn Citizen*, September 30, 1977.

Gelber, Steven. *Hobbies: Leisure and the Culture of Work in America*. New York: Columbia University Press, 1993.

Gimigliano, Michael Nicholas. "Experiences Along the Cherry Valley Turnpike: The Education of a Traveler." PhD diss., Syracuse University, 1979.

Gladding, Effie Price. *Across the Continent by the Lincoln Highway*. New York: Brentano's, 1915.

Gladwell, Malcolm. "The Science of the Sleeper: How the Information Age Could Blow Away the Blockbuster." *The New Yorker*, October 4, 1999.

Gladwell, Malcolm. *The Tipping Point: How Little Things Can Make a Big Difference*. New York: Little, Brown, 2002.

"Glencroft Coppersmiths Follow Family Roots." Unidentified clipping, Clarence History Museum, dated May 16, 1984. Email to Bruce A. Austin, November 26, 2018.

"Glidden Pottery Plant Being Extensively Enlarged." *Alfred Sun*, October 5, 1944.

"Glidden Pottery Plant has Doubled Production." *Alfred Sun*, May 7, 1942.

Goffman, Erving. *The Presentation of Self in Everyday Life*. Garden City, NY: Doubleday, 1959.

Goller, Robert Lowell. East Aurora Town Historian. Email to Bruce A. Austin, including photographs of the 1927 telephone directory and 1930 East Aurora census, September 25, 2019.

Goller, Robert Lowell. East Aurora Town Historian. Email to Bruce A. Austin, August 6, 2020.

"Good and Bad Tourist Camps." *Literary Digest*, October 26, 1929.

"Grand Opening of Egypt Valley Camp & Recreation Center" (advertisement). *Rochester Democrat and Chronicle*, June 24, 1949.

Green, Harvey. "Culture and Crisis: Americans and the Craft Revivals." In *Revivals! Diverse Traditions: The History of Twentieth-Century Craft, 1920–1945*, edited by Janet Kardon, pp. 31-54. New York: Harry N. Abrams, 1994.

Green, Harvey. "The Promise and Peril of High Technology." In *Craft in the Machine Age: The History of Twentieth-Century Craft, 1920–1945*, edited by Janet Kardon, 36–45. New York: Harry N. Abrams, 1995.

Green, Nancy E., ed. *Byrdcliffe: An American Arts and Crafts Colony*. Ithaca, NY: Herbert F. Johnson Museum of Art, Cornell University, 2004.

Greenfield, Briann G. *Out of the Attic: Inventing Antiques in Twentieth-Century New England*. Amherst: University of Massachusetts Press, 2009.

Grieve, Victoria. *The Federal Art Project and the Creation of Middlebrow Culture*. Champaign: University of Illinois Press, 2009.

Gudis, Catherine. *Buyways: Billboards, Automobiles, and the American Landscape*. New York: Routledge, 2004.

Gutfreund, Owen D. *20th-Century Sprawl: Highways and the Reshaping of the American Landscape*. New York: Oxford University Press, 2004.

"Had Two Cousins Named George Haltiwanger." *Hamlet* (NC) *News-Messenger*, September 1952.

Halbert, Ward K. "Oil Jobbers Provide Tourist Camp Ground Along Dixie Highway." *National Petroleum News*, October 5, 1921.

Hamell, George R. "Earthenwares and Salt-Glazed Stonewares of the Rochester-Genesee-Valley Region: An Overview." *Northeast Historical Archaeology* 9, art. 1 (1980): 1–14.

Hand, Jon. "Avon Fire is Determined to be Arson." *Rochester Democrat and Chronicle*, March 27, 1998.

"Happening Around Penn Yan." *Penn Yan Democrat*, December 6, 1910.

Hart, Val. *The Story of American Roads*. New York: William Sloane Associates, 1950.

Hedglon, Mary. "The Road Less Traveled." *Rochester Democrat and Chronicle*, October 20, 1991; November 5, 1991; December 17, 1991; February 18, 1992; May 28, 1992; June 18, 1992.

Hedglon, Mary. "Area Shop Keepers Try to Thrive in Shadow Cast by Retail Giants." *Rochester Democrat and Chronicle*, January 21, 1992.

Hedglon, Mary. "Along the Way: Routes 5 & 20 Offer Slice of Finger Lakes Life." *Rochester Democrat and Chronicle*, September 6, 1992.

"Hemlock Forge is Opening New Service Division." *Lima Recorder*, April 7, 1960.

"Hemlock Man Establishes Traditional Southern Pottery Near East Bloomfield." *Livonia Gazette*, June 24, 1932.

"Hemlock Ye Observer." *Livonia Gazette*, July 23, 1953.

Henry, Lyell. "Camps of Crime: Exposing the 'Motel Menace.'" *SCA Journal* 29, no. 1 (Spring 2012).

Hewitt, Mark Alan. *Gustav Stickley's Craftsman Farms: The Quest for an Arts and Crafts Utopia*. Syracuse: Syracuse University Press, 2001.

"High School Note." *Livonia Gazette*, April 13, 1906.

Hill, Jeffrey. "Albert Berry: A Northwest Craftsman." *Arts & Crafts Quarterly* 2, no. 4 (1989): 4–5.

Hintze, Stephen Brandon. "Cultivating the Crafts: Aileen Osborn Webb and the Instituting of American Craft, 1934–1964." MA thesis, Corcoran College of Art & Design, 2008.

"History of the Branchport Baptist Church." *Penn Yan Yates County Chronicle*, October 9, 1873.

Holbrook, Morris B., and Elizabeth C. Hirschman. "The Experiential Aspects of Consumption: Consumer Fantasies, Feelings, and Fun." *Journal of Consumer Research* 9, no. 2 (September 1982): 132–40.

Hoover, J. Edgar. "Camps of Crime." *American Magazine*, February 1940, 14–15, 130–32.

Horowitz, Daniel. *The Morality of Spending: Attitudes Toward the Consumer Society in America, 1875–1940*. Baltimore: Johns Hopkins University Press, 1985.

"How 'Mission' Furniture Was Named." *The Craftsman*, May 1909.

Howard, Kathleen L., and Diane F. Pardue. *Inventing the Southwest: The Fred Harvey Company and Native American Art*. Flagstaff: Northland Pub. Co., 1996.

Howland, Lance. "Route 20 is for Travelers Who Want to 'Stop and Smell the Roses.'" *Syracuse Herald American*, June 24, 1984.

Hunt, Wendy Arndt. "Let's Go Behind the Scenes at a Coppersmith Shop." *Buffalo News*, May 25, 1980.

"In Area Churches." *Rochester Democrat and Chronicle*, May 2, 1959.

Isenberg, Alison. "'Culture-A-Go-Go': The Ghiradelli Square Sculpture Controversy and the Liberation of Civic Design in the 1960s." *Journal of Social History* 44, no. 2 (Winter 2010): 379–412.

Jaramillo, Melissa. "Roadside Attractions." *Glens Falls Post Star*, January 18, 1991.

"Jermyn-Miller Case Settlement Reported After Jury was Drawn." *Batavia Daily News*, May 26, 1926.

Jessup, Elon. *The Motor Camping Book*. New York: G. P. Putnam's Sons, 1921.

Johnson, Keith F. "Cinema Advertising." *Journal of Advertising* 10, no. 4 (1981): 11–19.

Jowett, Garth. *Film: The Democratic Art*. Boston: Little, Brown, 1976.

Kammen, Michael. *In the Fast Lane: Historical Perspectives on American Culture.* New York: Oxford University Press, 1997.

Kaplan, Wendy. *"The Art That is Life": The Arts & Crafts Movement in America, 1875–1920.* Boston: Little, Brown, 1987.

Kardon, Janet. "Within Our Shores: Diverse Craft Revivals and Survivals." In *Revivals! Diverse Traditions: The History of Twentieth-Century Craft, 1920–1945,* edited by Janet Kardon, 22–30. New York: Harry N. Abrams, 1994.

Kates, William. "Preserving a Trip Across N.Y." *Ithaca Journal,* September 2, 2000.

Katz, Elihu, and Paul Lazarsfeld. *Personal Influence.* New York: Free Press, 1955.

Kay, Jane Holtz. *Asphalt Nation: How the Automobile Took Over America, and How We Can Take It Back.* New York: Crown, 1997.

Kessler, Jane. "From Mission to Market: Craft in the Southern Appalachians." In *Craft in the Machine Age: The History of Twentieth-Century American Craft, 1920–1945,* edited by Janet Kardon, 122–33. New York: Harry N. Abrams, 1995.

"Keuka College Girls List Hints for Home Ceramic Manufacture." *Geneva Daily Times,* March 24, 1950.

"Kick-Wheel Potter Exhibits at Fair." *Rochester Democrat and Chronicle,* August 25, 1941.

King, Floyd. "Through the Skioscope," *Rochester Democrat and Chronicle,* February 27, 1949.

Kolb, J. H., and Edmund de S. Brunner. "Rural Life." In *Recent Social Trends in the United States: Report of the President's Research Committee on Social Trends,* 497–552. New York: McGraw-Hill, 1933.

Kornacki, David. "The Secret Life of Karl Kipp." *Style 1900* (Fall 2009): 56–63.

Kornacki, Jon A. "Fulper's Marking System." *Journal of the American Art Pottery Association* 33, no. 1 (Winter 2017): 6–15.

Kowalczyk, Susan E. Curator of Collections/Director of Research, Alfred Ceramic Art Museum. Email to Bruce A. Austin, September 11, 2018.

Kransler, Ronald J. *Glidden Pottery: Alfred Mid-Century Highstyle Stoneware.* Boca Raton, FL: Universal-Publishers, 2011.

Kurp, Patrick. "Road to History." *Albany Times-Union,* April 30, 1989.

Lamoureux, Dorothy. *The Arts & Crafts Studio of Dirk Van Erp.* San Francisco: San Francisco Craft & Folk Art Museum, 1989.

"Large Crowd on Closing Night; Arts and Crafts Exhibit Complete Success." *Rochester Democrat and Chronicle,* April 26, 1903.

Larson, Erik. *Dead Wake: The Last Crossing of the Lusitania.* New York: Crown, 2015.

Lasch, Christopher. *The Culture of Narcissism: American Life in the Age of Diminishing Expectations.* New York: W.W. Norton, 1979.

Lauria, Jo and Steve Fenton. *Craft in America: Two Centuries of Artists and Objects.* New York: Clarkson Potter, 2007.

Lazarsfeld, Paul F., Bernard Berelson and Hazel Gaudet. *The People's Choice: How the Voter Makes Up His Mind in a Presidential Campaign*. New York: Columbia University Press, 1944.

Lears, T.J. Jackson. "From Salvation to Self-Realization: Advertising and the Therapeutic Roots of the Consumer Culture, 1880–1930." In *The Culture of Consumption: Critical Essays in American History, 1880–1930*, edited by Richard Wightman Fox and T. J. Jackson Lears, 1–38. New York: Pantheon, 1983.

"Legion Meeting." *East Aurora Advertiser*, January 19, 1928.

Lewis, Tom. *Divided Highways: Building the Interstate Highways, Transforming American Life*. Ithaca, NY: Cornell University Press, 2013.

Liebs, Chester H. *Main Street to Miracle Mile: American Roadside Architecture*. Boston: Little, Brown, 1985.

Lippincott, John. "Arts in My View." *Batavia Daily News*, March 26, 1977.

"Little Known Industry." *Avon Herald-News*, July 22, 1948.

Livadas, Greg. "Gift Shop Owner Mourned." *Rochester Democrat and Chronicle*, March 24, 1998.

"Livingston County Sheriff's Report." *Genesee Country Express*, April 16, 1998.

Livingstone, Karen, and Linda Parry, eds. *International Arts and Crafts*. London: V & A Publications, 2005.

"Livonia Man Found Dead at Fire Scene." *Genesee Country Express*, March 26, 1998.

"Local Brevities." *Cooperstown Otsego Farmer*, November 14, 1941.

"Local Brevities." *Cooperstown Otsego Farmer*, October 15, 1943.

"Local News." *Livingston Republican*, June 22, 1933.

Long, J. C. and J.D. Long. *Motor Camping*. New York: Dodd, Mead, 1923.

Lovelace, Joyce. "Who Was Aileen Osborn Webb?" *American Craft Magazine*, August/September 2011.

Ludwig, Coy L. *The Arts & Crafts Movement in New York State 1890s–1920s*. Hamilton: Gallery Association of New York State, 1983.

Lugowska, Agnieszka. "The Art and Craft Divide – On the Exigency of Margins." *Art Inquiry* 16 (2014): 285–96.

"Lulu Scott Backus." *Bulletin of the American Ceramic Society*, May 15, 1942.

"Luring the Tourist." *Geneva Times*, February 13, 1956.

Lynd, Robert S. "The People as Consumers." In *Recent Social Trends in the United States: Report of the President's Research Committee on Social Trends*, 857–911. New York: McGraw-Hill, 1933.

MacCannell, Dean. *The Tourist: A New Theory of the Leisure Class*. Berkeley: University of California Press, 1999 (first published by Schocken, 1976).

Machmer, Richard S., and Rosemarie B. Machmer. *Just for Nice: Carving and Whittling Magic of Southeastern Pennsylvania*. Reading, PA: Historical Society of Berks County, 1991.

Manchee, Doug. *Sutures and Spirits: The Photographic Illustrations of Lejaren a Hiller*. Rochester: RIT Press, 2018.

Manhart, Marcia Yockey. "Charting a New Educational Vision." In *Craft in the Machine Age: The History of Twentieth-Century Craft, 1920-1945*, edited by Janet Kardon, 62–73. New York: Harry N. Abrams, 1995.

Marek, Don. *Grand Rapids Art Metalwork, 1902-1918*. Grand Rapids: Heartwood, 1999.

"Market Building Starts at E. Avon." *Rochester Democrat and Chronicle*, May 21, 1956.

Markowitz, Sally J. "The Distinction Between Art and Craft." *Journal of Aesthetic Education* 28, no. 1 (Spring 1994): 55–70.

Mason, Philip P. *The League of American Wheelmen and the Good Roads Movement, 1880–1905*. Ann Arbor: University of Michigan Press, 1958.

Massey, Beatrice Larned. *It Might Have Been Worse: A Motor Trip from Coast to Coast*. San Francisco: Harr Wagner, 1920.

Massey, Jonathan. *Crystal and Arabesque: Claude Bragdon, Ornament, and Modern Architecture*. Pittsburgh: University of Pittsburgh Press, 2009.

Mayron, Amy. "Firefighters Find Body in Burned Avon Shop." Clipping (probably *Rochester Times-Union* or *Democrat and Chronicle*, n.d.), Avon Preservation & Historical Society, Avon, New York.

McCall, George. "Sticks Nix Hick Pix: Not Interested in Farm Drama." *Variety*, July 17, 1935, 1, 51.

McCarthy, John J., and Robert Littell. "Three Hundred Thousand Shacks: The Arrival of a New American Industry." *Harper's*, July 1933, 180–88.

McDade, Matt C. "New York State's New Main Street." *National Geographic Magazine*, November 1956, 567–618.

McFadden, Laurie Lounsberry. Interim Dean of Libraries and Alfred University Archivist, email to Bruce A. Austin, September 8, 2018.

McGovern, Charles. *Sold American: Consumption and Citizenship, 1890–1945*. Chapel Hill: University of North Carolina Press, 2006.

McKenzie, R.D. "The Rise of Metropolitan Communities." In *Recent Social Trends in the United States: Report of the President's Research Committee on Social Trends*, 443–496. New York: McGraw-Hill, 1933.

Merrill, Arch. "Wayland: Railroad Child, Potato Empire Capital." *Rochester Democrat and Chronicle*, August 17, 1947.

Merrill, Arch. "A Visit with Sally Patchin." *Rochester Democrat and Chronicle*, magazine section, May 21, 1950.

Moody, Jan. "Sears, Roebuck & Co.: America's Catalog (1888–2010)." *Journal of Antiques & Collectibles*, March 2019, 32–33.

"More About That Three-Wheeled Auto." *Livonia Gazette*, May 3, 1929.

"More Men Leave to Join Colors." *East Aurora Advertiser*, August 8, 1918.

"Mrs. Lulu Scott Backus Dies, Expert Ceramic Designer." *Rochester Democrat and Chronicle*, August 28, 1955.

"Mrs. Patchin Dies." *Rochester Democrat and Chronicle*, November 19, 1958,.

Mukerji, Betty-Lou. *Chinese Sewing Baskets*. Bloomington, Indiana: Authorhouse, 2008.

Murray, Lawrence L. "Complacency, Competition and Cooperation: The Film Industry Responds to the Challenge of Television." *Journal of Popular Film* 6, no. 1 (1977): 47–70.

"Neighborhood News." *Wayland Register*, February 21, 1924, 3.

"Neighborhood News." *Geneseo Livingston Republican*, April 29, 1937, 7.

Nelson, Mac. *Twenty West: The Great Road Across America*. Albany: State University of New York Press, 2008.

"New Building is Being Erected by C. E. Wemett." *Lima Recorder*, September 13, 1945.

New Hope Fellowship. East Bloomfield, New York. Historical documents, vertical file folder. Reviewed November 28, 2018.

"New Vacation Center Called Egypt Valley Has Just Been Completed in Bristol Hills." *Livonia Gazette*, May 26, 1949.

"Novelty Factory Located Here." *Rushville Chronicle and Gorham New Age*, 1925.

"Nunda Men Open Avon Supermarket." *Nunda News*, August 9, 1956.

"Obituary: Clarence E. Wemett." *Livonia Gazette*, November 9, 1961.

"Obituary: Mark Wemett." *Rochester Democrat and Chronicle*, January 7, 2015.

"Obituary: Mrs. Honni [*sic*] Coley." *Wayland Register*, September 17, 1953.

O'Connor, Lois. "Tompkins County Women on the Center Stage at State Fair." *Ithaca Journal*, September 5, 1952.

O'Connor, Lois. "State Fair: Ithaca JaynCees Do Well." *Ithaca Journal*, September 10, 1953.

"Oil Company Tourist Camp is a Good Advertisement." *National Petroleum News*, April 24, 1929, 93–94.

"Old Branchport Baptist Church is Razed on 100th Anniversary; Preserve Pulpit, Vane and Organ." *Elmira Star Gazette*, September 28, 1934.

"Old Branchport Church is Razed on 100th Birthday." *Geneva Daily Times*, September 28, 1934.

"'Old Halfway House' Former Collins Place, Being Revamped by C.E. Wemett." *Livonia Gazette*, April 22, 1937.

Olney, Martha L. *Buy Now, Pay Later: Advertising, Credit, and Consumer Durables in the 1920s*. Chapel Hill: University of North Carolina Press, 1991.

"On Japanese Art." *Rochester Democrat and Chronicle*, May 25, 1897.

"On Way to Federal Prison." *Burlington* (Vermont) *Daily Free Press*, November 26, 1906.

Osborne, Harold. "The Aesthetic Concept of Craftsmanship." *British Journal of Aesthetics* 17, no. 2 (1977): 138–48.

"Our Industries." *Wayland Register*, March 15, 1928.

"Out of Step." *Geneva Times*, September 10, 1955.

"Out of the Past." *Livonia Gazette*, August 6, 1953.

"Owner of Avon Copper Shop Dies." *Tonawanda News*, January 15, 1973.

Parker, Donald E. Death notice, *Rochester Democrat and Chronicle*, March 24, 1998(a).

Parker, Donald E. Death notice, *Mendon-Honeoye Falls-Lima Sentinel*, April 2, 1998(b).

Parry, Linda. *Textiles of the Arts and Crafts Movement*. New York: Thames and Hudson, 1988.

Parshall, Hannah. Email correspondence to Bruce A. Austin, November 30, 2018.

Patton, Phil. *Open Road: A Celebration of the American Highway*. New York: Simon and Schuster, 1986.

"Penn Yan Corporations." *Penn Yan Express*, December 18, 1924.

Perkins, Dorothy Wilson. "Education in Ceramic Art in the United States." PhD diss., Ohio State University, 1956.

Peterich, Gerda. "Cobblestone Architecture of Upstate New York." *Journal of the Society of Architectural Historians* 15, no. 2 (May 1956): 12–18.

"Plail Family Legacy Topic at Historical Presentation." *Dansville Genesee Country Express*, October 14, 1999.

Poling-Kempes, Lesley. *The Harvey Girls: Women Who Opened the West*. New York: Paragon House, 1989.

Pooler, Jim. *Why We Shop: Emotional Rewards and Retail Strategies*. Westport, CT: Praeger, 2003.

Porter, Daniel R. "Route 20 Ribbon of Memories." *Heritage*, NYS Historical Association, unpaginated, 1988.

Porter, Mark. "Avon Landmark Consumed in Tragic Fire," *The Mendon-Honeoye Falls-Lima Sentinel*, April 2, 1998.

"Pottery Making is Fun for Students at Keuka College Taking Part in New Program." *Corning Evening Leader*, March 24, 1950.

"Pottery Making to be Demonstrated for Federated Society." *Bath Steuben Courier*, July 2, 1937.

"Praise from Our Competitors" (advertisement). *New York Tribune*, January 7, 1915; also *New York Herald*, January 7, 1915.

"Prizes Awarded Winners at Fair." *Penn Yan Express*, September 4, 1924, and *Rushville Chronicle and Gorham New Age*, September 12, 1924.

Pye, David. *The Nature and Art of Workmanship*. Cambridge: Cambridge University Press, 1968.

Quinan, Jack. *Frank Lloyd Wright's Larkin Building: Myth and Fact*. Cambridge, MA: MIT Press, 1987.

Quinan, Jack. "Elbert Hubbard's Roycroft." In *Head, Heart and Hand: Elbert Hubbard and the Roycrofters*, edited by Marie Via and Marjorie B. Searl, 1–19. Rochester: University of Rochester Press, 1994.

Quinn, Sister Caitrona. "The League of American Wheelmen and the Good Roads Movement, 1880–1912, with Particular Emphasis on the Trans-Mississippi

West." Unpublished manuscript, August 1968. http://john-s-allen.com/LAW_1939-1955/history/quinn-good-roads.pdf. Accessed April 24, 2019.

Rae, John B. *The Road and the Car in American Life*. Cambridge: MIT Press, 1971.

Ramsaye, Terry. *A Million and One Nights: A History of the Motion Picture through 1925*. New York: Simon and Schuster, 1926.

Randall, Richard S. *Censorship of the Movies: The Social and Political Control of a Mass Medium*. Madison: University of Wisconsin Press, 1968.

Reece, William. Email correspondence to Bruce A. Austin, November 29–December 3, 2018.

Reports of International Arbitral Awards. "Elbert Hubbard II, Individually and as Executor of the Last Will and Testament of Elbert Hubbard, and Others (United States) *v.* Germany, and Elbert Hubbard II, as Executor of the Last Will and Testament of Alice Hubbard, and Miriam Hubbard Roelofs (United States) v. Germany." October 2, 1924, 452–56. United Nations, 2006.

"Resort Near Bushville Opened to the Public." *Batavia Daily News*, May 31, 1923.

"Restored White Horse Tavern at East Avon Will Be a Center of Interest." *Livonia Gazette*, August 6, 1953.

Revels, Tracy J. *Sunshine Paradise: A History of Florida Tourism*. Gainesville: University Press of Florida, 2011.

Reynolds, Carol. "Wayland Resident Keeps Patchin Legacy Alive." *Dansville Genesee Country Express*, August 6, 1998.

Rhoads, William B. "The Colonial Revival and American Nationalism." *Journal of the Society of Architectural Historians* 35, no. 4 (December 1976): 239–|54.

Rhoads, William B. "Colonial Revival in American Craft: Nationalism and the Opposition to Multicultural and Regional Traditions." In *Revivals! Diverse Traditions: The History of Twentieth-Century Craft, 1920–1945*, edited by Janet Kardon, 41–54. New York: Harry N. Abrams, 1994.

Riddle, Peggy. Director, Office of History and Culture, Denton, Texas. Email to Bruce A. Austin, August 14, 2018.

Risatti, Howard. "Metaphysical Implications of Function, Material, and Technique in Craft." In *Skilled Work: American Craft in the Renwick Gallery*, edited by Kenneth R. Trapp, 31–55. Washington, DC: Smithsonian Institution Press, 1998.

"RIT Honors 7 Upon Retiring." *Rochester Democrat and Chronicle*, June 13, 1952.

"Roadside Business Expanded Rapidly." *Batavia Daily News*, 1939.

"'Roadside Craftsmen' at East Bloomfield Leased to 'Woodcroftery Shops' of Wayland." *Livonia Gazette*, February 19, 1953.

"Roadside Handcraft Shop Extends Hearty Welcome." *Cooperstown Otsego Farmer*, July 17, 1942.

Roberts, Edna. Obituary. *Geneseo Livingston County Leader*, January 20, 1965.

Rogers, Everett M. *Diffusion of Innovations*. New York: Free Press, 1962.

Ronan, Kristine K. "Painting Print: N.C. Wyeth's Illustrations for The Last of the Mohicans (1919)" in *N.C. Wyeth: New Perspectives*, edited by Jessica May and Christine B. Podmaniczky, 44–57. New Haven, CT: Yale University Press, 2019.

"Rotarians Hear about Roadside Craftsmen." *Livonia Gazette*, November 16, 1950.

Rotzoll, Kim B. "The Captive Audience: The Troubled Odyssey of Cinema Advertising." In Vol. 3 of *Current Research in Film: Audiences, Economics and Law*, edited by Bruce A. Austin, 72–87. Norwood, NJ: Ablex, 1987.

"Route 20 Businessman Join to Combat Thruway Loss." *Fredonia Censor*, September 1, 1955.

"Route 20 Businessmen Plan 'Freeway' Brochure." *LeRoy Gazette*, March 29, 1956.

"Routes 5 & 20 Freeway Group Reports Membership of 1,000." *Geneva Times*, November 10, 1955.

"Rt. 20 Association Will Issue Brochure to Promote Highway." *Geneva Times*, February 28, 1956.

"Rt. 20 Freeway Assn. to Issue Advertising Book." *Fredonia Censor*, March 15, 1956.

"Rt. 20 Freeway Group Active." *Lima Recorder*, May 24, 1956, p. 4; also *Livonia Gazette*, May 24, 1956.

Roycroft Campus Corporation: http://roycroftcampuscorporation.typepad.com/roycroftcampuscorporation/2007/04/walter_u_jennin.html. Accessed May 2018.

Runyan, Kathryn. "A Content Analysis of Advertisements in *The Fra* and *Craftsman* Magazines, 1908–1916." MS thesis, Rochester Institute of Technology, 2013.

Rust, Robert, Kitty Turgeon-Rust, Marie Via, and Marjorie B. Searl. "Alchemy in East Aurora: Roycroft Metal Arts." In *Head, Heart and Hand: Elbert Hubbard and the Roycrofters*, edited by Marie Via and Marjorie B. Searl, 75–96. Rochester: University of Rochester Press, 1994.

Ryan, Bryce, and Neal C. Gross. "The Diffusion of Hybrid Corn Seed in Two Iowa Communities." *Rural Sociology* 8, no. 1 (March 1943): 15–24.

"Sally Patchin Funeral Tomorrow; Home Bureau Founder was 84." *Dansville Genesee Country Express*, November 20, 1958.

"Says Richcraft." *Cohocton Valley Times-Index*, November 12, 1947.

Schatz, Thomas. *Hollywood Genres: Formulas, Filmmaking, and the Studio System.* Philadelphia: Temple University Press, 1981.

Schinto, Jeanne. "Good Fellows: The Walpole Society." *Maine Antique Digest*, November 2015–March 2016.

Schlenker, Sandra Bortle. *Elton Park and the Monument of East Bloomfield.* East Bloomfield, New York: Historical Society of the Town of East Bloomfield, 2008.

Schmit, Henry. "Overnight Rest-Cabins Spreading." *Literary Digest*, June 9, 1934.

Schroeder, Virginia, and Marilyn Herr-Gesell. *Memories and Traditions of Bloomfield, 1789–1989, Sketchbook II.* East Bloomfield, New York: East Bloomfield Bicentennial Committee, 1989.

Schudson, Michael S. "Review Essay: On Tourism and Modern Culture." *American Journal of Sociology* 84, no. 5 (March 1979): 1249–58.

Schwartz, Barry. "The Social Psychology of the Gift." *American Journal of Sociology* 73, no. 1 (July 1967): 1–11.

Scott, Quinta, and Susan Croce Kelly. *Route 66: The Highway and its People.* Norman: University of Oklahoma Press, 1988.

Seiler, Cotten. *Republic of Drivers: A Cultural History of Automobility.* Chicago: University of Chicago Press, 2008.

Sennett, Richard. *The Craftsman.* New Haven, CT: Yale University Press, 2008.

Shelgren, Olaf William Jr., Cary Lattin, and Robert W. Frasch. *Cobblestone Landmarks of New York State.* Syracuse: Syracuse University Press, 1978.

Shell, Ellen Ruppel. *Cheap: The High Cost of Discount Culture.* New York: Penguin Press, 2009.

"Shell Service Station to Mark 18th Anniversary." *Mount Morris Enterprise*, June 22, 1949.

"Sheriff's Sale." *Penn Yan Democrat*, December 30, 1927.

"Should be in the Museum." *Livonia Gazette*, March 29, 1929.

"Silversmith at Hemlock Dies." *Livonia Gazette*, December 4, 1941.

Simmons, Becky. "Craft Education and the First Thirty Years of the School for American Craftsmen." In Bruce A. Austin, *Frans Wildenhain, 1950–75: Creative and Commercial American Ceramics at Mid-Century*, 79–121. Rochester: Printing Applications Laboratory, 2012.

Simonet, Thomas. "Industry." *Film Comment*, January–February 1978, 72–73.

Sklar, Robert. *Movie-Made America: A Cultural History of American Movies.* New York: Vintage, 1976.

Skvirsky, Salome Aguilera. *The Process Genre: Cinema and the Aesthetics of Labor.* Durham, NC: Duke University Press, 2020.

Smith, Mary Ann. *Gustav Stickley: The Craftsman.* Syracuse: Syracuse University Press, 1983.

Snow, Richard. "The Father of All Patent Trolls." Forbes Leadership Forum, July 30, 2013. https://www.forbes.com/sites/forbesleadershipforum/2013/07/30/the-father-of-all-patent-trolls/#379f413edcdf. Accessed February 25, 2019.

"Society of Arts and Crafts." *Rochester Democrat and Chronicle*, December 8, 1897.

Sontag, Susan. "Notes on 'Camp.'" *Partisan Review* 31, no. 4 (Fall 1964): 515–30.

"Spare Time Profits." *Geneva Daily Times*, April 17, 1947.

Stanger, Howard R. "From Factory to Family: The Creation of a Corporate Culture in the Larkin Company of Buffalo, New York." *Business History Review* 74, no. 3 (Autumn 2000): 407–33.

Stanger, Howard R. "The Larkin Club of Ten: Consumer Buying Clubs and Mail-Order Commerce, 1890-1940." *Enterprise & Society* 9, no. 1 (2008): 125–64.

"State Group to Plug Routes 5, 20." *Rochester Democrat and Chronicle*, March 6, 1956.

Steele, Lena S. "East Bloomfield Craftsman Produces Own Violins." *Rochester Democrat and Chronicle*, September 7, 1941.

Steiner, J. F. "Recreation and Leisure Time Activities." In *Recent Social Trends in the United States: Report of the President's Research Committee on Social Trends*, 912–57. New York: McGraw-Hill, 1933.

Stickley, Gustav. *New Furniture from the Workshop of Gustave Stickley, Cabinetmaker, Syracuse, NY*, 1900.

Stickley, Gustav. "The Use and Abuse of Machinery, and Its Relation to the Arts and Crafts." *The Craftsman*, November 1906, 202–27.

Stickley, Gustav. "Als ik Kan: Life on the Automobile Basis and Where it is Leading Us." *The Craftsman*, September 1910, 711–12.

Stickley, Gustav. "Als ik Kan: The Motor-Car and Country Life." *The Craftsman*, May 1911, 227.

Stickley, Gustav. "Als ik Kan: The Motor Car and the City Man." *The Craftsman*, July 1911, 420–21.

Stickley, Gustav. "Als ik Kan: A Vacation in a Motor Car." *The Craftsman*, August 1911, 527–28.

Stickley, Gustav. "Als ik Kan: The Motor Car for Hygiene and Humanity." *The Craftsman*, September 1911, 627.

Stillinger, Elizabeth. *The Antiquers: The Lives and Careers, the Deals, the Finds, the Collections of the Men and Women Who Were Responsible for the Changing Taste in American Antiques, 1850–1930*. New York: Knopf, 1980.

Surdam, David George. *Century of the Leisured Masses: Entertainment and the Transformation of Twentieth-Century America*. New York: Oxford University Press, 2015.

Swanton, Carolyn. "Arthur H. Cole of East Avon–Master Craftsman." *Avon Preservation & Historical Society Newsletter* (Spring 2009): 1.

"The Old Guard to Return to Roycroft." *Buffalo Evening News*, December 6, 1915.

"The Woodcroftery Now Located in Batavia." *Wayland Register*, February 20, 1936.

"35 Years Out of School." *The Saratogian*, December 3, 1935.

Thomas, Justin W. "Herber C. Kimball: A Mormon Potter from Western New York." *Maine Antique Digest*, April 2022, 138–41.

Thompson, Warren S., and P. K. Whelpton. "The Population of the Nation." In *Recent Social Trends in the United States: Report of the President's Research Committee on Social Trends*, 1–58. New York: McGraw-Hill, 1933.

"Thoughts by a Country Woman." *Wayland Register*, 1937.

"Three Firms OKd for SBA Loans." *Buffalo Courier-Express*, April 22, 1960, p. 19.

"Thruway and Freeway." *Rochester Democrat and Chronicle*, September 6, 1955, p. 22.

"Thruway and Freeway." *Albany Knickerbocker News*, September 9, 1955.

Thruway Chronology. Albany: New York State Thruway Authority, n.d.

Thwing, Lena M. "What's Business Reverse? Nothing to Youth Who Copies Ancestor Carving Art for Living." *Rochester Democrat and Chronicle*, June 2, 1935.

Till, Michael J. *Along New York's Route 20*. Charleston, SC: Arcadia, 2011.

Trapp, Kenneth. *The Arts and Crafts Movement in California: Living the Good Life*. New York: Abbeville Press, 1933.

Trietley, Virginia. "Artistry is Interesting Work for East Pembroke Woman," *Batavia Daily News*, April 7, 1951.

Tucker, Kevin W. *Gustav Stickley and the American Arts & Crafts Movement*. New Haven, CT: Yale University Press, 2010.

"25th Anniversary Sale." *Spencerport Suburban News*, August 7, 1990, and August 14, 1990.

"Unable to Use Autocamp." *Rome* (New York) *Daily Sentinel*, July 27, 1922.

"Vagabonds-deLux and the Plain of the Tourist Trails." *Literary Digest*, June 19, 1931, 36–38.

Via, Marie. "The Roycroft Pottery." In *Head, Heart and Hand: Elbert Hubbard and the Roycrofters*, edited by Marie Via and Marjorie B. Searl, 115. Rochester: University of Rochester Press, 1994.

"Visit Shop." *Canandaigua Daily Messenger*, September 20, 1948.

Wade, Diana J., comp. *The War Years in Bloomfield 1941–1945*. East Bloomfield: Town of East Bloomfield, October, 1988.

Ward, Hilda. "The Automobile in the Suburbs from a Woman's Point of View." *Suburban Life*, November 1907, pp. 269-271.

Ward, Ken. "Crafty Ads: Branding and Product Nesting in the American Arts and Crafts Magazine *The Craftsman*." *Journal of Magazine & New Media Research* 17, no. 2 (Winter 2017): 1–20.

"Wayland Industry Moves to Bushville." *Batavia Daily News*, February 21, 1936.

"Wayland Ready for 'Patchin Day.'" *Dansville Genesee Country Express*, April 1, 1993.

Weigle, Marta. "From Desert to Disney World: The Santa Fe Railway and the Fred Harvey Company Display the Indian Southwest." *Journal of Anthropological Research* 45, no. 1 (Spring 1989): 115–37.

Weinberger, Julius. "Economic Aspects of Recreation." *Harvard Business Review* 15 (Summer 1937): 448–63.

Weisberg, Barbara. *Talking to the Dead: Kate and Maggie Fox and the Rise of Spiritualism*. San Francisco: HarperOne, 2005.

Wells, Christopher W. *Car Culture: An Environmental History*. Seattle: University of Washington Press, 2013.

"Wemett Co. and Roadside Craftsmen Employees and Families Are Entertained at Egypt Valley." *Livonia Gazette*, October 13, 1949.

"Wemett & Co. Host to Shell Station Operators and Other Guests at Party in East Bloomfield Thursday Night." *Livonia Gazette*, May 6, 1937.

"Wemett Corp. Buys White Horse Tavern at East Avon." *Livonia Gazette*, May 28, 1953.

Wemett, Laurel. "The Roadside Craftsmen," typescript dated 1999 and included in New Hope Fellowship vertical file, East Bloomfield, New York, 2018.

Wemett, Laurel. "A Group of Spirited Workers: A History of the Roadside Craftsmen." DVD, 1999.

Wemett, Laurel. Email to Bruce A. Austin, October 17, 2018.

Wemett, Laurel. Email to Bruce A. Austin, June 29, 2020.

"Wemett Leases Shell Stations." *Livonia Gazette*, January 6, 1938.

"Wemett Pottery Has Moved to Rochester." *Livonia Gazette*, September 30, 1932.

"Wemetts Sell Camp to Ontario Scouts." *Livonia Gazette*, July 30, 1959.

Werbizky, Tatiana G. "Accommodating the Traveler: The Development of the Tourist Cabin Court on U.S. Route 20 in New York State Between 1925 and 1955." MA thesis, Cornell University, 1992.

"White Horse Inn at East Avon Destroyed in $100,000 Fire." *Buffalo Evening News*, August 1, 1955.

"White Horse Tavern." *Rochester Democrat and Chronicle*, August 2, 1955.

Wik, Reynold M. "The Early Automobile and the American Farmer." In *The Automobile and American Culture*, edited by David L. Lewis and Laurence Goldstein, 37–47. Ann Arbor: University of Michigan Press, 1983.

Wilensky, Harold L. "The Professionalization of Everyone?" *American Journal of Sociology* 70, no. 2 (September 1964): 137–58.

Willey, Malcolm M., and Stuart A. Rice. "The Agencies of Communication." In *Recent Social Trends in the United States: Report of the President's Research Committee on Social Trends*, 167–217. New York: McGraw-Hill, 1933.

Willms, Melinda Burris. "A Practical Spirituality: Merchandising Mountain Handicraft." *Style 1900* (Winter/Spring 1999): 61–66.

Wilson, Richard Guy. "Introduction." In *From Architecture to Object: Masterworks of the American Arts & Crafts Movement*, edited by Hirschl and Adler Galleries, 10–21. New York: Dutton Studio Books, 1989.

Wilson, Richard Guy, Shaun Eyring, and Kenny Marotta, eds. *Re-creating the American Past: Essays on the Colonial Revival*. Charlottesville: University of Virginia Press, 2006.

Witzel, Michael Karl. *Route 66 Remembered*. Osceola, WI: Motorbooks International, 1996.

Wolfe, Tom. "The 'Me' Decade and the Third Great Awakening." *New York Magazine*, August 23, 1976, 26–40.

Woloson, Wendy A. *Crap: A History of Cheap Stuff in America*. Chicago: University of Chicago Press, 2020.

"Woman Painter, 72, Finished Big Order." *Batavia Daily News*, December 6, 1941.

"Woodcraft Firm Dissolves." *Geneva Daily Times*, April 28, 1928.

"Woodcroftery in Wayland Plant." *Wayland Register*, July 23, 1942. http://www.wemett.net.

"Woodcroftery Shop Had a Busy Season." *Batavia Daily News*, December 23, 1936.

York, Hildreth J. "New Deal Craft Programs and Their Social Implications." In *Craft in the Machine Age: The History of Twentieth-Century American Craft, 1920–1945*, edited by Janet Kardon, 55–61. New York: Harry N. Abrams, 1995.

"You Sing America, Why Not SEE IT [*sic*]?" Advertisement for the Denver Tourist Bureau. *Chicago Daily Tribune*, April 27, 1921.

Zaiden, Emily. "An Unyielding Commitment to Craft: Aileen Osborn Webb and the American Craft Council." *Archives of American Art Journal* 50, no. 3/4 (Fall 2011): 10–15.

Index

Page numbers in *italics* indicate illustrations.

advertising, 112, 121, 125–46; billboard, 9, 40, 42, 199

Aerni, April Laskey, 172–73

Alfred University, 11, 90, 110, 188n23; Bloomfield Pottery and, 165–66, *167*; School for American Craftsmen at, 167, 168; Wemett and, 166, 168

Allen, Paul, 141

America House, 11, 173–74

American Craft Enterprises, 173

American Craftsman's Cooperative Council, 46

American Craftsmen's Educational Council, 173

American Hotel (Lima, NY), 22–24

amusement parks, 98

antique shops, 14–15, 54, 150, 182

art: categories of, 10; craft versus, 6, 10, 179, 211n9. *See also specific styles*

Art Deco, 23, 73, 126

Art Nouveau, 197n33

Arts and Crafts movement, 4, 52–61, 178; Colonial Revival style and, 3, 53–55, 57, 86; exhibitions of, 154–55; Hubbard and, 8; Ludwig's exhibition of, 11, 60; Modernism and, 3, 53–55, 57, 86; Morris and, 86; paradoxes of, 58–59; Plail Brothers and, 117–18; popularity of, 5; in Rochester, 160–63; scholarship on, 15, 55–56, 198n41; Shaker influence on, 52, 55, 56, 198n41; Webb and, 11–12; Wemett and, 52–53, 60–61, 82–83; Woodcroftery and, 117

Asawa, Ruth, 213n38

auto ownership, 9, 42

autocamping, 39–41

automobility, 2, 4, 78, 85, 171; Belasco on, 192n53; consumerism and, 29–31, 80, 184–85; road-building projects and, 9, 30–31; Seiler on, 193n13; tourism and, 7, 38–41

Avon Coppersmith, 2–6, 51, 99–100, 182; advertising of, *137*, 139–44; aesthetic appeal of, 178–79; bookends of, *181*; catalogues of, 15, 125, 133–39; Cole at, 97–103, 147; decorative styles of, 53–55; demise of, 144, 172; fire at, 63–64; legacy of, 176, 184–85; logo of, 133–34, *134*, *137*, 143, 150; pricing policies of, 80–81; product line of, 132–39, *135*; Roycroft products versus, 56,

Avon Coppersmith *(continued)*
133–38, 179, 209n12; sale of, 114,
147–48, 154; Shop One versus,
213n38. *See also* Wemett, Clarence
E.

Backus, Lulu Scott, 163–65, 168
Baggs, Arthur E., 164, 165
Baker, Ernestine, 46
basket-painting, 45, 47–48
Belasco, Warren, 41, 78, 83
Benedict Studios (Syracuse), 210n18
Berea Student Craft Industries (KY),
46, 188n24
Berean Gospel Church, 120
Berry, Albert, 158
bicycles, 29, 30, 191n39
billboards, 9, 40, 42, 199
Binns, Charles Fergus, 93, 162, 164,
165, 166, 212n29
Black Mountain College (NC), 172,
188n23
Bloomfield Pottery, 18, 21, *167*;
aesthetic appeal of, 178–79;
Alfred University and, 165–66,
167; brochure of, 91–93, *92*;
competitors of, 35, 45; creation of,
36–37; Daugherty at, 90–97, *92*,
95, *96*; history of, 204n2; labels
of, *96*; media coverage of, 90–91;
Rochester store of, 112. *See also*
Roadside Craftsmen
bookends, 15, 67, 180–81, *181*
Bourdieu, Pierre, 177
Boy Scouts, 78, 106
Bragdon, Claude, 161
Branchport (NY) Baptist Church,
48–50, *51*, 74
Braznell, W. Scott, 46
Briarcliffe (Ossining, NY), 172
broadcasting, 31, 33–34, 192n53
Brotherhood of the New Life, 8

Bullock, Homer, 38; bankruptcy of,
105, 107; Coley and, 118; family of,
106–8, 206n7
Bybee Cornelison Pottery (KY), 193n7
Byrdcliffe Colony (Woodstock, NY),
35, 60, 172, 193n2

camping, 39–41
Canadian crafts movement, 213n6
card game, 78, *79*
Carnegie Institute of Technology,
188n23
Castle, Wendell, 214n24
Cathers, David, 14, 198n34
Chautauqua Institution, 8, 111
Cherokees, 94
Chester, Eleanor, 37, 105, 106, 110
Chicago School of Design, 188n23
Chromewald, 86
Civil War monuments, 25–26
Civilian Conservation Corps, 172
Clark, Robert Judson, 155, 198n41
Cleveland School of Art, 188n23
Clingman, George, 197n33
cobblestone houses, 25–26
Cole, Arthur Harold, 2, 64–65, 71,
153–54; family of, 15, 147, 200n9;
Jennings and, 15, 70, 133–35, 179;
Kipp and, 15, 70, 72, 179; media
coverage of, 64–67, *66*, 200n9;
resignation of, 72; Wemett and,
73–74, 159
Cole, Don, 147
Cole, Jennifer, 136
Cole, Tom, 13, 134, 147
Coley, Johanna "Honnie," 48, 116–18
Coley, John Plail, 48, 116–20
Colonial Revival styles, 3; Arts and
Crafts movement and, 53–55, 57,
86
commercialization, 27, 42; aesthetic
values and, 178; Bourdieu on, 177;

gift-giving and, 6, 18; monetization versus, 187n5; of travel, 6–7, 9

Commission on Recent Social Trends, 193n15

consumerism, 42, 58; Arts and Crafts movement and, 3; automobility and, 29–31, 80, 184–85; broadcasting and, 33–34, 192n53

Corby, Mildred Esther, 200n9

Cowan, Guy, 165

Cox, Paul E., 163, 165, 212n29

Craft (capitalized), 2, 54, 81, 103; college curricula in, 172; definition of, 187n5; guildlike training in, 11, 70; Kessler on, 175–76; professionalization of, 3, 11, 172–73, 177, 213n6; tourism's influences on, 183

craft (lowercased), 173; art versus, 6, 10, 179, 211n9; folk art versus, 10, 187n7, 211n9

Craftsman Workshops, 81, 126

Cranbrook Academy, 172, 188n23

Crawford, Alan, 210n19

Croughton, Amy H., 36–37, 45, 93–94, 164

Crumrine, Chester W., 202n42

Cuba, 105, 106

Curtis, Clarence N., 111

Dartmouth College, 168

Daugherty, Guy, 2, 36, 38, 46; at Bloomfield Pottery, 90–97, *92*, *95*, *96*; celebrity of, 110; family of, 95; Wemett and, 159

Daughters of the American Revolution, 54

decorative arts styles, 3, 53–55

Delco Products (Rochester), 99

Denning, Gertrude, 110

Dennison, Kitty Ann Parker, 120, 133, 146

diners, roadside, 43

Disney Corporation, 157

Dispenza, Charles, 214n29

Dixie Highway, 39

do-it-yourself (DIY), 177. *See also* "see-it-made"

Drain, Hugh, 19, 193n7

drive-in movie theaters, 97–98, 103, 205n23

Drumm, Guy Merlin, *167*

Eastman, George, 169, 191n50

Easy Rider (1969 film), 195n47

Edison, Thomas, 8

Egypt Valley summer camp, 114–16, 159

Egyptianism, 54

Eldred Company, 19

Elim Bible Institute and College, 24

Ellis, Harvey, 161, 211n13

Elverhoj (Milton-on Hudson, NY), 172

Elwood, Marguerite, 111

Erie Canal, 9, 26, 27, 148

factory production methods, 4–5, 60, 122–23; Glencroft and, 145; Taylorism and, 2, 31. *See also* handcraftsmanship

Fairchild Award, 163–64

Federal-Aid Road Act (1916), 9, 29–30, 33

Federal Art Project, 54, 172

Federal Bureau of Investigation (FBI), 40

Federal Highway Act (1956), 9

Finch, Elnathan, 48–49

"Fletcherize," 103

Flink, James J., 193n13

folk art: categories of, 10; cobblestone houses as, 26; craft versus, 10, 187n7, 211n9; "Southern Pottery," 179

folk pottery, 205b18
Fonda, Henry, 195n47
Fonda, Peter, 195n47
Ford, Henry, 29–30, 54, 192n50
Fosdick, Marion, 166
Fox sisters (spiritualists), 8
Fulper Pottery Company, *59*
furniture manufacturers: Plail, 48, 116–18, 120; Stickley, 53, 55–56, 59; Tobey, 197n33

Genesee College (NY), 24
Genesee Wesleyan Seminary, 24
Genessee Country Village and Museum, 198n37
Gertz, Chester, 120
gift shops, 36, 45, 76, 84–85
Girl Scouts, 114
Glassgow School, 70
Glencroft Coppersmiths, 144–46, 210n17
Glidden Pottery (Alfred, NY), 133, 165–66
Goffman, Erving, 195n48
Good Roads Associations, 29, 191n39
Grapes of Wrath (1939 film), 195n47
Great Depression, 31–32, 83, 107; movie industry during, 44; unemployment during, 3
Greek Revival style, 26
Gregory, Waylande, 164
Grueby Pottery (Boston), 89, 162, 178
Gunlocke, William H., 117
Gurdjieff, George Ivanovich, 174

Hallmark card company, 84, 139
handcraftsmanship, 10, 59, 81, 122–23; Stickley on, 60. *See also* craft
Harris, Thomas Lake, 8
Hart, Val, 42–43
Harvey, Fred, 27, 157–58, 183
Hedglon, Mary, 7

Hemlock Forge, 54, 110, 111, 129, 153
Highway Act (1921), 30
Hill, John, 22, 29
Hollingshead, Richard, Jr., 97–98, 205n23
Hollywood. *See* movie industry
Hoover, Herbert, 33, 38, 191n39
Hoover, J. Edgar, 40
Hubbard, Elbert, 8, 56, 60, 67–69, 118; catalogues of, 138; death of, 71, 201n15; on Mission style, 197n33
Hubbard, Elbert "Bert," II, 71–72, 201n15
Hudson Motor Car Company, 9
Hunter, Dard, 70

International Style, 23. *See also* Art Deco
internet, 9, 31, 34–36
Interstate Highway System, 9, 86, 154, 159

Jennings, Ada, 204n18
Jennings, Anna, 204n18
Jennings, Rixford, 73, 133–34, *134*
Jennings, Walter, 71, 110; Cole and, 15, 70, 133–35, 179; Kipp and, 15, 68–69, 179; Wemett and, 73–74
Jermyn, William A., 208n63
Jessup, Elon, 39
Joy's Lamplight Shoppe, 63, 148

Kardon, Janet, 172
Kelly, Susan Croce, 30–31, 43
Kenzie, Ruth, 112–13, 114
Kessler, Jane, 175–76
Keuka College, 114
Kipp, Karl, 15, 68–72, 85, 138–39, 179
Kirkpatrick, Cornwall, 158

Larkin Soap Company, 28, 67, 80
League of American Wheelmen, 29, 191n39
Lewis, Sinclair, 75
Lima, NY, 22, 23
Limbert, Charles, 59
Ludwig, Coy, 11, 60
Lusitania sinking, 71, 201n15
Lynd, Robert, 42

MacCannell, Dean, 43, 76, 77, 195n48
mail-order companies, 8, 75–76, 151; catalogues of, 15, 67–70, 125, 171; Roadside Craftsmen, 125–32, *128–30*; Roycroft, 67–69, 126, 177, 209n12; Sears, Roebuck, 28, 80
Majestic Furniture (Mexico, NY), 118
Manchester, W. Eugene, 111
Marblehead Pottery, 164, 165, 212n18
March, Louise, 174–75
Marley, Doris, 166, *167*
Martin, Darwin, 55, 118
McCall, Jane Byrd, 35
McCaul, Stanley, 49
McDade, Matt, 159
McHugh, Joseph, 197n33
Mechanics Institute (Rochester), 11, 90, 111, 161–63, 188n23; Backus and, 163–65; Rochester Institute of Technology and, 163; Wemett and, 169
Merrill, Arch, 48
metropolitanism, 41, 194n15
Miller, Roger, 40–41
Mission style, 52, 55, 197n33
Modernism, 3; Arts and Craft movement and, 53–55, 57, 86
monetization, 187n5. *See also* commercialization
Montezuma Wildlife Refuge, 14
Morelli, Laura, 211n9
Mormonism, 8

Morris, William, 139
motels, 39–40, 44
movie industry, 3, 8, 42, 44, 192n53; commercialization of, 44; drive-in theaters and, 97–98, 103, 205n23
Museum of Contemporary Crafts, 46
museums, 43, 76, 173, 195n48
My Man Godfrey (1936 film), 2

Naples Mill School of Arts and Crafts (NY), 214n24
Natchez Trace, 43
Native American craftsmen, 43
Nelligan, William, *102*
Nelson, Mac, 7–8, 35, 190n22
New York State Thruway, 100–101, 116, 151, 154, 158–59
Newcomb College (New Orleans), 163, 206n18
Newell, Harriet Haskell, 200n9
Niederlander, Fred, 145
Nott, Raymond, 139
Noyes, John Humphrey, 8
Nutting, Wallace, 53, 86

O'Connor, Lois, 95
Ohr, George, 158
Old Mission Kopperkraft, 59
Old Town Collectibles (FL), 151
Olds, Alice Mae, 200n9
Oneida Community, 8, 55
Onondaga Metal Shop, 210n18
Orientalism, 54
Overbeck, Elizabeth, 165

Paley, Albert, 213n38
Park-In Theatres, 97–98
Parker, Clark, 148
Parker, Don, Jr., 151
Parker, Donald E., 64, 148–51
Parker, Erwin, 148
Parker, Glidden, 165–66, 168

244 | Index

Parker, Joyce, 148–51
Parker Brothers' "Touring" card game, 78, *79*
Patchin, Sally Nutall, 45, 47–48
Penland School of Craft (NC), 172
Pennzoil, 19
Peoples Oil Company, 39
Pewabic Pottery, 164
Philadelphia Centennial International Exposition (1876), 53, 54, 88
Plail, John, 116, 117
Plail, Joseph, 117
Plail Brothers Chair Co., 48, 116–18, 120
plank roads, 9, 22, 23. *See also* road-building
Ponce de León, Juan, 109
Pond, Theodore Hanford, 158, 161, 162
Pope, Albert Augustus, 29
postal service, 28, 79–80, 209n12. *See also* mail-order companies
Prip, Jack, 12
professionalization, 3, 11, 172–73, 177, 213n6
Ptolemy of Alexandria, 8
Public Works of Art Project, 172
Putnam County Products, 45–47, 188n24
Pyle, Howard, 193n8

radio, 31, 42, 44, 192n53–55, 199n44
Radio Act (1912), 33
Rago, David, 189n31
railroads, 9, 27, 31, 79–80
Rector, Mary, 106, 107
Reece, Glenn H., 144–46
Reece, Jim, 146
Reece, William, 146
Rhoads, William B., 53
Richcraft Pottery (Cohocton, NY), 214n29

road-building, 8–10, 30–31, 36, 42–43; Interstate Highway system and, 9, 86, 154, 159; New York State Thruway and, 100–101, 116, 151, 154, 158–59; roadside businesses and, 77–78. *See also* plank roads
Roadside Craftsmen, 2–6, 45; Alfred University and, 165–66, 168; baseball team of, 109–10; Bullock at, 105–9; business records of, 121–22; catalogues of, 125–32, *128–30*; as "cooperative," 109–11, 160; Cooperstown store of, 112–13, *113*; demise of, 115, 129, 159, 172, 174; display room of, *51*; fire at, 50; legacy of, 176, 184–85; predecessors of, 36–37, 46; pricing policies of, 80–81, 109; Rochester Folk Art Guild and, 174; shipping label of, *21*; styles of, 53–56; successor of, 48, 116–21; weavers at, 110; wrought-iron foundry of, 110, 114. *See also* Bloomfield Pottery; Wemett, Clarence E.
Roadside Woodcroftery, 116–18, 120
Robineau, Adelaide Alsop, 56, 165
Rochester Arts and Crafts Society, 162
Rochester Folk Art Guild, 174–75, 193n2
Rochester Institute of Technology (RIT), 163. *See also* School for American Craftsmen
Rockefeller family, 54
Rodies, Heinz George, 110, 166
Rogers, Elizabeth L., 91, 110, 166
Rogers, J. D., 106
Rookwood Pottery (Cincinnati), 89, 123, 178
Roosevelt, Eleanor, 47, 54
Roosevelt, Theodore, 41
Roseville Pottery, 78

Route 5, 22–24, 25, 63, 154
Route 15, 73, 154
Route 20, 6–7, 13–15, 22–24, 25,
    63; development of, 9; New York
    State Thruway and, 100–101; traffic
    volume on, 78, 154, 159
Route 66, 6–7, 195n47
Roycroft community, 67; Avon
    Coppersmith products versus, 56,
    133–38, 179, 209n12; baseball team
    of, 110; bookends of, 67, 180–81;
    catalogues of, 67–69, 126, 177;
    Coley and, 118; demise of, 67–68;
    leather goods of, 67, 68, 180; Coy
    Ludwig and, 60; pottery of, 60,
    199n43; production scale at, 177;
    Secessionist style at, 69, 70, 178,
    181; Wemett and, 60–61
Roycroft Copper Shop, 67, 68, 70–73,
    177
Roycroft publishing, 56, 67, 180, 189n35
rural free delivery (RFD), 28, 79–80,
    209n12. See also mail-order
    companies

Sargent, Irene, 162
Sarver, Elizabeth Rogers, 167
School for American Craftsmen
    (SAC), 46; at Alfred University, 167,
    168; faculty of, 214n24; Shop One
    of, 161, 167–68, 173–74, 188n26,
    213n38
Sears, Roebuck Company, 28, 80,
    191n32
Secessionism, 69, 70, 178, 181,
    197n33
"see-it-made," 5, 34, 36–38, 46, 58,
    158, 177
Seiler, Cotten, 193n13
Selden, George, 191n50
Shakers, 7, 35; Arts and Crafts
    movement and, 52, 55, 56, 198n41

Shelburne Museum (VT), 54
Shell Oil Company, 19, 73
Sheridan, J. K., 106
Shop One. See under School for
    American Craftsmen
Simmons, Ernest, 71
Skvirsky, Salome Aguilera, 195n48
Smith, Joseph (Mormon founder), 8
Smith, Warren, 97
Southern Highland Handicraft Guild,
    46, 172–73, 188n24
"Southern Pottery," 56, 179
souvenir shops, 7, 43, 85, 158
Steinbeck, John, 195n47
Steuben Historical Society, 48
Stevenson, Robert Louis, 139
Stickley, Gustav, 55, 56, 57, 153, 177;
    on automobility, 193n13; catalogues
    of, 126; on Colonial Revival style,
    86; on Craftsman style, 197n33;
    electrical fixtures of, 131; on
    handcraftsmanship, 60, 81; motto
    of, 138; on Shakers, 198n41; United
    Crafts of, 81, 162; Wemett and, 85
Stickley furniture company, 53, 55–56,
    59
Stieglitz, Alfred, 174
Stowell, M. Louise, 161–62
Stratton, Mary Chase, 164
Sullivan, Louis, 197n33
Sweet, Deborah, 110
symbiosis, 4
Syracuse University, 11

Taylor, Nora, 110
Taylorism, 2, 31. See also factory
    production methods
Teco Pottery (Chicago), 59, 89, 123,
    178
Tennessee Fabricating Co., 131–32
Texaco, 73
Thomas, Richard, 110, 166, 214n29

"tin can tourists," 5, 36, 38, 41
Titanic's sinking, 33
Tobey Furniture Company, 197n33
Tocqueville, Alexis de, 27
Tookay Shop, 69–70, 138–39. *See also* Kipp, Karl
tourism, 4, 83; automobility and, 7, 38–41; growth of, 42–43; railroads and, 9, 27; roadside restaurants and, 157–58; sightseeing and, 77
travel, 42, 75; commercialization of, 6–7, 9; plank roads for, 9, 22, 23; tourism and, 4
Troy School of Arts and Crafts, 11
Tubman, Harriet, 8
Turner, Frederick Jackson, 27, 193n13
turnpikes, 9. *See also* road-building

Underground Railroad, 8
United Crafts, 81, 162
United Society of Believers in Christ's Second Coming. *See* Shakers
Unverdorf, Henry, 134
utopian communities, 8, 35, 55, 58

Val-Kill Industries (Hyde Park, NY), 54
van Erp, Dirk, 153
Vanderbilt, Cornelius "Commodore," 46
Victorian design styles, 23, 52

Walpole Society, 54
Walrath, Frederick E., 162–63, 165, 212n18
Webb, Aileen Osborn Vanderbilt, 3, 11–12, 103; Canadian crafts movement and, 213n6; family of, 198n37; foundations of, 46; legacy of, 173–74, 182–83; Putnam County Products, 46–47; School for American Craftsmen and, 167; Wemett's approach versus, 183
Webb, Electra Havemeyer, 54, 198n37
Wehle, John "Jack," 198n37
Weinberger, Julius, 42
Wemett, Clarence E., 2–6, 17, 113–16; Alfred University and, 166, 168; Arts and Crafts movement and, 52–53, 60–61, 82–83; Branchport Baptist Church and, 49–50, *51*, 74; Bullock and, 107; business strategies of, 12–13, 35–36, 75–83, 171–72, 177, 188n26; businesses of, 18–19, 32, 61, 113–16, 121, 159–60; Cole and, 73–74, 159; employee benefits provided by, 20, 122; family of, 15, 17–18, 108, 112, 204n18; financial success of, 182; Florida trips of, 36–37, 46; Jennings and, 73–74; legacy of, 176; managerial style of, 121; Mechanics Institute and, 169; media coverage of, 17–20, *20*, 37, 87; obituary of, 18; pricing policies of, 80–81; Roycroft and, 60–61; Webb's approach and, 183
Wemett, Jean L., 190n16
Wemett, Mark, 111, 127, 204n18
Wemett, Mary, 114, 127, 204n18
Wemett, Norris G., 108, 166, *167*
Wheeler, William A., 99
White Horse Inn (East Avon, NY), 115–16
Whitehead, Ralph Radcliffe, 35
Wildenhain, Frans, 164, 213n38, 214n24
Williamsburg (VA), 54
Willis, Charles D., 106
Wilson, Woodrow, 9, 29
women's rights, 8
Woodcraft Products Corporation, 106–7, 206n7

Woodcroftery, 48, 116–21, *119*
Woodstock, NY, 35
Works Progress Administration (WPA),
    172; Design Laboratory of, 188n23;
    Federal Art Project of, 54, 172
World's Columbian Exposition
    (Chicago, 1893), 89–90

Wright, Frank Lloyd, 55, 118

yard sales, 15, 158
"Yellowstone Highway," 24
York, John M., 64

Zschiegner, Emil "Chick," 166, *167*